1985

LITERARY INHERITANCE

Roger Sale

The University of Massachusetts Press
Amherst, 1984

Library of Congress Cataloging in Publication Data
Sale, Roger.
Literary inheritance.
Includes index.
1. Influence (Literary, artistic, etc.) 2. English
literature—History and criticism. 3. American fiction—
History and criticism. I. Title.
PR401.S3 1984   820'.9   84-8757
ISBN 0-87023-450-1

For Alan Fisher

Contents

Preface

>>>> A READER of this book in manuscript wrote "it was difficult to perceive the audience you are writing for," since "parts appeared to be aimed at readers with fairly sophisticated backgrounds in literature and criticism" while other parts "seemed written for a much more general audience." I have written this book to give profit and delight. But to whom? Our terms for audiences of books about literature, like those above, or "students of . . ." or "specialists in . . ." seem to specify more than they possibly can. Most of those who pick up this book are, like its author, all these audiences, depending on the particular subject and the freshness of one's knowledge. No one will feel currently conversant with all the works and authors discussed here, and many will feel, with respect to certain authors and periods, that they know more, or see more deeply, than I do. A relatively short book about the literature of four centuries has no choice but to be "aimed at readers with fairly sophisticated backgrounds" *and* for "a much more general audience."

My argument can be simply stated: in recent centuries literary tradition has been made, or unmade, primarily by the relations authors have established with important writers in the immediately preceding generation. Since my aim has been to illustrate rather than to argue this point, and to avoid fighting its battles in favor of suggesting what can be seen when looking from its point of view, I have engaged little in polemics and have not sought to emerge with a theory. While for me this is mostly a tactic, for some it may well seem not only a complete strategy but an eva-

sive one as well, a means of avoiding saying where I stand in relation to others who have written on my subjects and of skimming
over the theoretical assumptions that underlie the proceedings. I
hope it is not ingenuous of me to say that, since most polemics
and theories give me little profit and delight, I cannot hope to give
these to others by such means. If I have one aim it is to suggest
how varied and complex our literary history is, and how flexible a
literary historian must be to attempt to respond to that variety. So
much has been lost one is often tempted to be elegiac, yet so
much has been gained in the wake of these losses as to rebuke
that tone, or any other encompassing one.

I am grateful to *National Forum* for asking me to write an essay,
"Literary History and Literary Criticism," which for me became
a kind of prolegomena to this book. My thanks also to the University of California at Santa Barbara, the University of British Co-
lumbia, and the University of Newcastle, where versions of parts
of the book were tried out as lectures.

A number of friends, especially Paul Alpers, Anne Howells,
Bill Pritchard, and Dorothy Sale, helped at various stages, and I
hope the work profited as much as the author from their generosity and tough-mindedness.

This is not the book on literary tradition that Alan Fisher would
have written, but I hope it is close to the one he wanted me to
write. In listening, arguing, correcting, and suggesting, he
helped me struggle to say what was on my mind, and he then insisted I keep working to say it better. One could not ask for, or receive, more from a colleague and friend.

R.S.

1 ∘ *Introduction*

T

⫸⫸⫸⫸ HIS is a book about literary tradition, and about changes in the nature of tradition, in England and America in the last four centuries. It does not, as Eliot did, see tradition as "the existing monuments" forming "an ideal order among themselves, which is modified by the introduction of the new (the really new) work of art among them." It sees, rather, tradition as something active, and changing, primarily as a relation of one generation of writers to those in the generation immediately preceding. I start with the seventeenth century because it was then that this way of enacting a relation of present to past became primarily a matter of one generation working with the one before it.

In earlier centuries, writers inherited the past as though it were timeless, its truths needing only to be spoken, or respoken, in order to be present truths. Commentators on the works of Aristotle, poets using the topos of the Golden Age, painters depicting scenes from the life of Jesus, worked in ways we must think of as unselfconscious, so complete was their assumption that the present and the past yielded the same truths. During the Renaissance, changes began to jeopardize this inheriting of tradition unselfconsciously, and one major change was the shift from seeing the present emanating from a timeless past to seeing the present as being immediately related to the preceding generation. Like all important changes, this one was gradual, so one cannot point to a moment, or generation, and say "*then* it happened." Mostly we must settle for saying "by then it *had* happened."

When tradition becomes a matter of relations between two

generations, then the term I most frequently use to describe those in the second generation, "heir," can begin to seem appropriate. Writers inherit, as blessings or as curses, their immediate predecessors. When the relation seems a blessing, the heir is enabled and grateful, and tradition itself is enabled, the past is more clearly seen and understood. When the relation seems more like a curse, one that makes the heir defensive and deflective, tradition itself is in danger of becoming discontinuous, and the past misunderstood. Something happened, for instance, to the understanding of pastoral poetry between 1637 and 1780 so that Johnson could call Milton's "Lycidas" "easy, vulgar, and therefore disgusting." Something then happened between 1780 and now so that we might not understand how Johnson could have judged "Lycidas" as he did. Here, though the gaps in time are longer than a single generation, is a classic instance of discontinuity gradually becoming loss. It then takes nothing less than dedicated and uncertain historical labor to try to recover enough from the loss to explain it. No longer anything like heirs to Milton, or Johnson, we must become historians to understand them.

Harold Bloom has often located the beginnings of modern, or "belated," poetry in Satan's declaration that "We know no time when we were not as now." It seems, however, that we always do know there was a time that is not as now, and know we must acknowledge that our relation to the past (any past much longer ago than a generation) is sufficiently endangered as to require work in order to gain any recovery. Insofar as literary theory attempts ahistorical formulations, literary history must resist theory; we can make the past present in some way only if we acknowledge the many other ways it must remain past, lost. We cannot write like Milton, or read with his eyes; we cannot do this with Henry James either, but the mere fact of time passing makes the latter recovery easier than the former.

I envisaged a triptych when I began this book, three writers or groups of writers, each facing in the generation immediately preceding a writer or writers too great to ignore: a seventeenth-century Before, an eighteenth-century During, and a nineteenth-century After. In the Before, an enabled inheritance, in the During, a crisis, and in the After, inheritors clearly suffering from what Bloom calls "the anxiety of influence" and what W. Jackson Bate calls "the burden of the past." My central documents were three sets of works, written about the immediately preceding generation: Thomas Carew's "To Ben. Johnson" and "An Elegie on the Death of the Dean of Pauls, Dr. John Donne" for my Before; Johnson's *Dictionary* and "Life of Pope" for my During; Shelley's *Peter Bell the Third* and Keats's letters about Wordsworth for my After. All these receive extensive treatment here, but they do not have quite the prominence I originally planned for them. First, I discovered that I needed some careful treatment of my three sets of predecessors—Jonson and Donne, Pope, and Wordsworth—so the panels in each picture began to seem more crowded than I first intended. Second, I felt the nineteenth century seemed distorted when considered only as an After, a time of belatedness. Shelley and Keats did indeed suffer as Wordsworth's heirs, so their poetry suffered, but in writing about Wordsworth they also created the possibilities for modern literary biography, a fact itself lost in subsequent discontinuities between generations.

Even more important, in the nineteenth century other inheritings, even kinds of inheriting, became possible. There are, for instance, the exciting cross-genre relations of Jane Austen to Johnson, and of Ruskin to Turner. In trying to see how the nineteenth could be called Wordsworth's century, the most exciting of these for me is the relation of *Great Expectations* to *The Prelude*. Here it is not a matter of direct inheritance, since there is no reason to believe Dickens ever even read *The Prelude*. It is a matter of Wordsworth's creating a kind of inheritance—the man as heir to the child—and Dickens's supremely exploiting it, in this novel above all, and harm has come to our understanding of *Great Expectations* when it has not been read as Wordsworth teaches us to read the childhood events in *The Prelude*.

Having brought in a novel, I realized I could not ignore fiction if I were to account for tradition, and changes in tradition, in the last two centuries. The history of the novel shows something very different from the history of poetry at the same time. Instead of embattled heirs, for more than a century after its inception in English, the novel and novelists seemed able not to have or need much sense of tradition, and there were no novelistic heirs of great importance. One senses it was a time similar to that in which Sophocles could know Aeschylus and say, in effect, "Yes, and this is what I'm going to do," and Euripides could look at both Aeschylus and Sophocles and say the same. There was a great outpouring, from Richardson to George Eliot, of fiction of great quality and variety, all written at a time when poets were becoming belated, anxious, burdened. Yet novelists did subsequently become self-conscious, and some of those most burdened were driven to the desperate idea that the novel was dead, or that the only novels left to be written were "experimental." In the crucial moment of transition one finds Henry James, and in James's coming to London to face the looming shadow of George Eliot one finds what may be the most interesting instance of anxious inheritance on record.

Yet James was no place to stop, since to do so would be to imply that the fate that had overtaken poetry had eventually, and alas, overtaken the novel: after James, Conrad, and Ford, and a long night. But, clearly, that did not happen, and, approaching the end of this century, we should be able to see that none of the usual descriptions of modern and postmodern will more than marginally account for what has happened, the great and indeed glorious burgeoning of fiction in America in the last generation, one that deserves any name rather than the tepid "postmodern." It seems too soon to attempt a careful study of this phenomenon, but we are not here dealing with a clutch of anxious heirs. Yet we are not dealing with America the new-found-land either, a place and a time when everything can be torn loose from the past and begun endlessly anew. It is still, as James said, a complex fate to be an American, because an American sense of the past both is, and is not, European. In a speculative last chapter, I want to begin to locate our current sense of the past, in which History has become a more looming ancestor than any individual precursor. Lawrence said, and rightly, that in America the cry of freedom is a rattle of chains. That, however, seems no longer true without being totally irrelevant either.

Thus the three original panels became four, plus an epilogue that itself dares not try to close the matter off. Whatever I have lost in neatness, I hope to have gained a fuller sense of our past and present means of being heirs. Since the literature of four centuries is under consideration, in a short book I cannot hope to be more than suggestive, concerning facts and achievements in the past and hopes in the future. A history of literature seen as a matter of inheritance should be able to contribute to a larger sense of the history of the literature of these centuries, but it is only in the persuasiveness of the accounts of individual cases that the persuasiveness of the overall design can exist.

Literary history seems always to have been a kind of stepchild, a Cinderella who never meets the prince, a way of considering literature that has never been central. One reason for this is that the best literary historians have usually been called by some other name, as though, if one were theoretical, or "a critic," a Marxist or a psychologist, one might better be able to get to the wedding. To end this introduction I would like to indicate some of my own bearings when I attempt to be a literary historian, and then to diagram some particular changes that confront any historian of our literature.

≫≫≫≫ We all know, and with a certain dread, what is meant by the term "standard literary history." An auxiliary of library science, a compilation of facts and marginal allegations made worse than a simple reference book by the pretense that no more than a crude understanding of literature, authors, and history is needed to do the job. I trust there is no need to cite examples. When I was coming of age, it was still a standard practice to urge students to read these compilations, and so I did, or read at them. It was some time before I realized that certain writers, then called "critics," were literary historians, and that I admired them most because that is what they were. I would like here only to cite two examples, one from the work of F. R. Leavis and the other from that of William Empson, to show my sense of the nature and value of literary history as they practiced it and introduced me to it.

Leavis came into a world that, he felt, was still tied to the nineteenth century, and to some of that century's more indolent ideas of what either literature or history was. In the twenties, thus, despite the presence of Eliot and Pound, despite the publication of Hopkins's poems, educated English university people were, in his view, still stuck somewhere between Lamb and Swinburne. He wanted not just to replace one taste with another, but to show the literary and moral superiority of his own, and to do this, he knew, he had to revaluate English literary history.

Eliot's early criticism helped give Leavis his bearings. Here he could find comparisons of Dryden and Marvell to Shelley; he could find it said that "the feeling, the sensibility, expressed in the *Country Churchyard* (to say nothing of Tennyson and Browning) is cruder than that in the *Coy Mistress*"; here he could find it said that "with our eye still on Marvell, we can say that wit is not erudition; it is sometimes stifled by erudition, as in much of Milton." Eliot had rattled the cupboards, and had been content to do no more. Leavis knew that while Eliot's method was perfect, his manner was keeping Eliot from being taken with the seriousness Leavis felt he deserved. So, in effect, he would redesign the room.

In "The Line of Wit," the opening essay of *Revaluation*, Leavis thus begins by praising Donne's originality, but soon insists that a true literary history of the seventeenth century, which Eliot had only suggested, must undertake a statement of the greatness of Ben Jonson. He slides from Donne briefly to Carew, and, by means of Carew, back to Jonson: "Jonson's effort was to feel Catullus, and the others he cultivated, as contemporary with himself; or rather, to achieve an English mode that should express a sense of contemporaneity with them." Eliot knew how much Jonson had been denigrated by the praise as well as by the castigation he had suffered, but he himself did no more than show how Jonson's plays work on different principles from Shakespeare's. True enough, but Leavis knew that those surrounding him had not heard, so he attempted to show what Jonson's poetry had done that Donne's had not:

> Whatever its relation to any Latin originals, it is indisputably *there*, an achieved actuality. It belongs, of course, to literature, and is the product of a highly refined literary sensibility; yet it is at the same time expressive, if to a large degree by

aspiration only, of a way of living. In it the English poet, who remains not the less English and of his own time, enters into an ideal community, conceived of as something with which contemporary life and manners may and should have close relations.

Starting just with this, Leavis can attempt to redraw the received map of the seventeenth century.

He can, first, establish Jonson's as a way of writing that is sufficiently supple and varied that it can often be like Donne's; this lets Leavis steer clear of those narrow considerations of style that call Donne "metaphysical" and Jonson "classical." He can, second, then establish Carew and Marvell as poets who are nurtured in the line of wit by both Donne and Jonson, and this is seeing the matter generationally as Eliot seldom was interested in doing. He can, then, third, come down to Dryden:

> The community to which Jonson as a poet belongs is, though (as we have seen) brought into relation with the life and manners of his time, predominantly ideal; membership is the achievement of creative effort. Jonson's greater fineness and his more assertive robustness go together. The community to which Dryden belongs as a poet is that in which he actually lives, moves, eats, and talks; and he belongs to it so completely, and, with its assurance of being sophisticated and civilized (it is on the point of considering itself truly Augustan—that is, as attaining and realizing afresh a kind of absolute of civilization), it is so completely engrossing that he has no ear, no spiritual antennae, for the other community.

Finally, he can say "In Pope the line ends," and show Pope's use of language and his concern for civilization linking him with Jonson, Donne, Carew, and Marvell; this helps establish Pope's greatness as something different from a great representative Augustan, to say nothing of different from representative of a great age of prose. This was truly reforming work Leavis was doing, and, I might add, is still doing; since specialists in these periods still happily cut themselves off from each other by making 1660 a crucial dividing line, Leavis's line of wit remains a major series of demarcations.

He does so much of his work with careful quoting of texts, however, that it would take a close examination of his words and those of his authors to do him justice. What the quoting gives him is the ability to say, concerning Dryden, "that he has no ear, no spiritual antennae," thereby making a literary matter historical and moral as well. History is enacted on a page, in poems, not something to be reduced to styles, schools, trends, and backgrounds. Leavis is such a familiar figure it is somewhat embarrassing to say this, to insist on his greatness being a matter of being simultaneously historical, literary, and humanly alive. He is not always, or even often, as great as he is in "The Line of Wit," but his best work is, for me, a kind of model of what it means to say a literary critic must be historical in order to be a critic at all.

William Empson, in this context at least, is not all that different, for all that Empson found himself tilting against Leavis over the years. Seen as literary historians, the difference between them seems primarily a matter of manner. If Leavis always is attacking the indolence of those whose sensibility remained that of adolescents in public schools, Empson employs the language, tones, and bits of learning of those schools and does something astonishing with it. Through a mimicry of the High Table he attempts to bring in, as if casually, ways of reading and understanding history that we might reject if stated more formally and straightforwardly. He wants to create a community—a "we," an "our," an "us"—that assents to being at one with Empson ("of course we all know," etc.) and then includes writers and characters of the past. It is a much trickier and more ambitious kind of writing than Leavis's, one almost impossible to imitate successfully, but so compelling when it works that anyone might wish to try.

So much of "Milton and Bentley" in *Some Versions of Pastoral* is taken up with Empsonian fun about the commentary of Bentley and Pearce on *Paradise Lost* that it is easy to lose sight of the way this chapter is part of a historical book about pastoral feeling. Bentley and Pearce seem to stand as eighteenth-century scholars foolishly trying to tidy up the rich wantonness of Milton's verse, but Empson uses them also as writers who are still enough in

touch with Milton's language and world to be able to read more
closely than many later readers. What might seem only to obscure is thus used also to illuminate Miltonian cruces, in order to
try to make a community out of the seventeenth-century writer,
the eighteenth-century scholars, and the twentieth-century critical historian. Thus joined, we are invited to consider Adam, Eve,
and Satan: "We first see Paradise through the eyes of the entering
Satan, seated jealously like a cormorant on the Tree of Life. Like
him we are made to feel aliens with a larger purpose; our sense of
its pathos and perfection seems, as he does, to look down on it
from above; the fall has not happened, and we must avoid this
sort of thing in our own lives." Satan now joins the community,
the first of the fallen; seeing as he sees, aliens with larger pur-
poses, we likewise are asked to downplay his wickedness, to see
him only as "one of us" whose example we had better not follow:
"Like so many characters in history our first parents may be
viewed with admiration so long as they do not impose on us their
system of values; it has become safe to admit that in spite of what
is now known to be the wickedness of such people they had a
perfection which we no longer deserve." We look back, Satan
now a modern like Milton, Empson, and the rest of us, and see
Adam and Eve as we might Alexander, or Moses; they are perfect
in their remoteness, but maybe it is only their remoteness that
hides a wickedness. Pastoral thus conceived may be only a trick.

Such figures, in such a landscape, cannot, thus, hold us; nor
could it hold Milton three centuries earlier:

> Without any reason for it in Milton's official view of the story
> this feeling is concentrated onto their sexual situation and
> the bower where Eve decks their nuptial bed (let not the
> reader think there is any loss of innocence in its pleasures)
> has the most firmly "pagan" and I think the most beautiful of
> the comparisons.
>
> In shadier Bower,
> More sacred and sequestered, though but feigned,
> Pan or Sylvanus never slept, nor Nymph
> Nor Faunus haunted.
> "*Pan, Sylvanus,* and *Faunus,* savage and beastly deities, and

acknowledg'd *feign'd*, are brought in here in Comparison, and their wild Grottos forsooth are sacred." "These three verses, after all his objections, were certainly Milton's, and may be justified though perhaps not admired."

The first of these comments is Bentley's, and the second is Pearce's.

Bentley has asked, as we might not have, if Milton's lines say that Pan and Sylvanus sleep in Eden, and Faunus haunts it. The grammar of the lines certainly supports such a reading, and Empson thus is readied to intone:

> Surely Bentley was right to be surprised at Faunus haunting the bower, a ghost crying in the cold of Paradise, and the lusts of Pan sacred even in comparison to Eden. There is a Vergilian quality in the lines, haunting indeed, a pathos not mentioned because it is the whole of the story. I suppose that in Satan determining to destroy the innocent happiness of Eden, for the highest political motives, without hatred, not without tears, we may find some echo of the Elizabethan fulness of life that Milton as a poet abandoned, and as a Puritan helped to destroy.

Having earlier allied us with Satan, Empson then allies Milton with him, seeing in the presence of the savage pagan gods an "Elizabethan fulness of life" that Milton, so the argument goes, both understood and abandoned, longed for as for an Eden, yet helped to destroy. Since we are inclined to feel Empson is right about Milton's sense of his immediate past, we may be tricked for the duration of that feeling into forgetting that Empson is also asking us to think of Satan as a Puritan apostle of liberty. No matter, truly—that being more central to the argument of Empson's later *Milton's God* than here; what is crucial is Empson's way of being literary, making us rivet on the lines he quotes—as a way of being historical, seeing Milton and ourselves looking back on Eden, a pastoral as pathetic as perfect, seeing in its lostness the lostness of the Elizabethan age as Milton can be imagined to have experienced it.

Empson is more powerful than Leavis because he wants not only to write his history but to create, in defiance of that history's implication, a community in which we, Bentley, Milton, and even Satan share that "pathos which is not mentioned because it is the whole of the story." Feeling all that those within the community share, all that the community stands as being later than, we seem to defy history, to be in Milton's century as well as our own; the next step will be to come down to Gay, and then to Lewis Carroll, and from the position of those writers we will also look back, sense loss, measure what is left. Since it is a community that is created, since history is thereby defied, the feeling of loss is made inspiriting, supportive, enhancing without losing its sadness and pathos.

What Empson most shares with Leavis is the knowledge that, in order to be simultaneously critical and historical, they must be writers, alive in the way they phrase everything so as to be expressive of when they are as well as of the literature that preceded them. In that spirit I have written this book. Though Leavis and Empson will make few explicit appearances in the pages that follow, they stand for me as a strong and, I hope, enabling presence.

Since this is not a fighting, or even a particularly arguing book, I have referred to more recent literary historians, like Bloom, Bate, Christopher Ricks, and Hugh Kenner, only when convenient for a point I am trying to make. They and many others have helped me especially when they forced me to ask what I most wanted to say. As will become apparent, I find Bloom's "anxiety" and Bate's "burden" to be much less pervasive in the literature of the last four centuries than they do, though both are especially pertinent to my consideration of Wordsworth's century. It was while reading their work that I began to formulate this one, but I see no reason to make my stance polemical for that reason; any reader of their work will easily see where we overlap and where we diverge.

Tu se' lo mio maestro e 'l mio autore
Tu se' solo colui da cu' io tolsi
Lo bellow stile che m' ha fatto honore.

Thus Dante to Vergil, and even one whose Italian is scanty can
make out what is being said:

> You are my master and my author
> And you alone are he from whom I learned
> The beautiful style which has given me honor.

This is a supreme instance of one of the prized and celebrated
abilities of older writers: to honor the predecessor, to let the predecessor be guide and creator. "All the world speaks a single language," wrote Baudri of Bourgueil at the turn of the eleventh century, "and all mankind shall teach us." Predecessors did not
loom, they taught and bequeathed—styles, stories, knowledge,
wisdom. For the learned person of the Middle Ages, E. R. Curtius
writes: "All *auctores* are of the same value, all are timeless. This is
and remains characteristic of the entire Middle Ages. No distinction is made between Augustan and late Antique literature, or between Theodolus and the early Christian poets. The passage of
time only increases the list of *auctores*." Dante makes his special
acknowledgment of Vergil out of gratitude, while Chaucer's
Chauntecleer plunders Cato for the arguments about the validity
of dreams. The gap between them is huge, but they share the
same sense of what the past and its writers could teach.

I offer this as a given, a sense of time when we were not as now,
one that extends back as though the mind of man could not run to
the contrary. The processes whereby all this changed is the subject of the chapters that follow. I want to conclude this introduction with a comparison of a Before and an After in order to indicate at the outset what may be the most important single fact
about this change. First, here is Marvell, at the opening of "A Picture of Little T. C. in a Prospect of Flowers":

> See with what simplicity
> This Nimph begins her golden daies!
> In the green Grass she loves to lie,
> And there with her fair Aspect tames
> The Wilder flow'rs, and gives them names:
> But only with the Roses playes;

And them does tell
What Colour best becomes them, and what Smell.

Marvell would have seen this prospect, if indeed he saw it at all,
in a real landscape. In the poem, though, T. C. is lying in the grass
and wild flowers, and she is playing with the roses, and we know
nothing of where the grass is in relation to the roses or wild flowers, or whether she does one thing before another, or both at the
same time. One could not take a picture of the prospect in the
poem. Further, in suggesting that T. C. names the wilder flowers
we are given a type of Eden, humankind given dominion by the
power of language, and T. C. is a kind of Eve. Then T. C. is said to
know what Eve did not, something special about roses, and by
raising them to the level of her playmate she becomes, presumably without her knowledge, intuitively sexual and passionate.

Marvell then teases out these suggestions by imagining that
T. C. will grow to be a chaste "virtuous enemy of Man" whose
eyes will be like a chariot driving "in Triumph over Hearts that
strive." Then he returns to the girl in the prospect:

Mean time, whilst every verdant thing
It self does at thy Beauty charm,
Reform the errours of the Spring;
Make that the Tulips may have share
Of sweetness, seeing they are fair;
And Roses of their thorns disarm:
   But most procure
That Violets may a longer Age endure.

Marvell could not have said, or at least need not have said, where
he learned his way of understanding our relation with flowers.
From his *auctores*. Marvell does not imagine that the spring makes
errors, but he does want to imagine that T. C. might not grow
from playing with roses into "the virtuous Enemy of Man." For
that not to happen, something extraordinary, something we
might name "unnatural" must happen: the tulip must smell
sweet, the rose must lose its thorn, the violet must outlive early
spring. That is, T. C. must become sweet, not dangerous, and

must not grow up. The wit insists that while this is impossible, only T. C. is powerful enough to do it.

In his ninety-fourth sonnet Shakespeare warns them that have power: "Lilies that fester smell far worse than weeds." His Perdita gives Mopsa and Dorcas daffodils because they are maids who "wear upon your virgin branches yet Your maidenheads growing." Herbert knows we are but flowers that glide, though he also knows that because we are not flowers we can evoke the wrath of God. A fairer flower than Proserpin, Milton's Eve after the Fall is "defac't, deflower'd, and now to death devote." Renaissance literature abounds with variations of this metaphor of human beings understood as flora, but, long before, Isaiah knew that all flesh is grass, and Jesus speaks of us as lilies of the field. That the metaphor was timeless gave it authority, and could not diminish its power. It could be a rose one wanted, a violet, a sprig of rosemary or rue, ivy, lilies, or a bulb that retreats in winter to its mother-root. Flowers did not exist as a taxonomy but as a range of references within the metaphor.

I would like to speak of this metaphor first in the context of "conventions," then in the context of the "real," in order to show its relation to both. I am leery of talking about conventions since to do so implies something more formal or rigid than older writers, who employed them, took them to be. We speak of conventions to cover a variety of uses: generic considerations for epic, tragedy, and pastoral, like "the Homeric catalogue," the "epic simile," "in medias res," the dramatic unities, the dialogue of shepherds; topics, like "the golden and the brazen age" or "the world is a stage"; the muses and the invocation thereof; "Once upon a time" and "they lived happily ever after" to begin and end fairy tales; stock figures, like the shiftless lad or the wicked stepmother in such tales, or the devil, the senex, and the lovesick young man on the stage. Many of these have origins in antiquity, many appear later, but it is the timeless nature of older bequests and inheritances that while the authorizing *auctores* were known and could be cited (except for fairy tales), any *auctore* would serve. All discussion of the drama being "Aristotelian," the dramatic unities of time, place, and action could be associated with his name, though his *Poetics* does not mention them.

If these are "conventions," then the metaphor about human beings and plants could exist within them or without them, in apparently pure or in mixed form. We may say that Marvell's flowers are "pastoral," or that "The Picture of Little T. C." is a pastoral poem, but it is not a Vergilian eclogue or a Spenserian calender—to name two versions of the convention—and it shares a good deal with conventions we call Petrarchan. Or, here is the opening of Shakespeare's thirty-fifth sonnet, no one's idea of a pastoral poem:

> No more be griev'd at that which thou has done;
> Roses have thorns, and silver fountains mud.

These roses are "the same as" Marvell's in their association with a sexual beloved, and the thorns are in each emphasized as much as the blossoms. The absence of a pastoral context, however, gives them a different use. Something we might think of as a convention and therefore as easily said—"Roses have thorns" —stands in apposition to something we associate with no convention at all—"and silver fountains mud." The speaking tone does not change, but we nonetheless recognize a shift, from saying "We all make mistakes" to "Your mistake is hard to forgive because it made something ugly of something beautiful." It achieves this shift because thorns "go with" roses, while mud had seldom been asked to "go with" silver fountains. There are no rules, no limits created by conventions, for Shakespeare's or Marvell's use of the received metaphor. "Roses have thorns" may have something like conventional status, but it need not be used conventionally.

Which leads us to the "real," a latter-day term to be sure, but since we are latter-day people, we can use it profitably if we are careful. The mud that results from the fountain's flowing may seem "real," but only because the language draws less from a tradition than does that of the thorn on the rose. Shakespeare need never have seen mud alongside a fountain, and roses and mud are, after all, equally "real." What he had seen, almost certainly, were harbingers of spring, so that in Perdita's reference to "the daffodil that comes before the swallow dares," Shakespeare is bringing in something observed, something not necessarily part

of the traditional language of daffodils. Nonetheless, the daffodil, once brought in, functions in a traditional way to specify the
age and sexual status of Mopsa and Dorcas. If we are inclined
to distinguish between traditional language about flowers and
"real" observable nature, earlier writers seldom were, and fussed
very little when they did. There may be no necessary connection
between roses and passionate men and women, but it is easy to
understand how the connection was made and how, when it
was, the observable fact that roses have thorns became important, more so in its ability to make the metaphor complex than,
I suspect, it is for most people in "real" life. The observable fact
could always be emphasized by any writer, but it could also be
almost forgotten in the writer's exploration of the metaphor's
possibilities.

Thus we can have something like this, a stanza from Ben Jonson's Charis poems that Hugh Kenner once called one of the high
points in the management of our language:

> Have you seene but a bright Lillie grow,
>> Before rude hands have touch'd it?
> Ha' you mark'd but the fall o' the Snow
>> Before the soyle hath smutch'd it?
> Ha' you felt the wooll o' the Bever?
>> Or Swans Downe ever?
> Or have smelt o' the bud o' the Brier?
>> Or the Nard in the fire?
> Or have tasted the bag of the Bee?
> O so white, O so soft! O so sweet is she!

Some of the language is Petrarchan, and the comparison of a
woman's skin to the white, the soft, and the sweet in nature is
a convention, if one likes. But Jonson inquires here as though we
were all citizens of an observable rather than a traditional inherited world. The wonder is that one could answer "no" to each of
his seven questions—and personally I must answer "no" to four
of them—without losing that sense of the observable that consorts in perfect ease with the conventional or traditional.

So we can distinguish between the conventional and the real,
but only roughly, and the ways of older writers with the meta-

phor of people and flowers is a good place to see the roughness. No longer heirs to that tradition, we can nonetheless learn much about that time when we were not as now, but there is always a danger of distortion, of not seeing the lurking possibility of historical provinciality. We know the older authors felt no discontinuity in time—I am using a dead author's language—or in space —I am like the flower. We know it, but because we can no longer use the metaphors as our own, we need to be careful how we speak of it.

Now then, what happened? Why is it necessary to speak of "older" and "latter-day"? What are the implications for us of the fact that there is an older and that we must be historians of its literature rather than heirs to it? Curtius says that "Keats and Wilde continue the line" of the "flower flora of the ancients," but here is the fourth stanza of the "Ode to a Nightingale":

> I cannot see what flowers are at my feet,
>   Nor what soft incense hangs upon the boughs,
> But, in embalmed darkness, guess each sweet
>   Wherewith the seasonable month endows
> The grass, the thicket, and the fruit-tree wild;
>   White hawthorn, and the pastoral eglantine;
> Fast fading violets covered up in leaves;
>   And mid-May's eldest child,
> The coming musk-rose, full of dewy wine,
> The murmurous haunt of flies on summer eves.

Like Marvell when he wishes T. C. would give the tulips a sweet smell, Keats is creating a condition contrary to fact, since he cannot see and so can only guess what flowers are at his feet. And like older writers, Keats does not hesitate to conflate his seasons, so that the "seasonable month," the mid-May when the poem was written—when the violet fades, the hawthorn blooms, and the muskrose is coming—slides easily into the summer eves of the last line.

But the pastoral metaphor that compares person to flower is gone. Two stanzas earlier Keats writes of the weariness, the fever, and the fret of his world where "youth grows pale, and spectre-thin, and dies." Here he speaks of "fast-fading violets."

For Marvell it would have been an easier leap than to pluck bright honor from the pale-faced moon to make the violets a metaphor for pale youth. It is unimaginable for Keats. We may say that Keats wants to keep the violets and the youth separate, inhabitants of different worlds, but that is beside the point, especially since he is about to imagine it were rich to become spectre-thin and die in the embalmed darkness of the nightingale's world. For Keats the flowers are useful as something lush and evocative, and he cannot imagine using them as a metaphor for the human. For all his imaginativeness, Keats's world, seen as a matter of the deployment of language, has been reduced to the real.

The resources available to a poet diminished between the seventeenth and the nineteenth century. Earlier writers could, of course, specify by means of the real and could, occasionally, write as lushly as Keats about the real; it is a sign of the shift that Shakespeare and, especially, Milton were prized in the nineteenth century for this lushness, while the sheep-shearing scene in *The Winter's Tale* or the description of Hell as seen by the exploring angels in Book 2 of *Paradise Lost* had to be diminished in order to be taken in. Later writers had to try to get some of the effects achieved by traditional metaphors in older poets by means of "symbol," like Keats's nightingale, or Shelley's west wind, or Arnold's Dover Beach. The easy and flexible converse between the real and the metaphoric no longer available, poets had to become more elaborate, more atmospheric, more "poetic," the language of the real strained to create the world of an urn, a bird that never was, a land of lotus eating, real waves bringing in the eternal note of sadness. Earlier poets who had no semblance of this use of language, like Jonson and Marvell, inevitably were misunderstood or ignored. The strain on the language to gain some of the old effects without the old means is accompanied by the strain to be original, to be inspired. The result is anxious, unfree, unenabled heirs, in poetry at least. The great explorers of the world reduced to the real are the novelists.

If it would distort to say there is a single line of inheritance that runs from Homer and the Hebrew scriptures down to Marvell and Milton, it would not distort to say that for us now, looking back, there is the strong appearance of such a continuity. By the time of Keats, clearly, it was lost, and for all his labor to reinvent it, not Eliot nor anyone else could get it back. Keats knew that modern poets were only little electors of small provinces, and that Wordsworth therefore could only offer the egotistical sublime. But he was effectively cut off from the old culture; for him the world in the time of Milton was only awakening from a long age of superstition, for him the older poets was not a tradition but a few isolated great writers. Coming later, we can see the tradition that was there ourselves, but only as historians.

2 ∘ *Carew as Composer*

WHAT were Virtue, Love, Patriotism, Friendship—what were the scenery of this beautiful Universe which we inhabit; what were our consolations òn this side of the grave, and what were our aspiration beyond it, if Poetry did not ascend to bring light and fire from those eternal regions where the owl-winged faculty of calculation dare not ever soar? Poetry is not like reasoning, a power to be exerted according to the determination of the will. A man cannot say, "I will compose poetry." The greatest poet cannot say it: for the mind in creation is as a fading coal, which some invisible influence, like an inconstant wind, awakens to transitory brightness.

⨠⨠⨠⨠ T HIS is Shelley in *A Defence of Poetry,* offering the terms for the exercise of a poet that have, well into this century, endured as something like articles of faith. Shelley could not "compose" poetry. Nor could Keats. Nor, so far as they knew, could Wordsworth.

A considerable vocabulary had to be built to consort with this idea of the origins of poetry—and of virtue, love, patriotism, friendship, and all else that mattered. Words like "genius," "creative," "imagination," "natural," and "original" were made terms of high praise, and in order to do this each of these words often had to be wrenched in meaning from what preceding centuries understood by them. The After had begun, and the terms of its beginning had to be invented and reinvented.

Romantic poetry and aesthetics held sway for so long that it has often been difficult to see how blurred a glass they offered a reader of earlier poets. Metaphors became symbols, symbols became the uniting power of "the shaping spirit of imagination," poets became isolated, meditative, the godlike voices bringing light and fire from the eternal regions—or else poets lamenting that they could no longer do so. When this happened, earlier poets were in danger of being distorted, slighted, or forgotten. Chaucer was admired, but only patronizingly. *Sir Gawain and the Green Knight* and *Beowulf* were recovered and quickly buried in scholastic commentary. Spenser became a patron saint of the dreamy, his alert and vigorous grimness lost. Shakespeare was enthroned, beyond our question, for reasons no one between Ben Jonson and Samuel Johnson would have understood. Milton became a looming figure, as he had not been for Dryden, Pope, or Johnson. In claiming a new power for poetry, the past had to be rewritten.

Ben Jonson has never seemed to register on a scale established to read Keats's odes, Yeats's Byzantium poems, or *A Defence of Poetry*. Gradually, since the early running tide of Romanticism, other poets of Jonson's century have been fruitfully reclaimed. First Donne, never really lost, then Marvell, then Herbert, have been reestablished, or, better still, have become poets in constant need of being reestablished. This has never really happened to Jonson. The praise and terms of reunderstanding offered by Eliot, Leavis, Wesley Trimpi, Jonas Barish, and others have been ignored or have themselves offered invitations to further slighting. For most, Jonson remains owl-winged, unsoaring, and calculated; he is a great proclaimer whose constant proclamation is "I will compose poetry," but that has limited his appeal rather than defined his greatness. That Jonson might be a greater poet than Keats or Yeats seems not to have crossed anyone's mind. Nor is it generally acknowledged that the gap between Shakespeare and Jonson as dramatists is not as great as that between Jonson and whomever one wants to name next.

Jonson is the most important single figure whom later writers ignored. As a living force in poetry, or in conversations and dissertations about poetry, Jonson barely survived the seventeenth century. This is an aberration, a failure of tradition to maintain itself, the result of not knowing a time when we were not as now.

Jonson made himself into a great heir, and for a generation after his death he was a great enabling ancestor. Shadwell worked well with Jonsonian drama, and Herrick with Jonsonian lyric, but Jonson's finest heir is Carew, and it is a sign that we have lost touch with what it meant to be an enabled heir that Carew remains virtually unknown, a resident of anthologies as one of the Cavaliers alongside Lovelace and Suckling. Carew might have said to Jonson: "You alone are he from whom I learned / The beautiful style which gave me honor," except the honor was never really given, and not just because Dante is a much greater poet than Carew.

⧽⧽⧽⧽ Ben Jonson is a man speaking to someone; his verse is always social. He invites a friend to supper, he addresses the Sidney estate at Penshurst, he wonders if he is scorned because a woman in Scotland saw his picture and therefore ignored his verses to her. He replies to one who asks to be sealed in the tribe of Ben. He writes to himself, in odes. He never turns inward. "And why to me this, thou lame lord of fire," he demands of Vulcan after his house has burned. "'Tis true, I'm broke," he confesses to his "offended mistress." "Wake, friend from forth thy lethargie," he admonishes one reluctant to be a soldier.

Having thus begun, he goes on as people do when following a train of thought in another's presence, and when he has said his say, he stops. He may rise to grave or lofty language, sing a song, or bite off an epigram, but always tone and form are at his disposal, not he at theirs. He extols Donne in an epigram, then breaks off after eight lines:

> All which I mean to praise, and yet, I would;
> But leave because I could not as I should!

There is ambiguity in such phrasing, no doubt more clearly intended than would be the case were Donne actually with him. He stops his epigram because he cannot praise Donne properly, and he stops because he knows he should praise Donne more highly than he wants to, or can at the moment. This is not all he has to say about Donne, but all he needs to honor the occasion.

Such insistent addressing has struck many as a sign of great egotism, which it is, and some turn away from Jonson, not exhausted necessarily but nonetheless feeling the heavy impress of Jonson's boundless assurance that he can make an occasion out of any need or situation. It is the mastery, the apparent lack of any need to turn within as if confused, that creates the limited admiration he has so often received. Yet his is always a controlled egotism, controlled by a need to express a situation, the one being addressed, and the motions of a mind that delights in what it can do. Seldom need one know or care who the people are whom he speaks to, since Jonson's confidence allows him to assume that what is important about a situation is what he makes of it. Yet, as a result, the one addressed is never denigrated and never scraped or bowed to beyond the demands of dignity, as is so often the case in Donne.

Jonson wrote verse letters, the best in English, but in a sense everything he wrote might be called a verse letter:

> Since you must goe, and I must bid farewell,
>   Heare, Mistress, your departing servant tell
> What it is like: And do not think they can
>   Be idle words, though of a parting Man:
> It is as if a night should shade noone-day,
>   Or that the Sun was here, but forc't away;
> And we were left under that Hemisphere,
>   Where we must feel it Darke for half a yeare.
> What fate is this to change mens days and houres
>   To shift their seasons, and destroy their powers!
> Alas I ha' lost my heat, my blood, my prime,
>   Winter is come a Quarter e're his Time,
> My health will leave me; and when you depart,
>   How shall I doe sweet Mistris for my heart?
> You would restore it? No, that's worth a feare,
>   As if it were not worthy to be there:
> O, keepe it still; for it had rather be
>   Your sacrifice, then here remaine with me.
> And so I spare it: Come what can become
>   Of me, I'le softly tread unto my Tombe;

Or like a Ghost walke silent amongst men,
　　Till I may see both it and you agen.

On first reading, this may seem a halting version of something
Donne does better. Especially in the lines beginning "It is as if a
night should shade noone-day," Jonson takes a metaphor that
Donne might have pulled tautly through the grip of his intelligence, and does no more than play with it briefly before moving
on. Whatever Jonson may lose writing this way, he gains a shifting play of mind that allows him to be extravagant and to acknowledge that extravagance for what it is.

The parting is an end, and not an end. Jonson will go to his
grave because his mistress is gone, yet he will be a ghost only as
long as she is gone. It will be dark, or winter, and he will lose his
powers, when she goes, just as he has already lost his heart; but
by adding "And so I spare it," he asserts his power, if not over her
parting, then over his attitude toward it and his future. Love is
crucial, and turns noonday to night, yet life goes on, and his egotism becomes an acknowledgment that anyone but a youthful
lover must make. The lavish language, so familiar in Elizabethan
love poetry, is never allowed to overtake or obscure Jonson's
sense of his situation. Should Jonson have had such a mistress,
and should she have received this elegy, she might well be
pleased, and assured, and feel the assurance as something more
valuable than flattery.

"Since you must goe" is not a great poem; no one would think
to call it that. But it is made with a great kind of poetry, as one can
more easily see by reading many Jonson poems than by a long
study of any one poem. Jonson has few individual poems one
must know, and he is represented close to his best by many
poems that seldom or never make their way into anthologies. "To
Celia" and "Drinke to me, onely, with thine eyes" are acknowledged to be exquisite, as though Campion might have written
them. "To Penshurst" and the Cary and Morison ode are both
splendid performances, but "An Epistle to Master Arth. Squib" is
as good, and is given little attention. Ours is not an age that pro-
duces a book like *Bartlett's Familiar Quotations*, but it still tends to
judge poets and poems by their brief heights, and, as a result,

Jonson's more even performance, his inability to write a bad poem, his genius' being more expressed in variety and flexibility than in spectacular bursts, all tend to count against him.

Rather than saying what he can do, the world in the last two centuries has been generally happier saying what he cannot do. He lacks Donne's tautness and desperate adventurousness. He lacks Shakespeare's sensuality and ambiguity. Thus he is morose, or an inkhorn writer, or one with no access to the roots of feeling. If we believe, with Wordsworth, that darkness makes abode in the greatest poets, then Jonson acknowledges no such darkness, no division of self or doubt of God's mercy, that might help to create it or lead one to explore it.

What he created was irrelevant to the interests of Donne or Shakespeare, namely communities. His way of being social always includes another person or place and often extends outward to include an ideal community along with the stated immediate one. He was no gentleman, and personally seems to have been less than instinctively gracious, but his way of saying that he never sought to live above or apart from the world makes him always our potential companion, as Donne and Shakespeare are not. Even those poems where he seems to reject the world, like "False world, good night," or "Come leave the loathed stage," create an implied community of those who have known the pettiness or corruption to which human beings can descend. His learning helped him here, and it taught him much more than Donne's or Shakespeare's taught them. It gave him, first, access to an ideal relation implied by his relation to his *auctores;* it gave him then a way to express the immediate situations that are the social occasions of his poems; it gave him the ability to create relations with readers who see the ideal, know the real or actual, and join with Jonson in a new possible community.

Many have marveled at the way Renaissance writers gave us not only the last great expression of the long continuous tradition extending down from Homer and the Hebrew scriptures but also, in its expiration, a superb final flowering of that tradition. In "The Articulation of the Ego in the English Renaissance," William Kerrigan posits a time when young men, weaned early from the mother tongue of English, learned to imitate the father tongue of

Latin, and came, by their mastery of their male ancestors, to feel a power and confidence which they then could use to reenergize their mother, or native, language. Had Spenser, Sidney, Shakespeare, Donne, Jonson, and Milton continued to write in Latin after their schooling, they could only have followed, in the sense of imitated, their Latin authors, and would have been restricted, as Kerrigan calls it, to a kind of metonymy. Instead, learning led to artistic flourishing, the result of an ego that was made strong, and metonymy could burst into a full range of metaphor. Thus, in the Jonson stanza quoted in the introduction, from "A Celebration of Charis," we can say that Jonson learned to write:

> Have you seene but a bright Lillie grow,
> Before rude hands have touch'd it?

He then celebrates what that learning gave him in the equally beautiful but more homely:

> Ha' you mark'd but the fall o' the Snow
> Before the soyle hath smutch'd it?

"Smutch'd" is a word Jonson is empowered to use because of his mastery of the language of bright lilies.

Now Chaucer, we may say, is every bit as capable as Jonson of gaining this kind of effect, where the "learned" and the "native" are brought together easily, but he does it as if by breathing, while in Jonson this is celebrated, because the learning is the discovering, and exulting in the discovery, of the possibility. With Chaucer what feels as though it had never been lost was not then in need of being found. With Jonson, what feels as though what might have been lost is discovered, which is the source of the celebration.

Kerrigan does not discuss this possibility as such, but I think it consorts with his sense of what makes English Renaissance literature so rich, enabled, and excited. Not only is one enabled to mine the mother language by having learned the father language, but the sense of triumph this gives is accompanied by the sense that this might not have happened, and that anything less than such a triumph is decline and disaster. Nothing could contribute quite so much to a sense of an achieved, as opposed to a simply inherited, community as the sense that this was labor, and labor then rewarded with triumph. And in no one do we find this sense of achievement so delightedly expressed as in Jonson, except perhaps in the Milton of Book 7 of *Paradise Lost*. In Jonson we are constantly witnessing the way a triumph over potential loss animates a love of the past, yielding an excited sense of the present.

"To Celia," for instance, is altogether a lighter poem than Catullus's "Vivamus, mea Lesbia," on which it is based, and if we consider it only as a song, it would seem only a solid piece of imitative poetry. In *Volpone*, though, it works differently. Volpone leaps from his couch to announce to the wife of the man who would prefer any fate to that of cuckold that cuckoldry is stimulus to his lust:

> Cannot we delude the eyes
> Of a few poore household-spies?
> Or his easier eares beguile,
> Thus removed by our wile?

"Wile," of course, is what Celia has none of and no use for, but Volpone is not trying to fit his wooing to any sense of how this woman should be wooed. He relies on the elegance of his performance and the primacy of his own lust:

> I am now as fresh,
> As hot, as high, and in as jovial plight,
> As when, in that so celebrated scene,
> At recitation of our comedy,
> For entertainment of the great Valois
> I acted young Antinous; and attracted
> The eyes and ears of all the ladies present,
> T'admire each graceful gesture, note, and footing.

It is all wrong, since nothing will prove more revolting to Celia than this announcement that the ladies watching an entertainment were attracted when Volpone last felt this sportive, this jovial. "Come my Celia, let us prove, / While we can, the sports of love," but Celia knows no Catullus, and Volpone's rich sense of community is entirely wasted on her.

So Volpone is a poor lover, Celia protests, and Bonario soon enters to attempt a rescue. The libertine is shabby in his presumptuousness. The Latin imitator has run into the native literal puritan. But Volpone really implicitly acknowledges this; he can offer his richness of language and sensual delight only to one who knows the tradition and knows that its language is all that can be offered. As the Latin meets the puritan, it acknowledges its limit, and those who have wooed according to the ancient pattern are created in a community of lovers. Not to know Catullus, says Volpone, argues yourself unknown, and all those who feel that can rally round, even as they know that Celia does not mind in the least arguing herself unknown, or anything else rather than Volpone's accepted lover. These are all effects Catullus might not have known or needed, but Jonson uses them to show he is at one with Catullus, and yet at a much later date as well, so that his community of Volpone-Catullus creates also a community of post-Catullus performers, excellent poets but often failed lovers.

The drama was the perfect place to show this clash of tradition against latter-day fact, which creates its own sense of sharing among those who know these are latter days. In the opening scene of *The Alchemist*, Dol Common empties her arsenal of language to find some way to stop the quarreling between Face and Subtle. "Gentlemen," she tries, "what mean you? Will you mar all?" Subtle shouts, then Face, and Dol interrupts again: "Will you undo yourself with this civil war?" To no avail, so Dol tries, in order, "sovereign," "general," "masters," then "gentlemen" again. By this point Face and Subtle are reduced to epithets: "Cheater," "Bawd," "Cow-herd," "Conjuror," "Cut-purse," "Witch." Dol tries one last time:

> O me!
> We are ruin'd! lost! Ha' you no more regard
> To your reputations? Where's your judgment? 'Slight,
> Have yet some care of me, o' your republic—

To call the union of a shaman, a rogue, and a whore a "republic" is a joke, the word too big for Dol's mouth. But Dol has in fact hit upon the right word, though none of the three believes it. When "republic" is not enough to stop the quarrel, Dol then launches into a speech that offers no such ideal term for their game and its stakes.

But the play then reverberates the joke, and we are left to do more than laugh at the fact that this con game is no republic. When the game is at its best, the players are a republic, expressing in their ways the ideal of preimperial Rome; then Subtle is indeed an alchemist, Face his acolyte, and Dol the Queen of the Fairies, because others think they are, which is all that is necessary for this con game to be a republic. Thus, when first gulling Ananias, Face and Subtle offer a catechism about something every bit as mysterious as the Eucharist:

> *Subtle.*   Your magisterium now?
>   What's that?
> *Face.*   Shifting, sir, your elements,
>   Dry into Cold, cold into moist, moist into hot,
>   Hot into dry.
> *Subtle.*   This's heathen Greek to you, still?
>   Your *Lapis philosophicus?*
> *Face.*   'Tis a stone
>   And not a stone; a spirit, a soul, and a body;
>   Which, if you do dissolve, it is dissolv'd,
>   If you coagulate, it is coagulated,
>   If you make it to fly, it flieth.

It is a play about belief, not just about the clash of belief against fact, but of the triumph of belief over fact, and of the surliness of those who believe that is not possible. Jonson moves among motives for believing, and the lore of believers, with an ease that never regards its learnedness; he triumphs by sustaining a large number of traditions even as he creates a realistic London scene of 1611.

Above all, he shows that Subtle and Face fail when they fail their republic, cheapen the game, doubt the magic, and fall into a scramble for control of a republic-turned-empire. The community here, however, is not only the one enacted between Face, Subtle, and Dol, but also between Jonson and his audience. It consists of those who laugh when Dol says "republic," and when

Face and Subtle preach the Eucharist to Ananias, but its central members are those who know that all republics and all Eucharists are created by communities that know that fictions sustain, and traditions hold, even as they are shown to fail. No nostalgist, no snob, Jonson knows that when fictions sustain and traditions are strong, then the present is a rich time. Which is why *Bartholemew Fair* is the greatest of all holiday works, the holiday-maker-author himself not once going on holiday.

The poems, not often needing this great comic sense of clash and upholding, can work differently, since they require no Celia, no Surly, to carp or refuse, and need only a rich sense of a present occasion to call forth extravagant and decorous responses. One such occasion is the publication of the first folio of Shakespeare's plays. No need to collide learned tradition against fact, or to list faults that Shakespeare committed and Jonson abhorred. No need either to flatter or to lie, and all in Jonson's ideal community and perhaps many in his actual one would know why. Shakespeare was not just for an age, but for all time. That is what Jonson meant, if not all that he meant, and so his praise remains, the simplest and truest truth ever said about his subject.

An even more telling display of extravagant decorousness can be seen in the most striking moments in Jonson's three poems on the death of children. His daughter, dead at six months:

> This grave partakes the fleshly birth.
> Which cover lightly, gentle earth.

His son, dead at seven years:

> Rest in soft peace, and, ask'd, say here doth lye
> *Ben. Jonson* his best piece of poetrie.

Solomon Pavy, a child actor:

> And know, for whom a teare you shed,
> Death's selfe is sorry.

Each is so responsive to its situation that the lines of one poem would be out of place in either of the other two. In each case, an audience is created in Jonson's typical sense of the social, with slight, telling verbal gestures—"cover lightly, gentle earth,"

"And ask'd, say," "And know"—but readers of all three poems in the context of all Jonson's poems have a fuller sense of audience than this. Lord Herbert of Cherbury, in "Elegy over a Tomb," Henry King in his "Exequy," and William Browne in "On the Countess Dowager of Pembroke," each wrote a poem celebrating a death that can match any of these of Jonson's, and Carew on the death of Donne outdoes them all. But these writers, by comparison with Jonson, had a simple felt sense of occasion as something that could compel verse. Jonson had this, to be sure, but for him being a poet of occasion was a full-time and lifelong occupation. So, looking at his entire output, which of course the careful preparation of his works for publication insured inasmuch as this was within Jonson's power to achieve, we can see variety in tone matching variety in occasion, extravagance coming to seem a way of being decorous, by turns coarse, dignified, ribald, warm, austere, noisy, terse. Gentlemen versify, often superbly; Jonson, no gentleman, is a poet.

He is the essential Renaissance writer, claiming and reclaiming, acknowledging loss and disappearance but discovering triumphs over these. The long continuity had been sufficiently endangered that it could not be had for the asking, but could still be regained. Jonson had been a pupil of William Camden's at Westminster School, though how he got there is a mystery, and after he left he became apprentice to a bricklayer. Hugh Kenner, whose instinct for the ways writers adjust to gaining and losing is unparalleled, describes Jonson's response:

> But Camden's precepts stayed by him: not only the injunction to work out his sense in prose before turning it into verse, but the conviction that a man was obliged to acquire all the learning he could master, and the vocation of bringing to the workings of the mind, even its casual or ephemeral workings, whatever analogies were discernible with all that antiquity had thought and said.

Had Jonson become a university scholar or a churchman, he would have left his learning halfway complete, content that the father tongue had taught him all he needed to know to say what it had revealed to him. But these professions were, fortunately given the outcome, closed to him, and he ended up in the theater, *the* place in the late 1590s where the mother tongue was being renewed by men who had learned their humanistic father tongue. There everything learned had to be made active, and expressed in a vital English. At the outset, in the Humour and theater war plays, Jonson is a little stiff, stating his learning as a kind of ideal only. But first in *Sejanus,* and then triumphantly in *Volpone* and *The Alchemist,* the learning is made instinct, part of gestures made by everyone, knave and fool, the wooing Volpone and the would-be-wooed Lady Pol.

Jonson was rightly proud of his achievement, but in the same years of his great comedies he had the good fortune to be asked to write masques for the court of James I. He wrote these creations of real communities transformed into ideal ones so well he might have made a career of writing them alone. Instead, he moved into the Great World, his success on the stage and at court giving him a confidence most gentlemen found hard to come by: "Poets are far rarer births than kings," he wrote, boldly, and truly. The result was the great set pieces like "To Penshurst" and the Cary and Morison ode and "An Elegie on the Lady Jane Pawlet." It was also something that could be expressed as well in a slight poem:

> Madame, I told you late how I repented,
>> I ask'd a lord a buck, and he denyed me;
> And, ere I could ask you, I was prevented:
>> For your most noble offer had supply'd me.
> Straight went I home; and there most like a Poet,
>> I fancied to my selfe what wine, what wit
> I would have spent: how every Muse should know it,
>> And Phoebus-selfe should be at eating it.
> O Madame, if your grant did thus transferre mee,
>> Make it your gift. See whither it will beare mee.

Looking at those rhymes, and seeing the gracefulness of the mocking, respectful playfulness of the created relation of poet to patron, one sees the impropriety of speaking of Jonson's "major" or "minor" poems when all that ever alters is the occasion. To the same Countess of Bedford to whom this is addressed, Samuel Daniel could only bow, and Donne could only be learned and nervous. Here everything except the parsimonious lord is made to shine: the generous countess, wine, wit, the feast for Apollo, and above all, the created community. He did not give, you gave, I give in return; whatever Jonson's actual relations with the countess were, here they are worldly and ideal simultaneously.

⫸⫸⫸⫸Jonson's was such a commanding presence, his tongue was so sharp, his sense of himself so secure, his temper so uncertain, that it might seem he would cast a long shadow, especially over younger writers who sought to be sealed in the Tribe of Ben. For these writers in the next two generations, he was there, certainly, as no one had been for him, but it was an ideal as well as a real community he had made, and those who shared his ideal of poetry could therefore be nurtured by him.

Thomas Carew's antecedents were different from Jonson's. He was born in 1595, when Jonson was in his twenties and beginning his work in the theater; he was the son of a landed gentleman and faintly related to many distinguished Caries. He resembled Jonson most in succeeding by assuming he would. At a time when his father's fortunes were collapsing, and young Carew could count on nothing from him, he managed to get himself cashiered from a post with Sir Dudley Carleton, ambassador to Venice. He did it by making fun of Carleton in a piece of writing, and by not caring if Carleton saw it. But somehow this same arrogant insouciance worked to obtain him a position as Sewer to Charles I, and Carew spent his last fifteen years at court, where he could be idle, woo women, and write poems.

Little is known of Carew's personal relations with Jonson, but we can say he was not the most ardent member of the Tribe. One James Howells, in a letter of April 5, 1636, offers this description of an evening:

> I was invited yesternight to a solemn Supper, by B. J. . . . there was good company, excellent cheer, choice wines and jovial welcome: One thing intervened, which almost spoil'd the relish of the rest, that B. began to engross all the dis-

course, to vapour extremely of himself, and by vilifying others, to magnify his own Muse. T. Ca. buzz'd me in the ear, that tho' Ben. had barrell'd up a great deal of knowledge, yet it seems that he had not read the *Ethiques* which, among other precepts of Morality, forbid self-commendation, declaring it to be an ill-favour'd solecism in good manners.

That Jonson could, especially when relaxed, puff himself tiresomely is well known, and by 1636, aged sixty-four and with only a year to live, he was perhaps more given to vaporing than earlier. Carew's response shows a wit and an insolent assurance characteristic of him; he would buzz Howells rather than be bothered with the consequences of confronting the great man. But this was not Carew's only, or most important, attitude toward Jonson.

Much earlier, in 1616, Jonson had written a play, *The Devil Is an Ass,* that was ill received, and he resolved to write no more plays. After James I died in 1625, however, Jonson's pension was reduced, and the invitations to write new masques became infrequent, so Jonson returned to the stage. He wrote three plays in the next six years: *The Staple of News, The New Inn,* and *The Magnetic Lady.* Dryden refers to these plays as Jonson's dotages, and if they aren't that, they certainly are inferior, and nowhere near as good as his poems and masques of the same time.

When *The New Inn* was coldly received, Jonson replied with his second "Ode to Himself," a much better work than the play that occasioned it:

> Come leave the loathed Stage,
> And the more loathsome Age,
> Where pride and impudence in faction knit,
> Usurpe the Chaire of wit:
> Inditing and arraigning every day,
> Something they call a Play.
> Let their fastidious vaine
> Commission of the braine,
> Runne on, and rage, sweat, censure, and condemn,
> They were not made for thee, lesse thou for them.

He appended this fine outpouring to his edition of the play, which carried the following on its title page: "A Comedy. As it was never acted, but most negligently play'd, by some, the Kings Servants, and censured by others, the Kings Subjects. Now, at last, set at liberty to the Readers, his Majesties Servants, and Subjects, to be Judg'd."

For Carew, or any member of the Tribe, the prudent thing to do would have been nothing at all, but Jonson demanded more than that. He demanded homage, but being better than his vanities, he demanded "to be Judg'd." So Carew wrote "To Ben. Johnson. Upon Occasion of his Ode of defiance annext to his Play of the New Inne." Just as there is point in saying Beethoven's First Symphony is one of Mozart's best, so there is point in saying that Carew's is one of Jonson's finest verse letters:

'Tis true (deare Ben) thy just chastizing hand
Hath fixt upon the sotted Age a brand
To their swolne pride, and empty scribbling due,
It can nor judge nor write, and yet 'tis true
Thy Commique Muse from the exalted line
Toucht by thy Alchymist, doth since decline
From that her Zenith, and foretells a red
And blushing evening, when she goes to bed,
Yet such, as shall out-shine the glimmering light
With which all stars shall guild the following night.

The verse is so easy and casually polished that a more slavish member of the Tribe might have found it impudent. All the opening concessions—"thy just chastizing hand" laid on "the sotted age" of "swolne pride and empty scribbling"—are made under the aegis of the opening " 'Tis true (deare Ben)," so we then wait for a second and modifying " 'tis true," which comes in the fourth line. Carew's tone is unanxious; he no more needs elaborate foot-scraping indirection than Jonson did when addressing the Countess of Bedford. Your greatest play was written years ago, and you have declined from your zenith. You are the sun still, to be sure, and your sunset will be "red and blushing"— from diffusion of your light, perhaps, or from silly rage, or even from chagrin at having to admit the justice of what I say.

These opening lines are bold, respectful, and grateful. Those who are growing old, or whose powers are diminishing, receive this news in many ways, but they usually try to work around the obvious facts, by little acts of self-deception, by emphasizing the compensations of age, by making it hard for others to notice. Those who write, especially those who write a great deal, have no desire to think their masterpiece was completed years earlier, though it is clear that only a few write their best works late. And as we settle into the truths by which we discover we live, we find it hard to imagine someone younger coming up with truths that can replace our own. How, then, to tell Jonson what he must in honesty be told? The best way is to dare to appeal to his best self, knowing that his vanity could not easily admit what his best self might. But it does take daring.

Carew can hope to succeed, however, not just by various acts of boldness and tact. He can do it only if he can, in his verse, compose Jonson, show how he has derived his own poetic strength from his master. I call this "composing" here rather than imitating not to make a distinction in kinds of act; "To Ben. Johnson" is clearly an imitation, but C. C. Colton's famous statement about the sincerest form of flattery can get in our way, as can the Augustan usage of "imitation." We need not worry if Carew is "sincere" in this poem, if he actually believes the age cannot judge or write or that Jonson's sunset will outshine all the stars that will follow. To compose is to honor, to repay, to take the gift Jonson gave him and make it serve the ideal community into which Jonson had ushered Carew. It is what many often find easier to do for their chosen parents than for their blood parents.

It is tempting to try to say what historical conditions may have been at work to allow such composing; Leavis, whose pages on Carew are among the best on record, puts it this way:

> What it represents is something immeasurably finer than, after the Civil Wars and the Interregnum, was there—was there at all, by any substitution—for the mob of gentlemen who wrote with ease: it represents a Court culture (if the expression may be permitted as a convenience) that preserved, in its sophisticated way, an element of the tradition of chiv-

alry and that had turned the studious or naively enthusiastic Renaissance classicizing into something intimately bound up with contemporary life and manners—something consciously both mature and, while contemporary, traditional.

This formulation is very suggestive, and accurate too, as a way of praising Jonson's achievement and, by extension of that, Carew's. It *is* an element of the tradition of chivalry that is at work in much of Jonson and in "To Ben. Johnson," and it *is* true that after the Civil War the court culture was by comparison crude, complacent, or, at best, worried. Furthermore, while Leavis is blind to the ways Sidney, Spenser, and Greville, those studious or naively classicizing poets, were themselves bound up with contemporary life and manners, one sees what the comparison is getting at. It is what Swift and Dr. Johnson meant when they wrote that the English language reached its apogee in the years just before the Civil War.

Yet, however suggestive Leavis is, he does not here seem good enough. He implicitly slights Carew's personal achievement by making it a matter of the court culture. The homage and assessment Carew offers here was not within the reach of Donne, in his verse letters at least, to say nothing of courtiers like Suckling and Lovelace. Of all Renaissance writers the only other who could have begun a letter this way is Jonson himself. Nor does it account for the fact that, at this same time but removed from the court culture, Herbert is taking what he learned, primarily from Donne we may assume, and making poetry as great or greater than Donne's, and more original than Carew's. Nor does Leavis seem adequately aware of other kinds of enrichment that had been possible for centuries, though often with centuries rather than a single generation intervening: for Vergil, Homer; for Dante, Vergil; for Ariosto, Boiardo; for Spenser, Ariosto. Finally, it ignores the huge reworking of traditional materials that Milton was beginning to undertake at this same time.

Of course these matters were not of immediate concern to Leavis when he was seeking to praise Carew's representative quality as a poet in the line of wit. Nor do I intend to pursue all the matters named above here, because to do so would be to distract us from Carew's way of composing Jonson. Perhaps I can, however, use another passage from Leavis's great chapter to indicate a necessary emphasis: "Donne, Ben Jonson, Herbert, Milton, Marvell, Dryden—it is a matchless array; and the lesser figures show, by their number and quality, how remarkably favourable to the development of its talent the century was. To start with Donne and Ben Jonson together was luck indeed; either was qualified to be a decisive force." All true. But I think there was something at work, in Donne, in Jonson, and in Shakespeare and Spenser too, that Leavis saw no need to get at. Kerrigan speaks of the great ambitiousness of many English Renaissance authors; as I have suggested, one ingredient in that ambition is a sense that tradition is something that must be *made,* and if it is not, chaos may well be come again. The confidence of those mighty egos had something to be urgent about. The case represented by each of the writers just mentioned is sufficiently different from that of the others that it would be beyond the powers of this essay to attempt to treat them all. For my purpose, the emphasis can fall on Jonson and Donne, and to add that no one was *there* for them as *they* were for Carew, Herbert, Marvell, and the young Milton. So that these second- and third-generation seventeenth-century writers enact relations with their immediate predecessors that are more direct and personal than what is involved in the inheritance of a mode. One reason, perhaps, for Leavis's sense of the century as offering a matchless array is that we are seeing here something that both continues the long line of tradition extending down from Homer and the Hebrew scripture and something new, a nurturing, an enabling, of children by their parents.

"I will compose Ben Jonson," Carew offers at the outset of his letter, to make his major point first so Jonson would know his follower had been enabled. He then proceeds to explore the implications of this composing:

> Nor thinke it much (since all thy Eaglets may
> Endure the Sunnie tryall) if we say
> This hath the stronger wing, or that doth shine

> Trickt up in fairer plumes, since all are thine;
> Who hath his flock of cackling Geese compar'd
> With thy tun'd quire of Swans?

The New Inn is minor stuff, its wings are weak and its plumage less than gorgeous. Yet it is Jonson's, not Richard Brome's or Thomas Killigrew's, and as Beatrix Potter once wrote: "A great master's worst pictures have generally something in them which is wanting in the best works of his inferiors." Coleridge also acknowledged this in a different way when he wrote marginal commentary for this very inferior Jonson play in question. If this is true, why then should Jonson rail:

> Why should the follies then of this dull age
> Draw from thy pen such an immodest rage
> As seems to blast thy (else-immortal) Bayes,
> When thine owne tongue proclaimes thy ytch of praise?
> Such thirst will argue drouth.

The itch of praise—for many, including Jonson, it is, more than fame, the last infirmity of a noble mind. Jonson was lordly, but incurably social too, and accustomed as he had been to the patronage of royalty, the hospitality of the landed, and the homage of the young, he itched for it and could not easily move into his last years without it.

If this was Jonson's besetting weakness, however, then say so and have done, because the real task is to show why the mob of hissers does not count. It may have been right about *The New Inn,* but it does not understand you, and so it seeks to expose as your weakness what is in fact the major source of your strength:

> . . . let the Rowte say,
> The running sands, that (ere thou make a play)
> Count the slow minutes, might a *Goodwin* frame
> To swallow when th' hast done thy ship-wrackt name.

From different angles, Shelley and the mob make the same mistake about Jonson: he wrote slowly, composed, deliberated. The hourglass drops so much sand before Jonson finishes a play that great sandbars—like the Goodwin in the English Channel—

could be made of it, and they might seem then dangerous enough
to wreck you. But:

> Let them the deare expence of oyle upbraid
> Suckt by thy watchfull Lampe, that hath betray'd
> To theft the blood of martyr'd Authors, spilt
> Into thy inke, whilst thou growest pale with guilt.

No scoffer ever put the case against Jonson so wittily: he increases the national debt by burning so much oil; his thefts from
other authors kill them and, rather than live off their blood, Jonson is pale with guilt.

This passage puts us in a good position to understand something important about the nature of tradition, and of inheritance,
in the English Renaissance. If we say of the eagle in "The Hus of
Fame," or of Chauntecleer in "The Nun's Priest's Tale," that they
are pedants, we are saying something about the spirit in which
they work, the results they seek to achieve, and not something
distinctive about their method. These birds are heirs to a tradition, and they pile up arguments to display their learning or to
enforce an argument. Chaucer, and all other medieval writers,
did the same; everyone was an inkhorn—so too, we might add,
were the authors of the four gospels, and so too, they claim, was
Jesus. There is little need at this point to say that for many centuries the argument from authority, the reference to earlier *auctores*
as sources of knowledge and wisdom, was the nerve and sinew of
discourse.

But something happened during the Renaissance. In his elegy
on the death of Donne, Carew speaks of Donne's predecessors as
overspreading "The Muses garden with Pedantique weedes"
planted by "the lazie seeds of servile imitation." In William Kerrigan's terms, humanist education often had the effect of leading
students from their mother tongue, teaching them their father
language, and leaving them there, either to continue their imitations in Latin, or in crudest English. Not everyone, in effect, fully
made the move back from metonymy to metaphor. There was a
puffing up, perhaps, similar to what we find in Chaucer's eagle
and rooster, made more extravagant but no more interesting by

the creation of an arena that seemed to admire such preening.

In the early 1590s, Thomas Nashe, in his preface to the *Menaphon* of his friend Robert Greene, spoke of "how eloquent our gowned age is grown of late," so that

> every mechanicall mate abhorreth the English he was borne too, and plucks, with a solemne peraphrasis, his *ut vales* from the inkehorne: which I impute, not so much to the perfection of Arts, as to the servile imitation of vaine glorious Tragedians, who contend not so seriously to excell in action, as to embowell the cloudes in a speech of comparison, thinking themselves more then initiated in Poets immortality, if they but once get *Boreas* by the beard and the heavenly Bull by the deawlap.

Later, in a passage made famous by its apparent reference to a play called *Hamlet* before Shakespeare's, Nashe contends:

> It is a common practise now a dayes amongst a sort of shifting companions, that runne through every Art and thrive by none, to leave the trade of Noverint, whereto they were borne, and busie themselves with the indeavours of Art, that could scarcely Latinize their neck verse if they should have neede; yet English *Seneca* read by Candlelight yeelds many good sentences, as *Blood is a begger*, and so forth; and if you intreate him faire in a frostie morning, hee will affoord you whole Hamlets, I should say handfuls of Tragicall speeches.

The immediate subject for Nashe, as for Carew in his poem to Jonson, is dramatists, but they clearly are not the only culprits.

It need not be that Renaissance inkhorns were different from earlier ones, but their particular odiousness, when they were odious, may have resulted from a different sense of their conditions. If Latin was not a living language for Chaucer, it was not yet dead, enshrined, entombed, a matter of books and learning, as it was for the Renaissance schoolboys. It could exist as a separate, father tongue, only if it were that. Ascham's *The Schoole-Master*, in that sense, could not have been written a century earlier. Much of the Elizabethan outpouring was, Nashe contends, bogus. Imitation in this bad sense represented an abortion of the maturing, ego-developing process Kerrigan sees when looking at Renaissance writers at their best. Most of the verse in most plays, and in most poems, in the years Jonson was growing up, was bad in just the way Nashe describes.

What Jonson saw was that the need was not to escape the process, but to do it right, which meant not to stand, hopelessly, in the position of one receiving an education and then mimicking in English what one had learned in school, but instead to work, long and hard, to find ways to make the glory of Latin literature—and, where it mattered, Italian literature—a glory of one's own:

> Repine not at the Tapers thriftie waste,
> That sleekes thy terser Poems, nor is haste
> Prayse, but excuse; and if thou overcome
> A knottier writer, bring the bootie home;
> Nor think it theft, if the rich spoyles so torne
> From conquered Authors, be as Trophies worne.

Carew's military language shows his sense of what had happened. Simple inheritance had become inkhorn hackwork, or else polite scribbling. Jonson had to create his tradition because it was no longer there, simply, to be inherited. It took all that oil, and a great conqueror, to make Latin antiquity part of Jonson's, and therefore Carew's, tradition. Just in the twenty years between Spenser and Jonson, the whole enterprise of English humanism had become sufficiently unglued, sufficiently in danger of being overtaken by grown-up schoolboys, so that the need of an heir to make had become urgent:

> Thy labour'd works shall live, when Time devours
> Th' abortive offspring of their hastie houres.
> Thou art not of their ranke, the quarrel lyes
> Within thine owne Virge, then let this suffice,
> The wiser world doth greater Thee confesse
> Then all men else, then Thy selfe onely lesse.

Leave the loathed stage if you will, accept my judgment of *The New Inn* only within your own virge (the twelve-mile limit established by the king's steward to proclaim the jurisdiction of the royal court). Remember there is a wiser world, know that I know it because you have taught me so, know that your lesser work must be judged by your greater, your sunset by your zenith, your itch of praise by your own condemnation of those you would have yourself be praised by.

The relation this fine poem establishes between Carew and Jonson is so strong one can easily become nostalgic about it, as implicitly Leavis becomes in "The Line of Wit." Nor, knowing what we know of later literary inheritances, is that nostalgia misplaced. Compared to the relation of many earlier writers to their predecessors, it is one that had to be created, earned, insisted upon; compared to many later inheritances, it is graceful and gratifying. For example, in 1805 Wordsworth visited Coleridge and read aloud parts of *The Prelude,* which he had just completed. Coleridge replied in "To William Wordsworth," and in the midst of his praise of Wordsworth's achievement, and his gratitude at having been part of its making, we see insidious comparing, sibling rivalry:

> Ah! As I listened with a heart forlorn,
> The pulses of my being beat anew:
> And even as Life returns upon the drowned,
> Life's joy rekindling roused a throng of pains—
> Keen pangs of Love, awakening as a babe
> Turbulent, with an outcry in the heart;
> And fears self-willed, that shunned the eye of Hope;
> And Hope that scarce would know itself from Fear;
> Sense of past Youth, and Manhood come in vain,
> And Genius given, and Knowledge won in vain;
> And all which I had culled in wood-walks wild,
> And all which patient toil had reared, and all,
> Commune with thee had opened out—but flowers
> Strewed on my corse, and borne upon my bier
> In the same coffin, in the selfsame grave.

Coleridge's composing in the blank verse of *The Prelude* is itself his homage, as Carew's verse letter couplets are his. But how sad, how needless, one wants to say, is Coleridge's use of Wordsworth to excoriate himself. Yet how much more familiar it is, too, than is Carew's strong gratitude that does not for a moment make him feel diminished. For Coleridge to attempt to compose Wordsworth is to collapse, to imagine his own death. Harold Bloom might cite Carew as the weaker poet of the two, but Carew's is incomparably the stronger poem.

But what it was possible for a writer to do as heir in 1629 was not, therefore, something easily done by many. Another comparison, offered by Herrick's "The Welcome to Sack":

Have I divorc't thee onely to combine
In hot Adult'ry with another Wine?
True, I confesse I left thee, and appeale
'Twas done by me, more to confirme my zeale,
And double my affection on thee; as doe those,
Whose love growes more enflam'd, by being Foes.
But to forsake thee ever, co'd there be
A thought of such like possibilitie?
When thou thy selfe dar'st say, thy Iles shall lack
Grapes, before *Herrick* leaves Canarie Sack.

There, if one likes, is an invitation to nostalgia. This is no inkhorn imitation, but tradition living on. If Herrick cannot be thoughtful about what he learned from Jonson, he can write Jonson poems cheerfully and splendidly, the placing of "Grapes" in the last line being especially felicitous. It was this that was lost by the time of Shelley's exaltation of the poet, this ability to adapt, almost to revel in being an excellent minor poet. Carew, I think, is better than this, but there is no difference in kind; Herbert's homage to Donne, if we should choose to call it that, is something far more original. Carew's specialness lies in his explicitness, in his social enactment of a relation to his master that confronts as well as embraces, but he too is content to walk in tracks already trod by another.

Nowhere, perhaps, is the excellence of his having learned Jonson's essential lesson more apparent than in his other critical masterpiece, "An Elegie upon the Death of the Deane of Pauls, Dr. John Donne." To understand Jonson, and his ideal of poet and poetry, is also to recognize Donne's importance. Though Jonson and Donne were exact contemporaries, the poetry for which Donne was, and is, best known had mostly been written before Carew was ten. That poetry had never been published, but for thirty years it had been the admired possession and plaything of gentlemen poets. Donne himself had not gone from zenith to sunset but from songs and sonnets to the pulpit, so that during Carew's maturity the libertine Jack Donne was a legendary figure in the background of the grave and witty dean of St. Paul's. There is no evidence that Carew knew Donne, and it is hard to imagine their relation, since Donne had long since left the kind of life Carew was resolutely continuing to live.

Carew, though, knew what he knew, and knew that admiration of Donne was his finest homage to Jonson:

> Can we not force from Widdowed Poetry,
> Now thou art dead (Great Donne) one Elegie
> To crowne thy Hearse? Why yet dare we not trust
> Though with unkneaded dowe-bak't prose thy dust,
> Such as the uncisor'd Churchman from the flower
> Of fading Rhetorique, short liv'd as his houre,
> Dry as the sand that measures it, should lay
> Upon thy Ashes, on the funerall day?

This is not the easy conversational opening of Carew's letter to Jonson. The occasion is different, and Donne is not Jonson.

Thus one is struck by the way it is difficult here to make out the plain sense of things, just as it often is with Donne himself. The second sentence snakes, piles up, reconsiders, and refuses grammar in the act of refusing to write dough-baked prose. Jonson might have deplored having "Why yet dare we not trust" followed by such a hefty subordinate phrase that "thy dust" is not easily identifiable as the object of the trust, or objected to having "Churchman" followed by three subordinate phrases before it gains its predicate. But Carew is doing it Donne's way, holding images and grammar in suspension, the mind taut and able to hold the language thus. By letting the dry-as-sand rhetoric stand analogous to and also against the dust and ashes of Donne, Carew takes us back, by the time we have finished the sentence, to the need for the hearse to be crowned by widowed poetry.

The next lines are difficult, but once we locate their intricacy, the major terms of Carew's praise will be clear:

But the flame
Of thy brave Soule, (that shot such heat and light,
As burnt our earth, and made our darknesse bright,
Committed holy Rapes upon our Will,
Did through the eye the melting heart distill;
And the deepe knowledge of darke truths so teach,
As sense might judge, what phansie could not reach;)
Must be desir'd for ever.

Carew will elucidate "our darknesse" later, and the "flame" of
Donne's soul is clarified in the next sentence where the fire heats
the "Delphique quire" that "kindled" the "Promethean breath"
of Donne; it "Glow'd here a while," but now lies quenched. But
one feels instinctively that the key phrase here is "Committed
holy Rapes upon our Will." It comes as a forced and unlikely appositive to the image of the bright fire lighting the dark earth, and
is followed by another unlikely appositive concerning the eye's
distillation of the melting heart. In forcing us to consider apparently dissimilar acts as though they could occur simultaneously
in a Donne poem, Carew himself performs the famous act of yok-
ing heterogeneous ideas together by violence.

Since "melting heart" is parallel to "our darknesse" and "our
Will," we may say that our will, and our darkness, is for a poetry
of the melting heart, and that that is a secular wish. Donne's rape
of our will is holy, casts an eye that distills the melting heart. But
we can also read the lines to say that Donne's flame melted his
own heart, brightened his own eye, which enabled him to rape
our wills. If we need an instance of this, we might cite "The Bait"
as a holy rape of those poems of the melting heart, Marlowe's
"Come live with me and be my love" and Ralegh's "If all the
world and love were young." But "The Bait" is small beer, and, as
we will see, trying to plug particular Donne poems into the context of Carew's argument is being more literal than the elegy really allows.

The couplet that closes the parenthesis offers a clarifying
paradox:

And the deepe knowledge of darke truths so teach,
As sense might judge, what phansie could not reach;)

We are familiar with the terms of the praise: Donne makes us think, and the poetry of "our darknesse" was a poetry of fancy that could not reach the dark truths lit by Donne's flame. But Donne's knowledge was so deep he could not only teach dark truths, but could make them so clear, or so palpable, that sense could understand them though they remain dark, or hidden, still. One hesitates to point to a passage and feel confident it is what Carew is thinking of, but this, from the end of "Satire iii" may help:

> As streames are, Power is; those blest flowers that dwell
> At the rough streames calm head, thrive and prove well,
> But having left their roots, and themselves given
> To the streames tyrannous rage, alas, are driven
> Through mills, and rockes, and woods, and at last, almost
> Consum'd in going, in the sea are lost:
> So perish Soules, which more chuse mens unjust
> Power from God claym'd, then God himselfe to trust.

Crudely put, the dark truth is this: acts that seem natural and easy can also be self-destructive and contrary to God's will; worse, at the time we perform these acts it may seem there was nothing we could have done about it. The flowers growing near the calm source of the stream of power thrive, but then, in the really dark phrase of the passage, "Having left their roots," they are doomed to a journey that leads to mauling and being swallowed by the sea. The power of the phrase lies in its ease and calmness. It is no act of rebellion or high ambition the flowers commit, just a "natural" going, giving themselves to the force of the water, a sign of shallow rootedness. Neither the danger nor the disobedience appears until the flowers have left, which of course is the way it usually is. The dark truth is there, and sense can judge it, see the ease of the flowers leaving their roots and the fatal consequences of their having done so.

But the fullest praise of such poetry demands we remember the context in which it was written:

> The Muses garden with Pedantique weedes
> O'rspred, was purg'd by thee; The lazie seeds

Of servile imitation throwne away;
And fresh invention planted. Thou didst pay
The debts of our penurious bankrupt age;
Licentious thefts, that make poetique rage
A Mimique fury, when our soules must bee
Possest, or with Anacreons Extasie,
Or Pindars, not their owne; . . .

Not just English Seneca read by candlelight, yielding *Blood is a begger*, but a whole generation of mimics incapable of understanding, or indifferent to knowing, that poetry is holy, a rage. " 'Fool,' said my Muse to me, 'look in thy heart and write!' " Yet Sidney was not often fool enough. Donne "open'd Us a Mine / Of rich and pregnant phansie," Carew goes on, "drawne a line / of masculine expression." Another comparison suggests itself. Here is part of one of Astrophil's Cupid poems:

On Cupids bow how are my heart-strings bent,
That see my wracke and yet embrace the same?
When most I glorie, then I feele most shame:
I willing run, yet while I run, repent,
My best wits still their owne disgrace invent,
My verie inke turnes straight to Stella's name;
And yet my words, as them my pen doth frame,
Advise themselves that they are vainely spent.

These are not the laziest seeds of servile imitation by any means, but we note that Sidney's fancy moves as a means of staying in the same place, as though the form were a vessel to be filled, an image to be sketched in. Now here is the end of Donne's meditation of Cupid, and failed love, "Love's Deitie," the poem that begins "I long to talk to some old lovers ghost / Who dyed before the god of Love was borne":

But every modern god will now extend
    His vast prerogative, as far as Jove.
To rage, to lust, to write to, to commend,
    All is the purlewe of the God of Love.

> Oh were wee wak'ned by this Tyrannie
>   To ungod this child againe, it could not bee
> I should love, who loves not mee.
>
> Rebell and Atheist too, why murmure I,
>   As though I felt the worst that love could doe?
> Love might make me leave loving, or might trie
>   A deeper plague, to make her love mee too,
> Which, since she loves before, I'am loath to see;
> Falshood is worse than hate; and that must bee,
>   If shee whom I love, should love mee.

Donne mines his "phansie," turns and turns on himself to see what it means to say there is a god of love, a need to be rid of that god, a deeper need to acknowledge there are pains in not loving. Thus exploring, he discovers an uncharacteristic truth: better that she hate me than she be forced to love me when she loves another. Spared that, he is spared the worst. The lines of masculine expression strike and strike, opening the mine, revealing the riches. No wonder someone in Carew's position could see only that nothing like this had happened before, which it hadn't, and could not see the greatness, or even the merit, in the poetry Donne was supplanting, which we can find occasionally in "Astrophil and Stella," occasionally in Marlowe's *Hero and Leander*, more frequently in Shakespeare's sonnets, and in long stretches of Spenser's *The Faerie Queene*.

Many in the century before Carew had felt the fault with English poetry lay not just in the servile imitation of ancient models, but in the language itself. The nature of modern English meter kept turning out to be intractable to notions of quantity, and could not be made to yield the ease of rhyme one could find, say, in Italian. Donne changed all that, at least as best he could:

> Thou shalt yield no precedence, but of time,
> And the blinde fate of language, whose tun'd chime
> More charmes the outward sense; Yet thou maist claime
> From so great disadvantage greater fame,
> Since to the awe of thy imperious wit

Our stubborne language bends, made only fit
With her tough-thick-rib'd hoopes to gird about
Thy Giant phansie, which had prov'd too stout
For their soft melting Phrases.

To make our language work, all sense of literal adaptation of antique models must be relinquished. Jonson is a warrior, conquering his knotty ancient authors; Donne is a cooper, bending the
staves of his language, too stout for the melting phrases of imitators, into barrels to hold his giant fancy.

Yet all that was a generation ago, and now "thou art gone,"
and those who cannot hope to match Donne can thrive by outliv-
ing him, by ungodding the god and once again putting up the
older, moldy ones:

. . . and thy strict lawes will be
Too hard for Libertines in Poetrie.
They will repeale the goodly exil'd traine
Of gods and goddesses, which in thy just raigne
Were banish'd nobler Poems, now, with these
The silenc'd tales o' th' Metamorphoses
Shall stuffe their lines, and swell the windy Page.

Libertines, who had had to acknowledge Donne as king, won't
wait long to rejoice in his departure, and to make a new anarchy,
a new apostasy. Carew was wrong; there were libertines in poetry, to be sure, but few even of them went back to sixteenth-
century "naive classicizing," and Herbert was at that moment
composing Donne with brilliance, and Marvell and Milton were
beginning. In fact, tradition had altered, what there was to be
handed down had changed.

But that matters little, since it is the occasion, not the impulse to
satire, that must govern here:

Oh, pardon mee, that breake with untun'd verse
The reverend silence that attends thy herse,
Whose awfull solemne murmures were to thee
More than these faint lines, A loud Elegie.

After Donne, it will be stuffed lines or else; much better silence. Yet Carew seeks pardon for his noise in a marvelous Donnean analogy and explanation:

> So doth the swiftly turning wheele not stand
> In th'instant we withdraw the moving hand,
> But some small time maintain a faint weake course
> By vertue of the first impulsive force:

Just as inertia will keep the wheel turning after the hand that impels it is removed, so will Donne's force allow for Carew faint lines while the wheel of the hearse still moves:

> And so whil'st I cast on thy funerall pile
> The crowne of Bayes, Oh, let it crack a while,
> And spit disdaine, till the devouring flashes
> Suck all the moysture up, then turne to ashes.

The image of the crown of bay leaves had had a long and honored history, one that would not last much longer, but perhaps never in that time had it been used so well. Donne is the monarch of wit during his own funeral, and spits disdain at Carew's homage; the flame is still there, and poetry is dying along with the poet, wit announcing its own last hour. Jonson would not have spit disdain at praise of him, but Donne would.

It is a poem worth going through with care many times. The argument is taut, the lines are difficult but they always reward, and the image of Donne that Carew creates here has never been improved upon. It is a great critical achievement, and should serve as a benchmark for critics and all others who necessarily come later, and whose subject must therefore be, in part, what it means to come later, to inherit, to compose with materials not one's own. Praise Jonson for his triumph over earlier poets, and for creating tradition; praise Donne for gleaning after others had harvested, a flame, an original, who cannot be said to be an heir and, so Carew thought, would have no heirs. Carew discovers who he is as he discovers them, creates them in the verse each taught him. If literary study were able to begin with these two honoring poems of Carew's, the result would be better criticism, better history, and a stronger sense of what a strong tradition is.

Carew's occasions were Jonson's ode and Donne's death, but I hope I have said enough of my sense of the whole period to be able to say that the fact of Jonson and the fact of Donne were the real occasions which Carew could not but honor. It is to our advantage that at least this one poet did his honoring with such loving explicitness. In the great writers just before and just after the turn of the seventeenth century—Spenser, Shakespeare, Donne, Jonson—we have many signs of an impending crisis. In Spenser, they are present only in the last book and a half of his massive poem; what precedes them in *The Faerie Queene* is perhaps the last serene celebration of the old tradition, and, because Shakespeare, Donne, and Jonson followed so soon after, Spenser quickly became an "older" poet, and his contribution to living poetry has never been large. Shakespeare, perhaps because his work was almost entirely done for the public stage, perhaps because his relation to the past was always somewhat sporadic and incidental, did become the first looming shadow, and his immediate heirs, Webster, Beaumont and Fletcher, Ford, and Massinger, were the first writers to feel an anxiety of influence; what blank verse, or what drama had been before Shakespeare ceased to matter for Jacobean and Caroline tragedians.

With Jonson and Donne we see the need for them to be conquerors and monarchs. In the sixteenth century, imitation in the narrow sense yielded only a schoolboy's relation to the past; the deadness of Latin did not mean that it was lost, but that for it to be a vital literary and human force more had to be done than can be found in all but the best Elizabethan poetry, almost all of which was written by Spenser. This is Jonson's achievement, not to look like the great original he was, just as Donne's was to be anyone's idea of a great original. But the originality of both lay in a kind of revitalizing of poetic possibility, using the language, the conceits, the ideas that had accumulated for upwards of two thousand years, but reworking their relevance—Jonson in his lifelong dedication to making all human situations an occasion for poetry,

Donne in his insistent probing, so that his mind seems both taut and leaping, of the latent possibilities in his received metaphors.

But because their energy and originality lay in no new materials, no search for yet newer materials was incumbent upon their successors. What there was to be said, as it were, was what there had always been to be said. The fidelity to thought and feeling, as Eliot called it, the insistent tracings of a mind's workings, and the creations of forms that might help shape but could never dictate those workings—these anyone might do who had mind and imagination worthy the task: for this the seventeenth century is remarkable. When Dapper can court his mistress out of Ovid, more is called for than imitation, and more was at hand.

If one were to attempt anything like a full description of inheritance after Jonson and Donne—in Herbert, and then in the followers of Herbert, in the superb assimilating poetry of Marvell, and in the massive instance of Milton—then choosing an admittedly minor poet like Thomas Carew to serve as a central figure would have to seem evasive. But my intention has been to show how, in the midst of what were to be decisive changes, a writer was enabled by large predecessors who were clearly his superior —and for this Carew offers a shining instance. And it helps, too, to find in this instance one who wants to be explicit about his debt, a critic who can thereby show the way in which criticism can be most valuable when it is most accurate, most grateful, most intimately related to its subjects, strong because weak. In a book dedicated to finding such strength out of such weakness, Carew is the patron saint.

≫≫≫ The two great occasional poems of the middle of the seventeenth century are Milton's "'Lycidas" and Marvell's "Horatian Ode upon Cromwell's Return from Ireland." In both poems is a sense of strain, of the poets' having to do many things at once in order to hold poet, poem, and occasion together, and this is the source of their greatness. Yet by comparison to Carew's verse letter and elegy, we see how the taking and seizing of occasions had become more effortful and self-reflexive. By the time we reach "To the pious Memory of the Accomplished Young Lady Mrs.

Anne Killigrew," the strain is gone, but something much less flexible and more hortatory has replaced it. A difficulty that Carew did not have is made evident in Milton and Marvell and then is covered over in Dryden. Occasion as Jonson and Carew had known it was lost.

Something happened around the turn of the seventeenth century, a crisis that Donne, Jonson, and Shakespeare announced and helped create. Something happened as well at the time of the Civil War and the Commonwealth, and attempts have been made from the Restoration to the present to say what this second change was, and what its consequences were. Something happened, too, in the middle of the eighteenth century, when Pope announced the onset of eternal darkness. It would be convenient if the Renaissance, and the much longer period of which it was the end, could have managed its demise more quickly, or if the more modern world that was to replace it had announced its coming with a single blast of a trumpet. But between the time that Hamlet said this goodly frame the earth was to him a sterile promontory and Pope lowered the curtain and darkness fell, each generation had to make a new assessment of what had happened, and of how to proceed. We need not trace all these changes, but some account, however brief, is needed before we can properly see why Pope is in important ways the last Renaissance writer and why Johnson wrote in darkness.

During the Restoration, one presumption was that writers like Denham and Waller, Suckling and Lovelace, had tamed English numbers and brought a grace and ease to poetry that it hitherto had little known. Carew's prediction of a time after the death of Donne when libertines in poetry would once again be set loose was not altogether wrong; Donne's dark truths were followed by poets who more charmed the outward sense, especially when "sense" could be made to include the lazier parts of the mind that simply ask an argument to follow along easily. Whatever was lost, it was incumbent on those who noted the changes to insist on what had been gained.

Johnson's *Lives of the English Poets*, reflecting the understanding of late eighteenth-century booksellers, effectively begins with the middle of the seventeenth century: Herbert, Jonson, Carew, and Marvell are unmentioned, and Donne comes in only as a way of describing Cowley. A century later, working much less copiously, Matthew Arnold calls Dryden and Pope poets of a great age of prose that had followed the great poetic age that, for him, had reduced itself to Shakespeare and Milton. Later still, Eliot posits a dissociation of sensibility that took place in the middle of the seventeenth century as the result of the massive influence of Milton and Dryden. Leavis adds that something went out of court life in the interregnum so that contact with an ideal community was lost. Hugh Kenner writes of Waller: "His poems have two salient qualities only; a readily paraphrasable argument, developed in easy steps, and a knack for fitting sentences which never arrest the mind to cadences which never impede the tongue. Both qualities recommended him to an age which strove toward other criteria than these, but judged these indispensable." Admiration of Waller did not last much more than a century, but it was long after that that a reasonable assessment of the Commonwealth-Restoration gains and losses became possible. It was easier to say that something had happened than to say what, how, or why.

Carew composed Donne in "An Elegie," while Pope wrote "The Satires of Dr. John Donne, Versified." Though it is significant that Pope could only call Carew "a lesser Waller," the attempt to achieve standards for an Augustan civilization did not lead Dryden or Pope to ignore, or denigrate, Chaucer, Shakespeare, Jonson, or Donne, but it did mean that, after the Restoration, many felt that a break had been made, and some improvements too. Since a readily paraphrasable argument and cadences that never impede the tongue were indispensable, earlier English writers came to be thought of as expressing themselves in an inferior language, or, at least, distinctly different and past. "We write in sand, our language grows," Waller writes,

> *Chaucer* his Sense can only boast
> The Glory of his Numbers lost;
> Years have defac'd his matchles Strain,
> And yet he did not Sing in vain.

Waller would never have dreamed of composing Chaucer, in the sense I speak of Carew doing with Jonson. Nor did Dryden compose Shakespeare, or Pope compose Donne. A break is there, a sense of lost continuity, and when the break came, the possibility of inheritance we have seen in Carew is at least distinctly altered.

One constellation of results has been very well identified by Christopher Ricks in "Allusion: The Poet as Heir." Noting Harold Bloom's tendency sometimes to speak of "the poet" as though all poets were "High Romantic" or "post-Cartesian," Ricks shows that in the cases of Dryden and Pope we have poets who gratefully acknowledge fathers and speak of themselves as heirs. They do this, very often, by means of allusions to their predecessors' work which express an inheritance while showing that their aims are both similar and different. Thus:

> High on a gorgeous seat, that far out-shone
> Henley's gilt tub, or Fleckno's Irish throne,
> Or that where on her Curls the Public pours,
> All bounteous, fragrant Grains and Golden showers,
> Great Cibber sate . . .

Here we not only have the long series of echoes of Satan on his throne at the opening of Book 2 of *Paradise Lost*, which acknowledge that in the creation of epic triumphant villainy Pope could not but rework Milton, but also the allusion to Flecknoe, which acknowledges that in the creation of mock epic triumphant villainy Pope could not but bow to Dryden.

This is different from what we have seen in Carew's letter and elegy, different from the relation of "Come my Celia" to "Vivamus mea Lesbia." Dryden and Pope allude so that the ancestor is acknowledged and "placed," as one belonging to an earlier era, an era, perhaps, less threatened by ignorance or vulgarity, by writers who imitated poorly or failed to see the need that allusion meets. Shadwell, as Dryden proclaims the matter, had failed to understand Jonson, and had thus become Flecknoe's true heir. Christopher Ricks points out that in the following lines Dryden was not only thus proclaiming, but stating his own ancestry:

> Nor let false friends seduce thy mind to fame,
> By arrogating Johnson's Hostile name.

> Let Father Flecknoe fire thy mind with praise,
> And Uncle Ogleby thy envy raise.

Jonson is hostile to Shadwell, and even Ogleby can only make him envious. But behind these lines also lies Vergil:

> ecquid in antiquam virtutem animosque virilis
> et pater Aeneas et avunculus excitat Hector?

We all have fathers, and uncles, the task being to say who is rightly whose.

In this there is a kind of embattled subtlety that Carew would not have seen the need for. Dryden and Pope approach their occasions more stiffly than Jonson or Carew did theirs; their couplets, which are among the glories of English verse, never can gain the adaptability of verse rhythms to spoken rhythms that one finds in Donne, Jonson, and Carew. Occasion tends toward formal occasion, especially in Dryden, so that Jonson's way of being social is soon misunderstood and then undervalued. Of course Jonson often felt beleaguered, felt that many around him were buffoons and scribblers, but that called for no cool reassessment from him, or for any response that indicated his sense of himself as poet was truly threatened. Of course, too, if we compare Jonson, Dryden, and Pope, considered as continuers of a traditional line of poetry, to nineteenth-century poets, then they all seem rather like each other in their aims, and often in their means. But the break is there nonetheless.

We do well to honor Eliot's choices of Milton and Dryden as the two inaugurators of change. Milton's relation to his poetic past was more intricate, more obscure, and far more voracious than Carew's, and he, like Jonson, had to triumph over those he most honored in order to redeem them. Feeling himself free, but feeling the world he faced to be everywhere in chains, he launched such a massive, and such a massively self-conscious literary effort, that he makes Jonson, in these respects like him, seem almost a singer of native wood-notes wild. He effectively cut off many later writers from earlier ones. The presence of Milton transformed Spenser into a specialized poet of dream allegory, a medieval to be honored when medieval was in vogue. If Milton could not cut later writers off from Shakespeare, he could alter the way they read him, especially in the years after Pope's death and the onset of universal darkness. He made literary poets of the eighteenth century seem small, and disabled. Blake and Keats wrestled with him as with a father, thus beginning that tradition of belatedness, as Bloom calls it. Though it was not a matter entirely of his own contriving, no one could be an heir to Milton, no one could compose Milton. What Carew had managed with Jonson and Donne could be managed no more.

Dryden was a more explicit critic and a more professional writer than Milton, and he said often what he was doing, and why, in many ruminations on literary tradition—most of our ideas of tradition were first formulated by him. W. Jackson Bate has made much of one of these ruminations, from the opening of "To my dear friend Mr. Congreve":

> Well then, the promis'd hour is come at last:
> The present age of wit obscures the past:
> Strong were our sires, and as they fought they writ,
> Conqu'ring with force of arms, and dint of wit;
> Theirs was the giant race, before the flood;
> And thus, when Charles returned, our empire stood,
> Like Janus, he the stubborn soil manured,
> With rules of husbandry the rankeness cured;
> Tam'd us to manners, when the stage was rude;
> And boistrous English wit with art indued.
> Our age was cultivated thus at length,
> But what we gain'd in skill we lost in strength.
> Our builders were with want of genius curst;
> The second temple was not like the first.

But this is not so much a statement of the past as burden as a way of establishing a comparison that will tilt the balance between Renaissance and Restoration, now favoring this, now that, in order to praise Congreve:

> This is your portion; this your native store;
> Heav'n', that but once was prodigal before,
> To Shakespeare gave as much; she could not give him more.

Bate is so intent on describing a neoclassic dilemma, a second temple not like the first, that he does not quote these lines, for Dryden the crucial ones in his praise of Congreve.

What Dryden does offer us, here and in many other places, is the sense of a break between his age and the former one; the past had passed. Near the beginning of his career, in "An Essay of Dramatic Poetry," he has Neander state this sense of the situation, in drama at least:

> Yet give me leave to say this much, without injury to their ashes; that not only we shall never equal them, but they could never equal themselves, were they to rise and write again. We acknowledge them our fathers in wit, but they have ruined their estates themselves, before they came to their children's hands. There is scarce an humour, a character, or any kind of plot, which they have not blown upon. All comes sullied or wasted to us: and were they to entertain this age, they could not now make so plenteous treatments out of such decayed fortunes. This therefore will be a good argument to us, either not to write at all, or to attempt some other way.

Though Neander is arguing only for the possibility of serious drama in rhyme, his sense of the race of giants before the flood is not, clearly, restricted to a matter of versification. They were, and they did so much we must acknowledge ourselves as their heirs, unable to do what they did.

Carew, or Herbert, or Marvell, or Milton would not have felt this way about any they acknowledge as masters, or fathers. Composing, in the sense I have used the term to describe Carew's imitations of Jonson and Donne, was possible, one presumes, for Dryden, but composing was what Shadwell had done. Dryden had to attempt some other way, and, it seems clear, he felt he and others of his time had found another way:

> Thus Jonson did mechanic humour show,
> When men were dull, and conversation low,
> Then comedy was faultless, but 'twas coarse:
> Cobb's tankard was a jest, and Otter's horse.

And as their comedy, their love was mean:
Except, by chance, in some one labour'd scene,
Which must attone for an ill-written play,
They rose, but at their height could seldom stay.

This comes from the "Epilogue to the Second Part of *The Conquest of Granada*" in 1672, and in his "Defense" of this epilogue, Dryden explains: "Yet would I so maintain my opinion of the present age as not to be wanting in my veneration for the past: I would ascribe to dead authors their just praises in those things wherein they have excelled us; and in those wherein we contend with them for preeminence, I would acknowledge our advantages to the age, and claim not victory from our wit." This was not his last word, as we know from the letter to Congreve, but it shows Dryden's characteristic measured sense as well as his nervousness about what he and his age could do. *All for Love* is aware of *Antony and Cleopatra* at every turn, as is *Truth Found Too Late* of *Troilus and Cressida*. In the one he deliberately wrote in blank verse "to imitate the divine Shakespeare," because he thought he could do something different in his management of character and action; in the other he used heroic couplets, neatened the action, pointed the moral, because he thought the work was part of Shakespeare's apprenticeship, something he wearied of long before the end.

In all this what one is most aware of is self-consciousness, a sense that one must always be comparing oneself to the past, weighing virtues and faults, making one's own way by doing better what the previous age had done ill or doing what it had left undone. But I have no sense that Dryden was crippled in all this, that he wrote less well than he might have because of his self-consciousness. Carew's way, which is essentially to say, "Because you are, I am," seems unknown to him. Rather, Dryden's stance is "Because you were, I am grateful, I am aware of coming later, and here are my acknowledgments." Dryden's culture was, in important ways, still Homer's, and Vergil's, and Shakespeare's; if his was later, and necessarily different, he was not cut off from theirs, which is why his critical writings are so rich in offering us a sense of tradition, of long eras, classical and Christian, ancient,

French, and English, of gains and losses, of which he is the inheritor. To speak across a chasm is for Dryden a position that never implied he could not see what was on the other side.

Something happened, then, around the end of the sixteenth century, which created a strenuousness in the making and remaking of inheritance in Jonson, and, in different ways, in Donne and Shakespeare. By comparison with later eras, this strenuousness may seem as easy as breathing, though it could not have seemed so at the time. Jonson's contemporaries thought of him as labored, inkhorn; Dryden said of him in this respect only "you will pardon me, therefore, if I presume he loved their fashion, when he wore their clothes." Carew, though, knowing enough of this "something" to be grateful for what Jonson and Donne had given him, could make himself by remaking them. After him, another "something happened," a new sense of a break, of having to compare present and past, such that "the last age" comes into play as a critical historical term as never before, or since.

There was to be another "something" forty years after Dryden's death, not so much an event as the announcement of an end of millennia of events. On the one side of the announcement is the announcer, Pope; on the other side is the heir, Samuel Johnson. But to be on the other side of *that* was to be a different kind of heir.

3 ○ *Johnson in Darkness*

BOSWELL often asked Johnson to compare the present time with that of Johnson's youth. "Ah, sir," Johnson might reply, "hadst *thou* lived in those days! It is not worth being a dunce now, when there are no wits." But, more frequently, he will insist that the past not be automatically deferred to:

> I am always angry when I hear ancient times praised at the expense of modern times. There is now a great deal more learning in the world than there was formerly; for it is universally diffused. You have, perhaps, no man who knows as much Latin and Greek as Bentley; no man who knows as much mathematicks as Newton; but you have many more men who know Greek and Latin, and who know mathematicks.

Or:

> BOSWELL. "Is there not less religion now in the nation, than formerly?" JOHNSON. "I don't know, Sir, that there is." BOSWELL. "For instance, there used to be a chaplain in every great family, which we do not find now." JOHNSON. "Neither do you find many of the state servants which great families used formerly to have. There is a change of modes in the whole department of life."

Johnson was well known as one who loved to argue on the other side of the question, to laugh, to be pugnacious, to show off his conversational skill. But this was only part of his tireless pursuit of cant, of easy attitudes, especially when they were solemnly expressed. There seemed to be so much dust on the furniture of most peoples' minds. He knew, in his early London years, that there were many who were outraged and alarmed at the excesses of Robert Walpole's government, and the corruption at the court of George II and Queen Caroline; he knew that such rage was mostly spite, and such alarm mostly pother, and he lived long enough to say, in the "Life of Thomson": "At this time a long course of opposition to Sir Robert Walpole had filled the nation with clamours for liberty, of which no man felt the want, and with care for liberty, which was not in danger." Or, when Boswell raised the subject of our feeling for the distresses of others: "Why, Sir, there is much noise made about it, but it is greatly exaggerated. No, Sir, we have a certain degree of feeling to prompt us to do good; more than that, Providence does not intend. It would be misery to no purpose."

Almost every one of Johnson's most famous statements is a cheerful and grim undermining, an exploding. There are no magical loyalties, there are no pastoral ties, Edward King and John Milton were never shepherds, and people who go to the theater know where they are:

> Delusion, if delusion be admitted, has no certain limitation; if the spectator can be once persuaded, that his old acquaintance are Alexander and Caesar, that a room illuminated with candles is the plain of Pharsalia, or the bank of Granicus, he is in a state of elevation above the reach of reason, or of truth, and from the heights of empyrean poetry, may despise the circumscriptions of terrestrial nature. . . . The truth is, that the spectators are always in their senses, and know, from the first act to the last, that the stage is only a stage, and that the players are only players.

The doctrine of dramatic unities had been cant for centuries, and Johnson refutes it *thus*. On the same day that he made his most famous refutation, of Bishop Berkeley's argument about the nonexistence of matter, he is also trying to clear Boswell's mind: "Don't, Sir, accustom yourself to use big words for little matters. It would *not* be *terrible*, though I *were* to be detained some time here." We are not the paragon of animals, like angels in apprehension, like a god, and please, Sir, remember that. The voice is gruff, alert, and compassionate, because there is nothing too little for such a little creature as man.

Johnson belonged to the old culture, and knew no other, but he came at its end, and, not realizing that, he knew that common sense and not poetry, empirical observation and not theory, cheerful opposition rather than applause, were essential. It was his way of being wise, and he seems not to have known that it was a way of being wise that he practically invented. Furthermore, since cant and camp following have not disappeared from the earth, the voice can still seem wonderfully bracing and useful; we quote Johnson more than anyone else as a way of stating the opposing case, or of reminding. Thus it may seem strange to say he could not see what perhaps many people later do not see, that Johnson comes at the end of the line, is the last great figure of the old culture.

Marvin Mudrick, who delights in creating historical figures with a minimum of surrounding historical context, describes Johnson as follows:

> Johnson reacts with a bang or merely broods, he doesn't dispose his efforts for the sake of sustained effects, he's a great writer only when he hasn't time to think. His sufficient provocation is any mass of particulars that will take his mind off itself: the words of his *Dictionary* demanding their definitions and illustrative citations; the *Lives of the Poets* compelling him to produce assessments of a miscellany of poems by his subjects and make practical inquiries in search of data, recollections, gossip, anecdote, "something to say [as he observes in a letter to Mrs. Thrale] about men of whom I know nothing but their verses, and sometimes very little of them"; Shakespeare's text, for which Johnson, assembling his edition of it, has to work up explanatory notes that from the day they were published have constituted the one readable book of Shakespeare commentary; or, best of all, conversation, in which, though the topics may be general, at all events his cronies are such specific and irresistible quarry that he can

run them down ("toss and gore" them, says Boswell) without even resorting to pen and paper.

As one might well imagine, to see Johnson's greatness in his
more improvised effects is to care little for *The Rambler* and *Rasselas:*

> "Every mind, however vigorous or abstracted, is necessi-
> tated by its present state of union to receive its information
> and execute its purpose by the intervention of the body," in-
> tones the Rambler, public monitor and scold, sicklied o'er
> with the pale cast of platitude, having to crank out one more
> weekly essay, indulging his weakness and sickness of spirit,
> the same mind abstracted and dim that in a tavern or draw-
> ingroom turns privately vigorous and incandescent.

Which seems to me true, but not true enough.

A Dictionary of the English Language is Johnson's masterpiece because in it he could "take his mind quite off itself" and also be
"public monitor and scold," and do both as a way of composing
much of the culture to which he fell heir. The circumstances of a
dictionary allowed, and even forced, Johnson to bring into play a
range of qualities that at other times he tended to compartmental-
ize. Johnson did not share Mudrick's distaste for being official,
and while he can be funny, compassionate, careful, learned,
subtle, and intense in the *Dictionary,* he also can be pious, grave,
and wise, heir to all the ages, over which he broods as well as
chuckles, intones as well as laments, as well as honors:

> When first I engaged in this work, I resolved to leave neither
> words nor things unexamined, and pleased myself with
> a prospect of the hours which I should revel away in feasts
> of literature, the obscure recesses of northern learning which
> I should enter and ransack, the treasures with which I ex-
> pected every search into those neglected mines to reward my
> labour, and the triumph with which I should display my ac-
> quisitions to mankind.

Since this is Johnson, we then expect and receive the *Rasselas*-like
sigh of regret: "But these were the dreams of a poet doomed at

last to wake a lexicographer," and a lexicographer is a harmless drudge. But a lexicographer, Johnson also tells us, is a philologist, and under "philological," Johnson quotes Watts: "Studies called philological are history, language, grammar, poetry, and criticism," and Walker: "Temper all discourses of philology with interspersions of morality." So if the poet is often doomed to wake a lexicographer, the poet's dreams can be realized by Johnson working as historian, grammarian, poet, critic, and moralist.

No one had thought before, and no one has thought since, that a dictionary was a way to compose or express the findings of a culture. Coming at the end of the Renaissance, and living in ages of polite learning, Dryden and Pope became translators, a task hitherto, and, for the most part, subsequently, not undertaken by the greatest writers of an age when they are at the height of their powers. Pope, and, following him, Johnson himself, had been "imitators" of the satires of Horace and Juvenal. These gestures represent a fully acknowledged laterness, a need for building bridges over a gap to the past, but celebrate not only their ability so to build but their assurance that, in some cases, improvements have been made, and in others a rescue operation has been performed so that Greek, Latin, Italian, and earlier English writers can be made vital in the accomplished Augustan idiom. A dictionary was a similar undertaking for Johnson. Johnson, and Swift before him, had felt that English had reached its apogee in the lifetime of Thomas Carew, and that it since was in danger, by means of proliferation in words and in those able to read and write words, of falling into the linguistic equivalents of cant. Johnson was in the acknowledged position of being later, but also in the position of being able to celebrate, in a vital eighteenth-century way, the best of all that had gone before. For all that the poet was doomed to wake a lexicographer, Johnson could say to Boswell about the *Dictionary*, "I knew very well what I was undertaking, and very well how to do it—and have done it very well."

Perhaps the hardest thing for people two centuries later to realize is that the *Dictionary* can be read not just as the reflection of a culture (the way we might read many documents) but as a large composing of that culture. One learns to read it first by seeing what Johnson does with a group of related words and ideas, concerning anything from food to time to chemistry to law. Johnson is never entirely consistent, and one soon recognizes that on some subjects he is quite content to quote the best current authorities: Mead on poisons, Miller on plants, Hill on fossils, Holden on Time, Ray on the Creation. In other places he will simply lift words and definitions from Chambers's *Encyclopedia* or Nathaniel Bailey's *Dictionary* of 1736. Poking around some more, one sees that on many words Johnson is content to bang together a definition, offer an illustrative quotation, and move on. Johnson worked by reveling in the feasts of literature, underlining passages he wanted and the particular words he wanted his clerks to list these passages under. He then went back and assembled his materials under individual words, and if nothing in the quotations he had interested him much, he was content to be a harmless drudge.

But here is Johnson with "dinner":

> Dinner. n.s. [*diner*, French] The chief meal; the meal eaten about the middle of the day.

No need to offer more than that, but Johnson gives us three quotations:

> Let me not stay a jot for *dinner:*
> Go, get it ready.   *Shakespeare's King Lear.*
> Before *dinner* and supper, as often as it is convenient, or can be had, let the public prayers of the church, or some parts of them, be said publicly in the family.   *Taylor*
> The jolly crew, unmindful of the past,
> The quarry share, their plenteous *dinner* haste.
> *Dryden's Aeneid.*

Being superfluous, the quotations call attention to themselves, and we see a moralist at work. First, the hasty Lear, then the pious Taylor telling him not to be hasty. But Johnson then uses Dryden to remind Taylor that the purpose of dining is not praying but eating, so, unmindful of the past, Aeneas's crew set to it. A neat construction of truths and priorities, not forcibly announced, but clear enough to alert us to other, larger possibilities.

Johnson's first definition for the word "solution" is "Disruption; breach; separation; disjunction," and we know "solution" carries no such meaning for us. Johnson then quotes Bacon's *Natural History:* "In all bodies there is an appetite of union and evitation, of solution of continuity," "evitation" being "the act of avoiding." So solution is a disruption because it breaks up continuity just as evitation avoids union. We can only glimpse properties of our meanings for "solution"; disruption is allied to our word "dissolve" and to the meaning for "solution" that involves dissolving. The second definition is "Matter dissolved; that which contains anything which is dissolved," and the two quotations are both scientific. One is from Dr. Arbuthnot, who speaks of a solution of opium in water, the other is from Newton's *Optics* and describes the result of pouring salt of tartar into the solution of any metal. These scientists lived almost a century later than Bacon, and we see the term is scientific for Johnson; "solution" begins as a word describing any breakdown or disruption and becomes a term specifying liquid for the breaking down to take place in.

Then the third definition: "Resolution of a doubt; removal of an intellectual difficulty." We recognize this as easily as the second definition; mathematicians and detectives find solutions, and we would seem to have a paradox: in one case a solution is made by dissolving, and in the other by resolving. Johnson's quotations show the paradox is not real, because resolutions are made by dissolutions:

> Something yet of doubt remains
> Which only thy *solution* can resolve.   *Paradise Lost*

The "doubt" here is like Arbuthnot's opium before it is dissolved in water, and when dissolving occurs here, so too does resolving. In a second quotation from Milton, it is "perplexities" that gain resolution by dissolution, and then, in quotations from Dryden and Watts, the word has its sense of a problem solved and bears no trace of its heritage.

So Johnson does not just offer three definitions, which is all one is likely to find in a later dictionary, but an analysis of the word's history in the preceding century and a half. The two definitions we now accept as distinct are, he shows, the result of a scientific or philosophical term's becoming a metaphor for a mental activity, and eventually the metaphorical sense is obscured so the meanings lose their relation to each other. The quotations offered Johnson something of a jumble, which he dissolved in his definitions, thereby solving the problem.

Seeing he can work this way, one can then see him making fun of Swift in his handling of "explode." Swift had wanted, indeed Johnson himself had wanted when he began the *Dictionary*, to fix the language "and put a stop to those alterations which time and chance have hitherto been suffered to make in it without opposition." Johnson discovered, however, that to ask for a fixed language was like asking for an elixir to prolong human life; being less stubborn than Swift, he accepted that fact. Like "solution," "explode" was a word whose meaning had not been fixed. Johnson's first definition is "To drive out disgracefully with some noise of contempt; to treat with open contempt; to treat not only with neglect, but with open disdain or scorn." Six quotations follow, from Milton down to Swift, and this last comes from the very treatise on language in which Swift asked the Earl of Oxford to organize a committee to fix the language: "Provided that no word, which a society shall give sanction to, be antiquated and *exploded*, they will receive whatever new ones they shall find occasion for." This use of "explode" is not entirely obsolete, though it is not the one we commonly recognize. "Our" usage was coming into existence in the eighteenth century, and Johnson must have loved finding Swift laying down rules where no rules could hold; he only has to offer a second definition: "To drive out with noise and violence":

> But late the kindled powder did *explode*
> The massy ball, and the brass tube unload.

Who should have written those lines but Swift's contemporary, the despised Richard Blackmore. Nor think the doom of man, or language, reversed for thee, Dean Swift.

In these workings, Johnson is historian, and moralist; to see the critic we can turn to his work with Shakespeare. Like Dryden, Johnson believed there had been a race of giants before the flood.

Take theology from Hooker and the King James Bible, take pol-
icy, war, and navigation from Ralegh, take the language of poetry
and fiction from Spenser and Sidney, take the language of common life from Shakespeare, and "few ideas would be lost to mankind, for want of English words in which they might be expressed." Since the language of common life offers many more
words than theology, war, and poetry, Shakespeare is much the
most quoted author in the *Dictionary*. But Johnson came two generations after Dryden, and felt no need to compare "the last age"
to his own. He can be both admiring and critical, as the edition of
Shakespeare shows; what the *Dictionary* reveals is that Johnson
could do what we do all too rarely: make Shakespearean usages
make sense. Under "pregnant," for instance, Johnson begins
by offering the obvious definitions: "1. Teeming, breeding, . . .
2. Fruitful; fertile; impregnating, . . . 3. Full of consequence." In
each case the quotations show the more metaphorical meanings
deriving from the more literal. But then we have three more definitions: "4. Evident, . . . 5. Easy to produce any thing," and
"6. Free, kind." The definitions look strange, and may have done
so to Johnson, but this is the kind of thing he was confronted
with: "My matter hath no voice, but to your own most *pregnant*
and vouchsafed ear." That is so much like Shakespeare that we
usually let that fact move us on to the next lines without asking
what the words mean. But, since "your own most *pregnant* and
vouchsafed ear" shows the usual meaning of the word only faintly, Johnson felt obliged to try a definition, and if "free, kind" is
not grand or elegant, it is hard to know what would have suited
more. Even more striking is Johnson's second definition of
"backwardly": "perversely, or with cold hope." The phrase itself
seems only piquant, but here is what Johnson was faced with:

> I was the first man
> That e'er received gift from him;
> And does he think so *backwardly* of me,
> That I'll requite it last?

Given that, "perversely, or with cold hope" seems brilliant, si-
multaneous testimony to Shakespeare's wayward genius and to

Johnson's ability to eulogize that genius in a definition. With it a bridge is built over a gulf, one that could not be built a generation or so later.

With "life," critic, moralist, and historian are all at work together:

> 1. Union and co-operation of soul with body; vitality; animation; opposed to an inanimate state.
>
>   On thy *life*, no more.
>
>   My *life* I never held but as a pawn
>   To wage against thy foes.   *Shakespeare's King Lear*
>   She shewes a body rather than a *life*
>   A statue than a breather.   *Shakespeares Antony and Cleopatra*
>   Let the water bring forth abundantly the moving creatures that hath life.   *Genesis* 1: 20
>   The identity of the same man consists in nothing but a participation of the same continued *life*, by constantly fleeting particles of matter, in succession vitally united to the same organized body.   *Locke*

The two Shakespearean passages by themselves seem to need no comment, but their presence under "union and co-operation of soul with body" shows that Johnson wants to make something of them, since we would not otherwise define "life" that way in either passage. Your life is in my hands, says Lear, and it may be paltry but surely you value it; yes, answers Kent, but its value cannot be measured by you, but only by my loyalty to you. The co-operation of soul with body, however considered, must be *considered*, however quickly Lear may bandy words. So too with Cleopatra in "an inanimate state"; a body is not to be preferred to a life, but the fact of Cleopatra challenges this, since she now is a statue, no longer a mere breather like the rest of us.

The union of the soul with body, thus, can be taken for granted or can be gravely considered, and we are asked to do both, in effect, with these Shakespeares; read them through, ask gruffly what the point is, and then discover the point. Then we are given the remote and powerful sentence from Genesis and the modern and trivializing one from Locke, whose sense of life leaves us with nothing to consider. Were it not for the context offered by Shakespeare and the Bible, we might not be able to say "modern and trivializing" about Locke, but look at Lear and Kent, look at Cleopatra, consider the miracles of God that gave these creatures life, and Locke becomes tinkling jargon. In the process, the critic slides off into moralist and historian without ever having to identify or restrict himself.

The climax of Johnson's work with "life" offers one last example of his brilliant composing, locating the past in a solution of consideration that instructs the present:

> 10. General state of man.
> Studious they appear
> Of arts that polish *life;* inventors rare!
> Unmindful of their Maker.   *Milton*
> All that cheers or softens *life,*
> The tender sister, daughter, friend, and wife.   *Pope*

The quotations are sufficiently divergent in tone and emphasis that only a large flat definition can hold them together. Michael is showing Adam in *Paradise Lost* the marriage tents of the sons of God and the "bevy of fair women." Adam is pleased because people here are following "the bent of nature," but Michael insists that while arts can indeed polish life, the price of such studious polishing is to be unmindful of the Maker. It is the general state of man to follow the bent of nature and to polish life with art; that is how the Fall took place. But if Johnson was mindful of his Maker, he was thereby afraid of God, and it was the bent of nature that took him away from the fear and toward human consolation, if not to a "bevy of fair women." The general state of man does not climb to Milton's lofty perch; we desert our master and return to our friends. What softens our general state is sister, daughter, friend, and wife. Johnson never had the first two of these, never had in the fourth much that cheered or comforted, so he threw himself into a life of friendship. Knowing what Milton knew, seeking thereby what Pope offers, Johnson shows us what we need to know to understand our general state.

Heir to all the ages, Johnson could not be diminished by the anonymity with which the lexicographer must work or the arbitrary structure of the work finally produced. Just as Carew could be most himself when working inside the clothes offered by the Jonsonian letter and Donnean elegy, so too Johnson is most fully expressed when the range of his learning and the fullness of his care for meaning and nuance can also be his signature for a whole culture. Of course there are hundreds of words with which Johnson is only being efficient or informative; these were not roles he scorned either. But these also serve to set off those many words where he is being more than this. One of Johnson's most spectacular moments comes with "fellow" which he treats as an Empsonian "complex word," capable of expressing whole doctrines and ranges of social feelings. His central definition of "fellow" is "the foolish mortal; the mean wretch; the sorry rascal," six more words he might well have treated as lovingly as "fellow," but when we go look them up, we are disappointed. One can find Johnson on God's harmony, but in quotations from Locke, Cheyne, and Atterbury, under "congruous"; Johnson on children is in an otherwise needlessly long quotation from Locke under "about." That the alphabet organizes his book, that the lexicographer cannot put an asterisk beside words or quotations where the critic, moralist, or historian is also at work, indicate the vanity of human wishes, and show he knew what he was doing and did it very well. To be tired of the *Dictionary* is to be tired of life, of the old culture and all that its last master could tell us about it.

But Johnson's great strength as an heir depended on his being able to work with a very rudimentary historical sense. Had he been much interested in the history of words, he could have gone back much further than he did and worked his way down with that in mind, but what he does with "solution" and "explode" is rare. He may have agreed with Swift that the language reached its apogee before the middle of the seventeenth century, but the large number of quotations from Shakespeare may obscure the fact that Johnson generally restricts himself to writers and usages after the Restoration. Sidney and Spenser are useful for archaisms; there is some Bacon, less Ascham and Hooker, and almost nothing of Marlowe, Camden, Drayton, Chapman, Donne, Jonson, Herbert, or Marvell. It is as though their language was not his, and needed to be consulted only for arcane or exotic usages. Dryden is used over and over to convey Johnson's sense of the polite or correct; he could not easily imagine anything had been lost in the language that was not, on the whole, well lost.

Thus, where Shakespeare is clearly presenting Johnson with a problem, as with "pregnant" and "backwardly," he can be brilliant, but where Shakespeare is embodying an idea common to his own time but alien to Johnson's, the *Dictionary* is innocent. Isabella's great lines in *Measure for Measure* about our being ignorant of what we are most assured, our "glassy essence," are quoted under "glassy," but Johnson's definition is "resembling glass, as in smoothness, or lustre, or brittleness," which conveys no sense of our being like a mirror, capable of being seen no matter in how much brief authority we are dressed, because that idea of our essence was no longer current. The distinct but often overlapping meanings of "kind"—as in Hamlet's "A little more than kin and less than kind," or Volpone's "Though nature lost her kind, she were our dish"—go unnoticed because the medieval sense of "kind" had gone by 1750. Supremely intelligent though he was, curious and learned though he was, it was wisdom, not history, that was Johnson's way of being wise. Something had happened, around 1600, and again in the middle of the seventeenth century, but Johnson was unaware of this, so inclined he was to be on guard for that form of cant that seemed to lament whatever had passed and to denigrate the present.

As a result, Johnson was totally unaware of the last great "something" that happened within his lifetime. In certain obvious ways, especially when we consider Johnson's poetry, his great ancestor was Pope, but Pope was a blind spot for Johnson, of all the great writers the one he may have known best and understood least. To consider their relation is to come to the fulcrum of this book, the crucial "during" of which the seventeenth century is the Before and the nineteenth and twentieth centuries the After. The Renaissance, and in some ways the ancient culture, ended with Pope, and Pope knew it, and spent his last great decade saying so. Johnson, disinclined to be historical and very much inclined toward a wisdom that leveled history, denied this. He lived in darkness, the first postmortem writer, the first disabled heir.

➥➥➥➥ In the "Life of Pope," Johnson describes Pope's removal to a house in Twickenham, paid for out of the subscriptions obtained from his announcement of his *Iliad:*

> Here he planted the vines and the quincunx which his verses mention; and being under the necessity to make a subterranean passage to a garden on the other side of the road, he adorned it with fossil bodies, and dignified it with the title of a grotto; a place of silence and retreat, from which he endeavoured to persuade his friends and himself that cares and passions could be excluded.
>
> A grotto is not often the wish or pleasure of an Englishman, who has more frequent need to solicit than exclude the sun; but Pope's excavation was requisite as an entrance to his garden, and, as some men try to be proud of their defects, he extracted an ornament from an inconvenience, and vanity produced a grotto where necessity enforced a passage. It may be frequently remarked of the studious and speculative, that they are proud of trifles and that their amusements seem frivolous and childish. . . .

The more Johnson contemplates Pope's grotto, the sillier he finds it. Of course cares and passions cannot be excluded just by going underground, of course it was vanity that tried to make a virtue of necessity ("he hardly drank tea without a stratagem"), of course a grotto in England is affectation or worse: "whether it be that men conscious of great reputation think themselves above the reach of censure, and safe in the admission of negligent indulgences, or that mankind expect from elevated genius an uniformity of greatness, and watch its degradation with malicious wonder. . . ." Johnson will allow no one of great reputation thereby to be above censure, nor does he imagine that genius can possibly produce uniformity of greatness. Item: the great Pope, with his invited lords about him, in this grotto.

Needless to say, the grotto was not this for Pope, though he too
imagined he was eagle-eyed in his ability to spot the puffed up
and the phony:

> And I not strip the gilding off a Knave,
> Unplac'd, unpension'd, no man's heir, or slave?
> I will, or perish in the gen'rous cause:
> Hear this, and tremble! you who 'scape the Laws.

This comes near the end of the first of his Horatian imitations.
Pope has been warned by Fortescue that stripping the gilding off
knaves could get him into trouble. Pope retorts that Boileau had
done the same under Louis XIV, that Dryden had done the same
under the later Stuarts, and, rather than be made to suffer, they
had been rewarded. Pope says he is "unplac'd, unpension'd" because, as a Catholic, he could receive no preferment, hold no office, and, indeed, could not live within twelve miles of the king.
That leads him to think of Twickenham:

> Yes, while I live, no rich or noble knave
> Shall walk the World, in credit, to his grave.
> TO VIRTUE ONLY AND HER FRIENDS, A FRIEND,
> The World beside may murmur, or commend,
> Know, all the distant din that world can keep,
> Rolls o'er my Grotto, and but sooths my sleep.
> There, my retreat the best Companions grace,
> Chiefs out of war, and Statesmen out of place.
> There ST. JOHN mingles with my friendly Bowl
> The Feast of Reason and the Flow of soul:
> And HE, whose Lightning pierc'd th' Iberian Lines,
> Now forms my Quincunx, and now ranks my Vines,
> Or tames the Genius of the stubborn plain,
> Almost as quickly as he conquer'd Spain.

Pope vaunts himself this way because he really believed that his
place of retreat and his friends gave him something special, but
Johnson thought no better of the friends than of the grotto:

> To his latter works, however, he took care to annex names
> dignified with titles, but was not very happy in his choice;

for, except Lord Bathurst, none of his noble friends were
such as that a good man would wish to have his intimacy
with them known to posterity; he can derive little honour
from the notice of Cobham, Burlington, or Bolingbroke.

As Johnson sees it, most of Pope's last dozen years were devoted
to projects designed to satisfy his vanity or to vent his anger; of all
the works of these years, it is Pope's shabby and highhanded way
of getting his letters published that most absorbs Johnson's attention and earns his scorn.

The house at Twickenham was not for Pope just a place to live,
or a place of retirement for himself and for chiefs out of war and
statesmen out of place. It was not a monument but an enactment
of an ideal celebrated in Vergil's *Georgics* and Horace's satires and
epistles, a place of human use where the natural is to be found in
orchard and kitchen garden, where the natural is made mysterious in the plays of light in the grotto, and where the life lived can
give Pope an angle to see court and politics, city and money, history and change, so that the pastoral retreat could be the home of
the heroic satirist. For Horace such a place offered equipoise and
grace impossible in a life more active or ambitious; for Vergil it included philosophical and scientific speculation, horticultural experiment, and enjoyment of the rapturous country gods.

Pope, however, soon discovered he was too anxious and embattled to exemplify Horatian equipoise or Vergilian speculation.
Outside the circle of Twickenham, the ideal offered by the Au-
gustans was becoming misunderstood, vulgarized, distorted,
and brutalized. At the end of the first dialogue of the *Epilogue to
the Satires* of 1738, Pope envisions Vice, in a triumphal car; it is
a passage Johnson admired, but only for its rhetorical grandeur
and not for its accuracy of description:

> Lo! at the wheels of her Triumphal Car,
> Old England's Genius, rough with many a Scar,
> Dragg'd in the dust! his arms hang idly round,
> His Flag inverted trails along the ground!
> Our Youth, all livery'd o'er with foreign Gold,
> Before her dance: behind her, crawl the Old!
> See thronging Millions to the Pagod run,

And offer Country, Parent, Wife, or Son!
Hear her black Trumpet thro' the Land proclaim,
That NOT TO BE CORRUPTED IS THE SHAME.
In Soldier, Churchman, Patriot, Man in Pow'r,
'Tis Avarice all, Ambition is no more!
See, all our Nobles begging to be Slaves!
See, all our Fools aspiring to be Knaves!
The Wit of Cheats, the Courage of a Whore,
Are what ten thousand envy and adore:
All, all look up, with reverential Awe,
At Crimes that 'scape, or triumph o'er the Law:
While Truth, Worth, Wisdom, daily they decry—
"Nothing is sacred now but Villainy."

By its very sweep, this seems hard to take literally enough to consider seriously. That it recalls Hebrew prophecy indicates its circumstances have long been with us. The world is the world, and the prince of darkness claims it. To sit in Pope's grotto and contemplate the East India Company and the ass licking of Walpole's followers (see a 1740 engraving, "Idol-Worship or The Way to Preferment," in Maynard Mack's *The Garden and the City*) is like being Juvenal in Rome, or Thomas Wyatt in Kent and Christendom, contemplating Henry VIII's court. It is an admirable passage, but we may be permitted to pull back and doubt that just *then* was Vice climbing into her triumphal car. For Johnson, who had lived through those years walking London streets all night with Richard Savage, and scrambling to get a few shillings together as a literary hack, and who had outlived that time to live in comfort, such a vision could only seem the rant of a spoiled and disappointed ass.

Pope meant it, though, and from this point on there was no regaining of Horatian equipoise. Ten years earlier he had attempted, with sporadic success, to versify the confidence of his friend Bolingbroke's philosophy of the divine plan, one that is only slightly coarsened in the famous summary: "Whatever is, is right." He had then, in the *Moral Essays*, the *Epistle to Dr. Arbuthnot*, and the *Imitations of Horace*—a huge body of verse, much of it brilliant—gradually found himself more mystified, more besieged, more disgusted and alarmed, close to saying "Whatever is, is wrong." The Man of Ross in "To Bathurst" is meant to balance the example of Sir Balaam; the example of Burlington is meant to balance the description of Timon's villa; the figure of Pope's father at the end of the *Epistle to Dr. Arbuthnot* is meant to balance Atticus and Sporus, but in each case it is the vision of the vulgar, the damned, and the wicked that we remember most, because there the verse is grand, ghastly, energizing. "In the worst inn's worst room with mat half hung," "Trees cut to statues, statues thick as trees," "She bears a Coronet and P-x for life," "And die of nothing but a rage to live," "And as the prompter breathes, the puppet squeaks," "Stoop'd at the ear of Eve, familiar toad"— a treasure house of great lines, but to contemplate these is far from having the distant din soothe Pope's sleep.

After the epilogue to the Satires came *The Dunciad* of 1742–43, first the separate publication of the new Book 4, then a revision of the first three books to conform to the final vision of the coming of universal darkness. Though Johnson could have his fun with Boswell—"Ah sir, hadst *thou* lived in those days! It is not worth being a dunce now, when there are no wits"—for him *The Dunciad* mostly was a sign of Pope's tireless malignity:

> But Pope's irascibility prevailed, and he resolved to tell the whole English world that he was at war with Cibber; and to shew that he thought him no common adversary, he prepared no common vengeance; he published a new edition of *The Dunciad*, in which he degraded Theobald from his painful pre-eminence, and enthroned Cibber in his stead. Unhappily the two heroes were of opposite characters, and Pope was unwilling to lose what he had already written; he has therefore depraved his poem by giving to Cibber the old books, the cold pedantry, and sluggish pertinacity of Theobald.

"Turn what they will to Verse," cries Bentley in Book 4, "their toil is vain; Critics like me shall make it Prose again." In this instance, Johnson seems to turn Pope's verse back into prose.

The secret to reading *The Dunciad* is to ask how Pope was right, not just about Cibber or Bentley, but about the relation of Chaos to Dullness and of both to the coming of the eternal dark. Simply considered as a vision, a literary outpouring, *The Dunciad* is as vast and precise as the House of Busirane in *The Faerie Queene*, or Hell in the first two books of *Paradise Lost*. But considered as an apocalypse of history it has the advantage over, say, the Revelation of John because time has shown Pope to have been, perhaps even increasingly to have been, right.

Johnson's comments on the feebleness of Pope's efforts when revising *The Dunciad* are somewhat inaccurate—the speeches of Theobald and Cibber in Book 1 are substantially different— and misleading, first because the role played by the king of the Dunces is not a crucial one in the original or the revision, second because for Pope the personal attributes of either Theobald or Cibber are not so important as the land over which either ostensibly reigns. And that land is not so much place as process:

> Here she beholds the Chaos dark and deep,
> Where nameless Somethings in their causes sleep,
> 'Till genial Jacob, or a warm Third day,
> Call forth each mass, a Poem, or a Play:
> How hints, like spawn, scarce quick in embryo lie,
> How new-born nonsense first is taught to cry,
> Maggots half-form'd in rhyme exactly meet,
> And learn to crawl upon poetic feet.
> Here one poor word an hundred clenches makes,
> And ductile dulness now meanders takes;
> There motley Images her fancy strike,
> Figures ill pair'd, and Similes unlike.
> She sees a mob of Metaphors advance,
> Pleas'd with the madness of the mazy dance:
> How Tragedy and Comedy embrace;
> How Farce and Epic get a jumbled race;
> How Time himself stands still at her command,
> Realms shift their place, and Ocean turns to land.
> Here gay Description Aegypt glads with show'rs,
> Or gives to Zembla fruits, to Barca flow'rs;

Glitt'ring with ice here hoary hills are seen,
There painted vallies of eternal green,
In cold December fragrant chaplets blow,
And heavy harvests nod beneath the snow.

The outpouringness of the verse is felt first, then the grotesqueness of some of the local detail—"Maggots half-form'd in rhyme
exactly meet," "And ductile dulness new meanders takes." This
seems like Chaos, but how and why it does not seem necessary to
inquire; here, the notes tell us, is Jacob Tonson the publisher, and
further on is some poetry making a ridiculous jumble.

What seems like list, or pile, however, is really process. How is
some mass, "a Poem, or a Play," formed? First "nameless Some-
things" sleep in the recesses of Chaos and become "scarce quick"
"hints"; the hints then are spawned into "new-born nonsense,"
having to be taught to cry, unlike the babes in *Lear;* the nonsense
is maggots—since these are scribblers producing, it takes them
only three days to make a poem, or three performances of a play
(the author getting a share of the profits on the third day), and the
process is like that of meat spoiling in "a warm Third Day"—perfect because they meet in exactly formed rhymes, then crawl on
poetic feet. In this smarmy swarm of military precision one word
is clenched by a hundred that pun with it, and dullness's forms
are flexible and aimless enough to meander, the order of dullness
being motley images, and similes in which there is no likeness.
One feels one is watching strange acts of propagation and growth
beneath a microscope. As they grow, the figures parade before
the goddess and become generic jumbles and careless pictures of
apparent precision in which Egypt has a rainy season and an arc-
tic region is rendered fertile; in a perfectly orderly fashion, the
whole globe becomes a jumble of inaccuracy and nonsense.

Pope has started with an image of Chaos known from Hesiod
to Spenser and Milton, a place of nameless shapes and forms. His
attitude seems to resemble Jonson's scorn of moldy tales like *Peri-
cles* or Carew's of an age that cannot judge or write. This is what
Johnson saw, Pope redecorating ancient figures and restating
familiar complaints. But while true enough, this is inadequate to

describe Pope's vision of a grotesque triumph of design, a miracle of perverse intention, a series of processes as orderly as Spenser's Garden of Adonis. What Jonson, or Carew, sees as aberration, ridiculous or disgusting, Pope sees as huge teeming achievement, not just something one sneers at, but stares at, in fear and awe.

The passage above comes early in Book 1, and the first three books as revised are content to make their poetry out of a criticism that is essentially literary, having poets, publishers, editors, and parasites for the original material. Without changing his original metaphors, in Book 4 Pope shows how Chaos and Dulness become one by becoming institutional, organized triumph. Dulness has a throne, and Cibber is king, but this hierarchy is more incidental than central; in the universe of Chaos, the triumphant voices exercise their will in ways that seem more appropriate, if that is possible, for the democratic twentieth century than the monarchical eighteenth. A world that knows a subject called Language Arts, another called Education, and a cluster called Sociology, Social Psychology, Social Anthropology, and Social Work has no trouble recognizing the boy-senator and the spectre who is his master:

> "Since Man from beast by Words is known,
> Words are Man's province, Words we teach alone.
> When Reason doubtful, like the Samian letter,
> Points him two ways, the narrower is the better.
> Plac'd at the door of Learning, youth to guide,
> We never suffer it to stand too wide.
> To ask, to guess, to know, as they commence,
> As Fancy opens the quick springs of Sense,
> We ply the Memory, we load the brain,
> Bind rebel Wit, and double chain on chain,
> Confine the thought, to exercise the breath;
> And keep them in the pale of Words till death."

There is process here too: the natural one of the learner asking, guessing, knowing, so that fancy can open the quick spring of sense; the schoolmaster's response: ply the memory, load the brain, bind the wit inclined to rebel, confine thought, teach elocution. When process is divorced from the natural, and comes to employ the natural as its raw material, it becomes habitual, dull, and pleased with itself.

That is pedagogy; here is philosophy, offered by a clerk who is a "Sworn foe to Myst'ry, yet divinely dark":

> "Let others creep by timid steps, and slow,
> On plain Experience lay foundations low,
> By common sense to common knowledge bred,
> And last, to Nature's Cause thro' Nature led.
> All-seeing in thy mists, we want no guide,
> Mother of Arrogance and Source of Pride!
> We nobly take the high Priori Road,
> And reason downward, till we doubt of God:
> Make Nature still incroach upon his plan;
> And shove him off as far as e'er we can:
> Thrust some Mechanic Cause into his place;
> Or bind in Matter, or diffuse in Space."

Here Pope's historical bearings are clearer than with Pope on literature or education. His note on the "high Priori Road" offers "Hobbs, Spinoza, Des Cartes and some better Reasoners" as the culprits, the philosophy we learn as part of the establishment of scientific method, rationalism, and the "modern world." Small human beings in a large universe could once learn of nature, and then of nature's cause, but on the high Priori Road one reasons "downward, till we doubt of God," denying the a priori, and beginning instead with "cogito, ergo sum." This is closely allied with the scholarly method of Richard Bentley:

> For thee explain a thing till all men doubt it,
> And write about it, Goddess, and about it.

Or, and here we can combine Bentley, the gloomy clerk, and the spectre schoolmaster with the horticulturist and lepidopterist who come later:

> How parts relate to parts, or they to whole,
> The body's harmony, the beaming soul,

Are things which Kuster, Burman, Wasse shall see,
When Man's whole frame is obvious to a *Flea*.

Method is constantly set over against method, the frail old
against the triumphant new.

Pope's sense of what was being overcome in the triumph of
Chaos has, unsurprisingly, a distinct eighteenth-century tinge to
it. It is hardly the religion of Paul, the philosophy of Aquinas, or
the humanism of Sidney that is felt in Pope's descriptions of parts
and wholes. It is nonetheless clear that it is an ancient culture and
a revered sense of knowing that Pope is honoring in its defeat. As
Reuben Brower has shown in *Alexander Pope: The Poetry of Allusion*, Pope reaches back to Homer, Vergil, Ovid, Spenser, Milton,
and Dryden to create his allies, and he sees himself as their last
true inheritor. If Pope's understanding of the architecture of the
old universe lacks the lustrousness of Hamlet's, or Dante's—if
his verse is most vivid when describing the symptoms of oncom-
ing darkness—his is sufficiently coherent with theirs that he can
show how they and theirs will be lost if he and his are lost. A
world of specialization, of jargon, of rationalism employed in the
service of complacent skepticism, of scholarship that sees no
need to distinguish Manilius from Horace, of philosophy that
swears itself foe to mystery and analogy—it is all coherent in its
bizarre jumbled way, and it is all coming to pass. In the face of
that, Pope, Socrates, and Isaiah are brothers.

A twentieth-century reader finds it hard to pick up *The Dunciad*
and naturally or instinctively understand it because one's eye is
too close to the object to see order, precision, and delineation of
process rather than a heap or jumble of "satiric targets." But the
poem is precise in every word, just as a curse of Lear's is a careful
anatomizing of terror and destruction, a call of Lady Macbeth to
the "murdering ministers" to unsex her is followed by a precise
description of what she wants to happen to her body, or the pen-
tangle on Sir Gawain's shield is something capable of being dis-
assembled by a scholar or reassembled by a fourteenth-century
reader. Metaphor, be it heightened or argued, shouted or hissed,
before Pope was always susceptible to the ministrations of sober

elucidation. Darkness for Pope was the loss of this way of seeing human beings thus at home in the created universe, and at home because we were not the creators but the elucidators.

What frightened Pope in *The Dunciad* was not just the triumph of some perverse values or some corrupt mongers of culture, but something deeper, something Pope was only coming to understand in the decade preceding. The very means of valuing had become perverse: the singer only sings notes, the spectre teaches only words, Bentley cares to dispute only of *Me* or *Te,* the horticulturist sees only the flower and the lepidopterist only the butterfly. For Pope this is proof that the universe is only fragments, and the mind, in metaphysics at a loss (because metaphysics will become a fragmented "subject") can only wander in a wilderness of moss. The refusal to ask, to guess, and thereby to know, by working from common sense to common knowledge, is seen by the dunces not as perversity but as triumph—the right divine of all these little kings to govern wrong. In *Dunciad* 4 Pope says that "art after art goes out, and all is Night," but he does so knowing that specialization, pedantry, and false method will soon not even know what he means by "art" or by "Night," or care to inquire, so great are their shouts of triumph.

> Lo! thy dread Empire, CHAOS! is restor'd;
> Light dies before thy uncreating word:
> Thy hand, great Anarch! lets the curtain fall;
> And Universal Darkness buries All.

What begins with the first verse of Genesis ends here, in a triumphal reversal of God's will. Darkness has fallen.

Hugh Kenner writes: "Yet it was easy to show that he was not exaggerating: the proof is that Pope himself became in fifty years all but unintelligible." If Kenner is wrong in his estimate, it is only because the process whereby Pope became unintelligible seems not to have taken fifty years:

> He repeated to us, in his forcible melodious manner, the concluding lines of the *Dunciad.* While he was talking loudly in praise of these lines, one of the company ventured to say "Too fine for such a poem—a poem on what?" JOHNSON.

(with a disdainful look) "Why, on *dunces*. It was worth while being a dunce then. Ah, Sir, hadst *thou* lived in those days! It is not worth being a dunce now, when there are no wits."

Pope was born in 1688, Johnson in 1709, Boswell in 1740. The concluding lines of the vision were grand stuff for Boswell, to be sure, but what was the poem about? The answer, from Johnson, who had been there: dunces. An answer, but one more relevant to the *Dunciad* of 1728 than to the *Dunciad* 4 from which Johnson was quoting. Pope announced there that he can have no heirs, that he is the last descendant, and in Boswell's question and Johnson's limiting answer we can see the way he was right.

Johnson, especially in his formal shapes, was so much an Augustan, heir to all the ages, that shortly after the turn of the nineteenth century he fitted comfortably into "the last age," the one eventually to be called "neoclassic," or "of prose." The fifty years between *The Dunciad* and the *Lyrical Ballads* had to be put somewhere because of the growing need, forecast so well in Pope's poem, to make categories, and because it was being discovered that the nineteenth century was Wordsworth's. Terms like "pre-Romantic" and "the Age of Johnson" came into use, on the general understanding that those who were to be caretakers of our knowledge of that half century were those who knew about Dryden and Pope, not those who knew about Keats and Tennyson. As a result, the great gap between Pope and Johnson, perhaps as great as that between any two generations on record, has only recently been imaginable. Understandably, Johnson did not see it, did not see the way in which he was living in darkness, and so in the history of literary inheritance he is a central and fascinating figure.

⪢⪢⪢⪢ As I noted earlier, Pope's way of describing what he saw as disappearing often had a pale, abstract, eighteenth-century cast to it. A universe of wholes and parts, in which one could be led through Nature to Nature's cause, is a twilight understanding compared to Hamlet's description of what is no longer available to him: "This goodly frame, the earth," "this most excellent canopy, the air," "this brave o'erhanging firmament, this majestical roof fretted with golden fire." Jesus' bright colorful way of describing the steadfast love of God for all creatures becomes, for Pope:

> Who sees with equal eye, as God of all,   '
> A hero perish, or a sparrow fall.

When one thinks of the thunderous prayer that closes *The Faerie Queen*, of the fierce intimacy of Donne's and Herbert's clashes with God, then Pope's "first Almighty cause" and his "gen'ral ORDER" seem Newtonian, flat, if not entirely stale or unprofitable. The processes Pope saw coming to a close in 1742 had been in motion a long time, a century's dying at least. What was possible for Spenser was not possible, as we have seen, for Donne and Jonson, and what was possible for them was not possible for Milton or Marvell and especially not for Dryden. *Paradise Lost* enacts the whole matter, beginning with the grand clashes of Satan with a God of infinite light and infinite creation, and ending with God retired, and Adam and Eve leaving Eden alone, guided only by a vague and benign Providence.

But with Pope the process comes to a close. "The weight behind that concluding passage of the *Dunciad*," Leavis writes, seeing the matter from a slightly different angle, "is greater than Marvell could supply and the urbanity has a different inflection, but the relation between wit and solemnity (Pope is deeply moved by his vatic nightmare—that is, by his positive concern for civilization) is essentially that of the Dialogue [Marvell's, between the soul and the body]." Johnson, coming a generation later, could affirm Pope's truth only to the extent of seeing that all around him there was cant, and that his task was his characteristic cheerful, grim exploding. But in order to see his own historical context clearly, Johnson would have needed to see Pope differently, or, to put it the other way around, the fact that Pope was a blind spot for Johnson is a sign that he did not see the darkness in which he lived.

Johnson's "Life of Pope" is much the longest of the *Lives*, and there are more references in Boswell's *Life* to Pope than to anyone else who was no longer living, but Johnson insisted this was not his doing: "Virgil is less talked of than Pope, and Homer is less talked of than Virgil; but they are not less admired. We must read what the world reads at the moment." In everything Johnson says or writes about Pope there is an air of having to put up with him because of his reputation and his undoubted genius. He always is looking for ways to level Pope with the stern gaze of his common sense. He would not see what Pope was saying, and so could not understand what he had achieved.

In his poetry, Johnson accepts Pope as the master of the couplet, but turns away from everything else. I would like to compare two passages to show Johnson in darkness. First, here is Pope's portrait of Narcissa in "To a Lady":

> Narcissa's nature, tolerably mild,
> To make a wash, would hardly stew a child;
> Has ev'n been prov'd to grant a Lover's pray'r,
> And paid a Tradesman once to make him stare;
> Gave alms at Easter, in a Christian trim,
> And made a Widow happy, for a whim.
> Why then declare Good-nature is her scorn,
> When 'tis by that alone she can be born?
> Why pique all mortals, yet affect a name?
> A fool to Pleasure, yet a slave to Fame:
> Now deep in Taylor and the Book of Martyrs,
> Now drinking citron with his Grace and Chartres:
> Now Conscience chills her, and now Passion burns;
> And Atheism and Religion take their turns;
> A very Heathen in the carnal part,
> Yet still a sad, good Christian at her heart.

Pope sets himself a mighty task: to move within the compass of sixteen lines from a Narcissa who would not quite stew a child to make a cosmetic to the "sad, good Christian" of the final line. Since the figure of Narcissa is legendary, and since this is a portrait rather than a narrative, Pope would seem to have restricted himself greatly.

The first six lines offer cameos of the character we expect, a woman of no malice, of no compassion, of easy fashionableness and shallow unscrupulosity; the tone is condescending, the caesura turns the line to break off a witty point. The turn comes in one of those great loaded Pope couplets:

> Why then declare Good-nature is her scorn,
> When 'tis by that alone she can be born?

"Why say Narcissa scorns good-naturedness, or the goodness of nature; it is only such feelings that can bear her, but they can do it"; "Why say she is an enemy of Nature, when it was, after all, Nature that gave her birth." In each case the second line does not so much answer the question of the first as indicate ranges of feeling and being that are beyond Narcissa, and beyond the vivid cameos of the first three couplets. One can hardly bear Narcissa good-naturedly, but we must remember that she too was born and is a fellow creature.

A mystery, then: how can such a one be? Why insult everyone, yet insist on the name that can be granted only by those insulted? The vivid pictures give way, Narcissa is her own enemy, not happy, a clown, a fool of pleasure. We can look back at, say, "And paid a Tradesman once to make him stare," and see that action as being compulsive, not truly willed, because Narcissa is a plaything of allegorical figures far more powerful than she:

> Now Conscience chills her, and now Passion burns;
> And Atheism and Religion take their turns.

As she was born like the rest of us, she has a conscience, but though it is strong enough to dominate her, it does so only as part of an awful pas-de-deux, cold giving way to heat since no one can stand to be as cold as her conscience makes her feel. Yet since she is without will, the rush from cold must be all the way to passion, at least to citron with his Grace and Chartres.

In the second line of the couplet, Atheism stands parallel to Conscience, and Religion to Passion. We can read this as a deliberate jumble, Pope describing a continued action in which there is no telling what comes first, and Narcissa bounces from one to the other. But we can keep hold of the parallels too, and ask how atheism is like conscience, religion is like passion. Now we have a narrative, atheism being a chilled response to passionate excess and religion a burning escape from the aridity of unbelief. After these powers have their way with her, who then is Narcissa:

> A very Heathen in the carnal part,
> Yet still a sad, good Christian at her heart.

Beyond being a victim and in need of attention and compassion, Narcissa is like all of us, in our carnality, heathen, in our hearts, good Christians, sad—not so much melancholy as wretched— because our obedience to our carnal part reminds us we are only would-be good Christians.

Pope at his most brilliant is found in the portraits of those who most frighten or disgust him: Atossa, Sporus, Timon, Bentley. Here that brilliance all goes into the first six lines as a picture of Narcissa that is then shown to be obvious, a mere noting of behavior, when what is needed is wonder and compassion, Narcissa as one of us, and all of us victims of a self-love we do not understand and cannot control. The hunchback dwarf looks at the shallow and willful woman of fashion and sees, in turn, child, lover, tradesman, widow, victim. But then he turns, and does so because his Lord had enjoined him to do so, and the passage becomes a fulfillment of Jesus' commandment to love one's neighbor as oneself.

Now here is Johnson's Charles XII of Sweden:

> On what foundation stands the warrior's pride?
> How just his hopes let Swedish Charles decide;
> A frame of adamant, a soul of fire,
> No dangers fright him, and no labours tire;
> O'er love, o'er fear, extends his wide domain,
> Unconquer'd lord of pleasure and of pain;
> No joys to him pacific sceptres yield,
> War sounds the trump, he rushes to the field;
> Behold surrounding kings their pow'r combine,
> And one capitulate, and one resign,
> Peace courts his hand, but spreads her charms in vain;
> "Think nothing gain'd," he cries, "till nought remain,
> On Moscow's wall till Gothic standards fly,

And all be mine beneath the Polar sky."
The march begins in military state,
And nations on his eye suspended wait;
Stern Famine guards the solitary coast,
And Winter barricades the realms of frost;
He comes, not want and cold his course delay;—
Hide, blushing glory, hide Pultowa's day:
The vanquished hero leaves his broken bands,
And shows his miseries in distant lands;
Condemn'd a needy supplicant to wait,
While ladies interpose, and slaves debate.
But did not Chance at length her error mend?
Did no subverted empire mark his end?
Did rival monarchs give the fatal wound?
Or hostile millions press him to the ground?
His fall was destin'd to a barren strand,
A petty fortress, and a dubious hand;
He left the name, at which the world grew pale,
To point a moral, or adorn a tale.

This is almost twice as long as Pope's portrait of Narcissa, yet asks
less of itself and less of us as readers. There is a story told, but because the question asked in the opening line is rhetorical, the effects offered in the tale are less active, more like decoration, than
anything in Pope. The line of wit, in which solemnity and wit
could nurture each other, had died with Pope. The greatness of
Charles is his frame of adamant, his soul of fire, and these must,
we know as we read of them, lead to triumph and then to down-
fall. The turning point—"Hide, blushing glory, hide Pultowa's
day"—does not need details since Johnson knows days like Pultowa must come, just as, if love, fear, peace, surrounding kings,
famine, and frost cannot stop Charles, something will. The pieces
are all fitted into prearranged places.

Of course that is what Johnson wanted. While Pope can use a
single line, and its caesura, to effect a turn—"To make a wash,
would hardly stew a child"—Johnson invariably uses the second
half of the line to pound, and reinforce—"And one capitulate,
and one resign," "While ladies interpose, and slaves debate,"

"To point a moral, adorn a tale." There is sober grandeur in "The Vanity of Human Wishes" that one does not find in Pope, but that is all there is in a hammered poetry of strong effects. In each extended passage in the poem, it is the second half, describing the fall, the vanity of the wish, that is strongest. Life is what it is, no surprises remain, and sober wisdom is all.

One cannot imagine Johnson innocent of all this, unaware of how much flatter his poetry is, how much more monochromatic. One can say that he saw, and then refused. Unable to compose Pope, unable to fathom what had happened—had not Pope praised his "London," had not his friend Savage been a some-time friend of Pope's and a recipient of his generosity, how could anything *have happened?*—Johnson's recourse was to diminish Pope: your grotto is no Horatian farm, your friends are but copies of what the great should be, your sense of disaster is vanity and spitefulness, your fancy portrait of Narcissa is contrary to what we know Narcissa to be. Is not the truth the truth? The very rich-ness of activity in a great passage of Pope's becomes something to mistrust, and, as if in response, Johnson makes his own couplets slower and more deliberate, his coins always coming up the same way. He could neither honor Pope nor avoid him, so a poetry of pointing morals and adorning tales would stand as all, and as enough, for him.

In the "Life of Pope," when Johnson comes to the passage on Timon's villa in "To Burlington," he can bring himself only to identify Timon as the Duke of Chandos—"a man perhaps too much delighted with pomp and show, but of a temper kind and benificent, and who consequently had the voice of the publick in his favour"—and then note that Pope was alleged to have re-ceived a thousand pounds from Chandos. When Pope then com-plains "of the treatment which his poems had found, owns that such criticks can intimidate him, may almost persuade him to write no more, which is a compliment this age deserves," John-son booms his cannons in reply:

> The man who threatens the world is always ridiculous; for the world can easily go on without him, and in a short time will cease to miss him. I have heard of an idiot, who used to

revenge his vexations by lying all night upon the bridge. There is nothing, says Juvenal, that a man will not believe in his own favour. Pope had been flattered till he thought himself one of the moving powers in the system of life. When he talked of laying down his pen, those who sat round him intreated and implored, and self-love did not suffer him to suspect that they went away and laughed.

Timon's villa is thus ensnared, but in the process, it is also ignored, and Johnson is the poorer for doing so, for thinking he does not really need to *read* "To Burlington," as "The Vanity of Human Wishes" shows. Johnson is wise—the man who threatens the world *is* always ridiculous—but the leap to the perch of wisdom is sometimes quick and easy.

In the *Dictionary* we can find many examples of this same kind of deflection from the greatness and the delicacy of Pope's poetry. There is a striking instance of this—striking because it comes in his work with "fellow," where he is at his best—when he is illustrating a definition I quoted earlier: "8. A word of contempt; the foolish mortal; the mean wretch; the sorry rascal." He begins with this from Sidney: "Those great *fellows*, scornfully receiving them, as foolish birds fallen into their net, it pleased the Eternal Justice to make them suffer death by their hands." Which gives us the proper sense of complication: those who died were foolish mortals and mean wretches, presumably, but so were those who killed them, which shows the wondrous ways of Eternal Justice. This is followed by five passages from Shakespeare, ending with this cheerful piece of gloom from Gonzalo in the opening scene of *The Tempest*: "I have great comfort from this *fellow*; methinks he hath no drowning mark about him; his complexion is perfect gallows." Nothing to fear from this storm, sail on; I feel much better since recognizing that this boatswain is not going to be drowned, since he clearly is born to be hanged; the fellow is not so much a person as a tea leaf. This is the kind of wonderful nuance Johnson can bring out when he loves his quotation and his definition. L'Estrange, Dryden, and Swift then echo this in more polite and offhand tones, but then, at the end, we have this, from *An Essay on Man*:

You'll find, if once the monarch acts the monk,
Or, cobler-like, the parson will be drunk,
Worth makes the man, the want of it the *fellow;*
The rest is all but leather or prunella.

Degree being vizarded, moral democracy will emerge, and not even the wide range of Johnson's definition will cover this usage. Pope's fellow had a chance to become a man by becoming worthy, but he failed. The social tones ranging around "fellow" are being, in effect, repudiated; to be a "fellow" in Pope's context is to fail morally, because social considerations there are only a matter of leather or prunella. Pope is fending off precisely those tones Johnson, not really attending to Pope's passage, asks us to include. It is as though Pope, for Johnson, is not worth the attention he accords Sidney, Shakespeare, or Dryden.

Or we might look at an extended passage, and see what Johnson in the *Dictionary* could make of it. Here is the soprano of *Dunciad* 4:

She tripp'd and laugh'd, too pretty much to stand;
Cast on the prostrate Nine a scornful look,
Then thus in quaint Recitativo spoke.
   "O *Cara! Cara!* silence all that train:
Joy to great Chaos! let Division reign:
Chromatic tortures soon shall drive them hence,
Break all their nerves, and fritter all their sense:
One Trill shall harmonize joy, grief, and rage,
Wake the dull Church, and lull the ranting Stage;
To the same notes thy sons shall hum, or snore,
And all thy yawning daughters cry, *encore.*
Another Phoebus, thy own Phoebus, reigns,
Joys in my jiggs, and dances in my chains.
But soon, ah soon Rebellion will commence,
If Music meanly borrows aid from Sense:
Strong in new Arms, lo! Giant Handel stands,
Like bold Briareus, with a hundred hands;
To stir, to rouze, to shake the Soul he comes,
And Jove's own Thunders follow Mars's Drums.

Arrest him, Empress, or you sleep no more"—
She heard, and drove him to th' Hibernian shore.

Though Pope here is not pushing the language around as power-
fully or extravagantly as he sometimes does, the passage offers
words one might well underline as being of interest to the lexicographer: quaint, chromatic, fritter, harmonize, joys in . . .
dances in, meanly, shake.

Johnson knew the passage, to be sure. One word, "fritter," is
quoted in the *Dictionary*, though his quotation begins "Joy to
great Chaos," and leaves out the next line, so the passage in Johnson makes little sense. The other words I noted are not in the *Dictionary* in their Popean usage. Johnson offers the following definitions for "quaint": "Nice, scrupulously, minutely, superfluously
exact"; "Subtle; artful. Obsolete"; "Neat; pretty; exact"; "Subtly
excogitated; finespun"; "Affected; foppish, this is not the true
idea of the word, which Swift seems not to have well understood." So Johnson is apparently hard at work with "quaint," but
Pope's sense of the word, while like some of these, and seeming
to include some of the meaning Johnson thought Swift should
not have given it, implies something more flamboyant than
"pretty" or "exact" can yield, something more of the velvet glove
that covers the iron fist. It is odd that "chromatic" is absent, since
Pope uses the word precisely, and Johnson's nearest definition is
far away: "Relating to a certain species of ancient musick, now
unknown." A meaning clearly available to Pope was clearly available to Johnson, but he refused the invitation. Johnson's one definition of "harmonize"—"To adjust to fit proportions; to make
musical"—works well enough for Pope; what is striking is that
the soprano's chromatic tortures harmonize "joy, grief, and
rage," which is to yoke discordant elements together by violence,
and to make anything but harmony. Johnson happened to pay
little attention to the preposition "in," but one can note that
thereby not only is Pope's switch in usages of "in" ignored, but so
too is each separate definition; Johnson does not come close to the
sense of "within, while wearing" that Pope essays in "dances in
my chains." "Mean" and "meanly" likewise did not attract much

attention from Johnson, so he has nothing like Pope's sense in "If Musick meanly borrows aid from Sense," of adding "slyly" or "stealthily" to "lowly" to indicate the danger represented by Handel's oratorios. Pope's sense that Handel can "shake" the soul is covered by the simplest literal definition, but Johnson never indicates that such shaking could be a good thing, inspiring.

Given the nature of the *Dictionary*, in which Pope need not be represented at all, one need not press the evidence into a distinct shape, and Johnson's lapses or ignorings there would never be noticed if one were not looking for them. But when one does begin to look, the evidence is everywhere that when Pope was in question, Johnson became strained, myopic, inattentive, acerbic, and liable to leap to the most easily available perch of wisdom.

Darkness had fallen, and Johnson did not know it because he refused to try to take Pope seriously. Looking back from a later time, we can think of countless figures who could, at best, guess what historical currents they were swimming in. How *can* one read the times in which one lives? But looking ahead, as it were, to Johnson, from the vantage points offered by earlier writers, we can see how much more easily they knew when they were. Dryden knew when he was, and assessed the matter with great, calm, anxiousness: *this* is what we must concede to the last age, *that* is what we must not. The historical instincts of Donne, Jonson, and, a generation later, of Carew, and, a generation later still, of Milton and Marvell, were excellent, available when needed, and imprecise only in details. Those of Pope were, at the last, uncanny. In the later stages of the Renaissance, it became increasingly important to have a clear historical sense, in order to see what had gone and what remained and what needed recovery.

But after Pope, darkness fallen, and none able to discern this clearly, it is as though two sets of responses were possible. The first was Johnson's, and, in a different but related way, Gibbon's: clear your mind of cant, know where you stand, explode the debris that the ages have accumulated. Be lowly wise, be majestically wise, be able to demolish history with wisdom. For contrast, we can offer this wisdom of Spenser:

> On either side of her, two young men stood,
> Both strongly arm'd, as fearing one another;
> Yet were they brethren both of halfe the blood,
> Begotten by two fathers of one mother,
> Though of contrarie natures each to other:
> The one of them hight *Love,* the other *Hate,*
> *Hate* was the elder, *Love* the younger brother;
> Yet was the younger stronger in his state
> Then th' elder, and him maystred still in all debate.

This is ancient, unembattled wisdom; Spenser is heir to all the ages, but what he knows anyone might easily know: Love and Hate are brothers, and Hate is prior, and therefore stronger in one sense, but Love, being love, can master the more primitive force. Spenser is rebuking no one, correcting no one, imagining no one in particular in need of his simple (or, as a friend of mine calls it, simpleminded) reminding. If what he offers here is not all ye know on earth or all ye need to know, then some other stanza of his vast poem may be better for you, or me, or some particular other member of the great human community.

Johnson's wisdom, by comparison, is grimmer, and more like an explosive, more aware that too many of us fill our minds with baggage that must, then, *be* exploded. Since I have already quoted much Johnsonian wisdom, let me here offer this, from Gibbon:

> Most of the crimes which disturb the internal peace of society are produced by the restraints which the necessary, but un-equal, laws of property have imposed on the appetites of mankind, by confining to a few the possession of those objects that are coveted by many. Of all our passions and appetites, the love of power is of the most imperious and unsociable nature, since the pride of one man requires the submission of the multitude. In the tumult of civil discord, the laws of society lose their force, and their place is seldom supplied by those of humanity. The ardour of contention, the pride of victory, the despair of success, the memory of past injuries, and the fear of future dangers, all contribute to inflame the mind, and to silence the voice of pity.

This is so much denser than the Spenser, so much more compli-
catedly thought through, and, though he might not have autho-
rized one word of it, so much like Johnson. Gibbon is clearing the
mind of cant in order to place before us a mystery: of course laws
of property create discord, of course the love of power places us
beyond the call of society or pity, where we feel only the pride of
victory or the despair of success. And as we assent, how then explain Commodus, the beast Gibbon has in view, the emperor
who inaugurated the decline of Rome, who had all the property
and power to begin with? Gibbon differs from Johnson only in
the way his great waves, as they beat against the shore, leave
a human iniquity unaccounted for, but what he seeks Johnson
seeks, a terrible, grim, witty reminding, not a simple, or simpleminded, statement of what we all know about the relation of loving and hating.

But to be complexly and ironically wise was something that
was forced upon both Gibbon and Johnson, and this they did not
know. Their very triumphs were in this sense beleaguered, and
that, too, it seems, they did not know. Gibbon, we may note, was
superbly alert to what possibilities were available to a person or
persons at any moment in the long epochs from A.D. 180 to 1453,
but his major unit of exploration was not the historical epoch but
the paragraph, and its majestic ironic possibilities. Johnson's assurance was that while this or that had changed, nothing in those
changes could alter his ability to know that where Juvenal might
show a Hannibal, he could show a Charles XII, or that while Pope
might announce a universal darkness, that was only the last great
outcry of a nature given over to rage and vanity. Gibbon and
Johnson are the great levelers of our literature, both living at
a time of diminished possibilities, both blind to that fact, both
thereby phenomenally alert to cant, to the need for wisdom when
it came to assessing the past, and, again without knowing it, to
shoring one's land against the ruins.

If the first possible response to the onset of darkness was Johnson's and Gibbon's, the second was Richardson's, and Fielding's. In the decade after *Dunciad* 4 we have, first, *Pamela, Sham-
ela,* and *Joseph Andrews,* and then the true inaugural of the novel
in *Clarissa* and *Tom Jones,* two huge works by antithetic geniuses,

about life lived in darkness, in which intelligibility is left to be created, and understood, as best as possible, by two late adolescents, their forebears having shown themselves ineffectual or bankrupt. Though both novels make large claims for themselves, their scope is mostly enclosed domestic space, so that heroism for Clarissa and Tom can only be the pursuit of virtue as a conception of self in relation to those few others one encounters. By comparison with many later novelistic heroes, Tom and especially Clarissa seem grand indeed, but, compared to Hamlet or Adam, they are domestic and ongoing.

When history is making one of its major turnings, proof often comes quickly, and none is perhaps more striking than this establishment of fiction as literature's major form in the immediate aftermath of Pope's vision of the unintelligibility of the created universe. For novels do not ask the universe to be intelligible, available, or responsive: "Stars, hide your fires! Let not light see my black and deep desires," says Macbeth; it is impossible to imagine Lovelace or Blifil contemplating their wickedness in such a large and responsive space. "Sweet is the breath of morn, her risings sweet," says Eve, apprehending her love of Adam in an apprehension of the splendid orderliness of God's creation; no such way of loving was open for Tom or Sophie. And what was left of such older ways of seeing and knowing was largely cant:

> Now the rake Hesperus had called for his breeches, and, having well rubbed his drowsy eyes, prepared to dress himself for all night; by whose example his brother rakes on earth likewise leave those beds in which they had slept away the day. Now Thetis, the good housewife, began to put on the pot, in order to regale the good man Phoebus after his daily labours were over. In vulgar language, it was in the evening when Joseph attended his lady's orders.

Fielding's mock epic bears none of the intimate relation of Pope's to Vergil or Milton. Hesperus, Thetis, and Phoebus are for him mere rhetorical flotsam left lying about, as they often are in the poems of literary late Augustan poets—see Gray's sonnet on the death of Richard West, for instance, that became cannon fodder for Wordsworth and Coleridge. Clarissa's bare announcement that she is going to her Father's house as she prepares to die may deceive her friends but has no echo in it of the witty, clashing journeys of Donne or Herbert speaking of or to God; even Macheath's "At the tree I shall suffer with pleasure" in *The Beggar's Opera* has more resonance. Words like "honest," "honor," and "virtue" become mere tatters of their former selves when spoken by Pamela or Lady Booby. In novels, the sky has been lowered, the units of consideration have become fragments, separate individuals leading daily lives, and lives begin to matter when they are more, not less, like our own.

Johnson was uninterested in doing something new as the printer Richardson and the hackwriter-magistrate Fielding did. But he faced the same world and had a similar task. He might hanker after originality in response to his wise sense that there was nothing new under the sun, but he was, always, a citizen of the old culture, never a seeker after the new. The figure he cuts in Boswell's *Life* is of a man always alert to the presence of the same kind of flotsam we can see in Fielding's paragraph above, but, a livelier, deeper, and gloomier man than Fielding, Johnson offers brief and telling sallies rather than whole sets of strategies and tactics for exposing cant. In his writing, even when he sustained himself over long periods of time at his labor, the work is fitful, rising to great heights, lapsing into the commonplace or the passable when his material did not inspire him. In the *Dictionary* he gave the past its space, lovingly let it shine, because he was essentially a private person, living a private life, in darkness, not in need of pointing out his wisest, cleverest, or funniest thoughts and maneuvers. And when we survey his writings, we see the same willingness to be fragmented, to do this then and that now, never offering himself—as Spenser, Donne, Jonson, Milton, Dryden, Pope had done—as a writer with ambition, with thoughts and feelings needing to become memorable words that will be accepted in the public world as the heir of a vast sustaining culture.

If we tried to inventory qualities that result from living in darkness, we could offer (without meaning to say people before 1742

were innocent of these ideas, feelings, or ways of knowing): frag-
mentation seen as specialization of knowledge, dislocation from
the past and an inability to see when one is; a sense that old materials have worn out and that new materials and new ways of seeing are essential; the breakdown of metaphor from a sense that
the creation created its own metaphors to a pressure put upon
writer and language to be "creative," or "original," or "imagina-
tive"; a habit of empiricism, common sense, and of making the
individual consciousness or character the major or even the sole
unit of inquiry.

Looking at Samuel Johnson with this inventory in mind, we
see what we might expect. Those habits of mind created triumphantly at the onset of Popean darkness, Johnson disavowed for
the most part, because he remained a citizen of the older culture.
But over and over he expressed the fact that the world had darkened. If Pope's use of abstractions like "Nature," "first cause,"
"parts" and "whole" is somewhat pallid, Johnson's reiterated
and at times almost forlorn use of the term "subordination" to describe how things came to be as they are places him at a still further remove from the earlier, denser, analogical understandings
of order. And, most of all, in his relation to Pope we see someone
cut off without knowing it. Here is our first major instance of a
large figure wrestling with a predecessor, and losing, because the
predecessor cannot be seen clearly, and the result is crippling,
though compared to what we can find in the last two centuries,
Johnson's failure with Pope seems more a matter of temperament
and less a necessary and diminishing tangle.

In his last work, Dryden had written: " 'Tis well an old age is
out / And time to begin a new." It was almost half a century before the old age was out, and almost another half century before
the new age truly began. The last great prose works of the old age
were Gibbon's history, Boswell's *Life*, and Burke's *Reflections on
the French Revolution*. The last great poem is Johnson's "On the
Death of Mr. Robert Levet." Here is the end of the line truly, a
poem that may never have had its due because the new age began
so soon afterward that it may have seemed outmoded while it
was still new. It is appropriate to end with it here as a way of hon-

oring Johnson, his best book a dictionary, his strongest appearance in someone else's book about him, his poems a few scattered things, his best prose work an homage to a friend whose life and work had come to nothing. Not so much a great writer, says Mudrick, as a great man writing. Which is true of his poem on the occasion of Levet's death, Levet aged seventy-nine, Johnson aged seventy-two, but the great man does wonderfully:

> Condemn'd to hope's delusive mine,
>   As on we toil from day to day,
> By sudden blasts, or slow decline,
>   Our social comforts drop away.

It is too bad Johnson did not discover the tetrameter quatrain earlier, for it is much more suited to his genius than the heroic couplet, where the solemnity invites grand sweeps and the sense of diminution from what Pope had achieved is always felt. In a pentameter line the crucial phrase, "social comforts," would have fared less well. Such comforts can seem a paltry concern, after all, but in the shorter line the phrases are fitted, and not swept along. After placing us in "hope's delusive mine," having shown that toilers in that mine can expect only blasts and decline, then "social comforts" seem pathetically weak and very important.

> Well tried through many a varying year,
>   See LEVET to the grave descend;
> Officious, innocent, sincere,
>   Of every friendless name the friend.

> Yet still he fills affection's eye,
>   Obscurely wise, and coarsely kind;
> Nor, letter'd arrogance, deny
>   Thy praise to merit unrefined.

Levet was disheveled and unlettered, not one who could be asked to join the Club, and he did not always get along easily with Anna Williams and Frank Barber and others in Johnson's household; given such an entourage, Johnson often preferred to live with the Thrales. But Johnson knew Levet as his fellow, obscurely wise because there was no wisdom in what he said, coarsely kind so that only those most in need of his kindness could recognize it for what it was. Worth makes the man; the rest is nothing but leather and prunella.

Above all, the poem can work the old culture's miracles with allegory:

> When fainting nature call'd for aid,
>   And hov'ring death prepared the blow,
> His vig'rous remedy display'd
>   The power of art without the show.
>
> In misery's darkest caverns known,
>   His useful care was ever nigh,
> Where hopeless anguish pour'd his groan
>   And lonely want retir'd to die.

Amidst the looming actions of the great prime movers—nature, death, art, misery, anguish, want—Levet himself moves, submerging himself into his "vig'rous remedy" and "useful care." But that is the praise of him, all claims of self and status irrelevant. Who else can move at all, to say nothing of vigorously and usefully, when nature faints, death hovers, hopeless anguish groans, and lonely want dies?

Johnson himself could, but only occasionally, and he knew it, just as he knew that hopeless anguish and lonely want can use Levet's care, can know its consolation after everything else has deserted or died:

> No summons mock'd by chill delay
>   No petty gain disdain'd by pride,
> The modest wants of every day
>   The toil of ev'ry day supplied.

It is wonderful to note the difference in tone and effect between "As on we toil from day to day" at the beginning of the poem and "The toil of ev'ry day supplied" here. The first is Johnson, *Rambler* wise and *Rasselas* weary; the second is Levet, always on call, turning toil to use, accepting whatever a patient could offer. Levet does not rebuke Johnson in this, but he forces Johnson to see how he could *be* rebuked:

His virtues walk'd their narrow round,
  Nor made a pause, nor left a void;
And sure th' Eternal Maker found
  The single talent well employed.

To take one talent, and with it to make oneself into one's virtues, so that it is the virtues who walk Levet's narrow round, may be more than Johnson, who had many talents and knew he had not turned them all into virtues, could claim. But he was a great man, and without him we never would have known Levet, and been thus humbled; the poem, says Christopher Hollis, is "one of the very few entirely sincere tributes paid by one whom the world calls a success to one whom the world calls a failure." Even the "Life of Savage," great as it is in this regard, cannot quite be called that.

It is usually deflecting to use "sincere" in working with the poetry of the old culture, but here it seems appropriate. We are never asked to inquire into the purity of Johnson's feeling—that is what the older poetry prevents—but we can see Johnson locating himself, and his stern loneliness, his comforts dropped once more at Levet's death, his feeling rebuked by Levet's life, because all these can be placed in the context of the looming allegorical figures that are so much more powerful than either Johnson or Levet. By showing how little Levet could do, Johnson makes us see how much he did.

Neither bang nor whimper but fitting close. No one could write this way with any success after Johnson. The next voice to be heard would be that of Blake's Piper.

SHELLEY knew more about poetry than that it brought light and fire from the eternal regions. He knew, for instance, that Wordsworth was more singular than any formula:

> He had a mind which was somehow
>   At once circumference and centre
> Of all he might or feel or know;
> Nothing went ever out, although
>   Something did ever enter.
>
> He had as much imagination
>   As a pint-pot;—he never could
> Fancy another situation
> From which to dart his contemplation,
>   Than that wherein he stood.
>
> Yet his was individual mind,
>   And new-created all he saw
> In a new manner, and refined
> Those new creations, and combined
>   Them, by a master-spirit's law.
>
> Thus—though unimaginative—
>   An apprehension clear, intense,
> Of his mind's work, had made alive
> The things it wrought on; I believe
>   Wakening a sort of thought in sense.

The lines were dashed off, Shelley in a Byronic *Don Juan* mood;
they come from *Peter Bell the Third,* written by one Miching Mal-
lecho. Leigh Hunt had sent Shelley an essay of his about *Peter
Bell,* along with a skit by Keats's friend John Hamilton Reynolds,
called *Peter Bell, a Lyrical Ballad.* Shelley had not seen Wordsworth's poem, and may never have, but he hardly needed to,
since he already had the Wordsworth he needed. "He was at first
sublime," he writes in his preface to *Peter Bell the Third,* "pathetic,
impressive, profound; then dull; then prosy and dull; and now
dull—oh, so very dull! it is an ultra-legitimate dulness." Hunt
and Reynolds would have been content with Shelley's fable
about the ultra-legitimately dull Wordsworth, but Shelley had to
get "sublime, pathetic, impressive, profound" in too.

"He had a mind which was somehow at once circumference
and centre of all he might feel or know"—one could hardly imagine a better first sentence to begin one's understanding of Wordsworth, the supreme poet of the darkened world. Wordsworth
knows what he knows because *he* knows it; he inherits almost
nothing. It is his strength to be able to say, and mean, and to be
able sublimely to get away with saying and meaning: "Lucy is
in her grave and oh! The difference to me!" The great egotists
Donne and Jonson would not have dared to imagine such lines.
Wordsworth had as much imagination as a pint-pot, and so could
not concern himself with the difference Lucy's death might make
to her; he could pass by *that,* as past darkest Erebus, unalarmed.
It was only what had happened to him that mattered.

Yet Lucy, so obscure she could tread untrodden ways and
leave them untrodden, can be a powerful figure for us, because
Wordsworth's mind could make "alive the things it wrought on;
I believe wakening a sort of thought in sense." How he did it
Shelley could not say, but that he did it Shelley was certain:

> At night he oft would start and wake
>   Like a lover, and began
> In a wild measure songs to make
> On moor, and glen, and rocky lake,
>   And on the heart of man—

And on the universal sky—
   And the wide earth's bosom green,—
And the sweet, strange mystery
Of what beyond these things may lie,
   And yet remain unseen.

Wordsworth had made words like "somehow," "something," and "sort of" part of his magical usage, his break from the centuries of metaphor of precise usage. He could write in "Tintern Abbey" of "the round ocean or the living air," so Shelley was free to echo with "And on the heart of man—And on the universal sky," because if the ocean is round and the air lives, the sky can undoubtedly be universal. Since Wordsworth, also in "Tintern Abbey," sees silent smoke, as though smoke could be other, and posits the fire had been lit by a hermit sitting alone, Shelley knew Wordsworth knew of what he could not see.

"For language was in Peter's hand / Like clay while he was yet a potter." True, though it is doubtful if even Shelley knew how strange and new Wordsworth's language was. Lucy is "Rolled round in earth's diurnal course," and we know, without knowing how we know, that suddenly Wordsworth needs that oddly precise "diurnal"—no mere "daily" will do. Or we can look at many lines and wonder if we are faced with precision or blank gestures: "With rocks and stones and trees," "sensations sweet, felt in the blood, and felt along the heart," "And with what motion moved the clouds!" Are rocks importantly different from stones? Are "in" and "along" directing us to some distinction between blood and heart? With *what* motion moved the clouds? Are the questions even relevant? Christ's blood, says Donne in "Good Friday 1613, Riding Westward," "made dirt of dust," and we know Donne is imagining a distinction, and a process of change that, even if we have to consult the *OED* to discover it, we can soberly understand. But we can ask and ask about "rocks and stones" and never be sure of an answer.

Furthermore, having no more imagination than a pint-pot, Wordsworth may not have known how striking, how impossible, in relation to the bearings offered by the old poetry, he could be.

He was a good critic, he read a lot, and he laid great stress on the need to be "original," yet he may not have seen himself as a great original user of words because he would have placed the emphasis elsewhere. One of his strangest, and most illuminating, statements about poetry comes at the end of Book 5 of *The Prelude:*

> Here must we pause: this only let me add,
> From heart-experience, and in humblest sense
> Of modesty, that he, who in his youth
> A daily wanderer among woods and fields
> With living Nature hath been intimate,
> Not only in that raw unpractised time
> Is stirred to ecstasy, as others are,
> By glittering verse; but further, doth receive,
> In measure only dealt out to himself,
> Knowledge and increase of enduring joy
> From the great Nature that exists in works
> Of mighty Poets.

It is an astonishing statement, blithely rendering as it does city types like Jonson, or Johnson, or Coleridge, into lesser readers of poetry. Centuries of poets and critics seem to disappear before Wordsworth's unblinking eyes, so intent is he on offering his qualifications for being a great reader, qualifications not so much special as uniquely his. Equally astonishing is what follows:

> Visionary power
> Attends the motion of the viewless winds,
> Embodied in the mystery of words:
> There, darkness makes abode, and all the host
> Of shadowy things work endless changes,—

Can one make any sense of the idea that darkness makes abode in Book 2 of *Troilus and Criseyde,* in Cleopatra's dream of her emperor Antony, in Adam's words to himself when he sees Eve and the eaten apple, in Pope on Narcissa? Is it not the case that in a chronologically arranged anthology of places where darkness *does* make abode in the works of mighty poets, the first entries are all Wordsworth?

As for the visionary power that attends the motions of the

viewless winds, it is Wordsworth's gentle breeze, his muse, which opens *The Prelude,* and what he describes in Book 5 is the power he feels in and around himself, no matter how little he could be imagined to have found it in earlier poetry:

> —there,
> As in a mansion like their proper home,
> Even forms and substances are circumfused
> By that transparent veil with light divine,
> And, through the turnings intricate of verse,
> Present themselves as objects recognised,
> In flashes, and with glory not their own.

Little as one knows what it means that in the mansion of darkness forms "are circumfused by that transparent veil with light divine," one knows this is a perfect *ars poetica* for a poet of darkness.

When faced with specific poems and passages, Wordsworth—and Coleridge too—often wrote well, like the well-educated eighteenth-century gentlemen they were. They knew when all that could be said of some lines was that they lacked sense. Wordsworth said of Johnson's redaction of a passage in Proverbs that it was a "hubbub of Words," and Coleridge could say of a line of Gray's that it has almost as many faults as words. Coleridge sounds like no one so much as Johnson when he responds to the "Best philosopher, Seer blest" passage in Wordsworth's "Ode." It would be possible, then, to say of this passage at the end of Book 5 that it wants sense, that it is a hubbub, that it has faults, if not as many faults as words. One blushes to imagine Johnson's comment on the special joys given to readers of poetry who in their youth had wandered among woods and fields. The analogical universe darkened, Wordsworth is naively literal. Yet "a master-spirit's law" is at work here.

If darkness makes abode in poetry—this is not Pope's darkness, yet how apposite they are—then the poet must put it there somehow, embody it in the mystery of words even as the poetry is being lit with a visionary power. For Wordsworth the darkness did not begin in poetry, but in the mind that was the haunt and main region of his song, and what haunted his mind was his past, especially his childhood. Wordsworth did not invent childhood,

but before him it is only one of the seven ages of man—"Thy in-
fancy, thy childhood, and thy youth," says Milton, and he might
have had something to say about the education proper to childhood, but he saw nothing special about it. It was Wordsworth
who invented the specialness, and what he took from his childhood were the famous spots of time.

So let us look at one of them. In Book 12 of *The Prelude* he recalls
a time when he rides into the hills with a servant, from whom he
suddenly is separated:

> and, through fear
> Dismounting, down the rough and stony moor
> I led my horse, and, stumbling on, at length
> Came to a bottom

The fear is natural, understandable, and likewise the description
of the descent and what he finds there:

> where in former times
> A murderer had been hung in iron chains.
> The gibbet-mast had mouldered down, the bones
> And iron case were gone; but on the turf,
> Hard by, soon after that fell deed was wrought,
> Some unknown hand had carved the murderer's name.
> The monumental letters were inscribed
> In times long past; but still, from year to year,
> By superstition of the neighbourhood,
> The grass is cleared away, and to this hour
> The characters are fresh and visible.

This could be the Wanderer beginning some "philosophic song of
Truth that cherishes our daily life," and the boy knows his lore,
knows the tale of the murderer and can say the bones and iron
case were gone but had once been there. But then:

> A casual glance had shown them, and I fled,
> Faltering and faint, and ignorant of the road.

Darkness makes abode here, surely. The boy has made some association with the murderer already, so that the "fell deed" is not
the original murder but the execution, and he makes some associ-

ation now, but what he does not know, or cannot say. All sense of understandable fear, or of lore, is lost.

We read of young Wordsworth stealing from another's traps, and stealing another's boat, after which he hears "low breathings coming after" him and he is haunted by "huge forms that do not live like living men." We can say we know what happened: the terror and guilt animate the surrounding world and the boy is powerless to escape. He was a child fostered alike by fear and by fear. We can also say that his greatness begins in his not flying to some rational explanation, or to adult patronizing talk of things that go bump in the night. The mystery remained mysterious, and thereby continued to haunt him. In this moment in Book 12, "somehow" the boy sees his own name as he reads that of the murderer; but that says little. If a guilty secret is being glimpsed, it is a secret and cannot feel the touch of earthly speculation. *Caverns* there were within his mind, he says, where sun could never reach.

The wonders of this episode, though, turn out to have just begun:

> Then, reascending the bare common, saw
> A naked pool that lay beneath the hills,
> The beacon on the summit, and, more near,
> A girl, who bore a pitcher on her head,
> And seemed with difficult steps to force her way
> Against the blowing wind.

As with the description of the legend of the murderer, Wordsworth flattens details and speaks calmly. Then another turn:

> It was, in truth,
> An ordinary sight, but I should need
> Colours and words that are unknown to man,
> To paint the visionary dreariness
> Which, while I looked all round for my lost guide,
> Invested moorland waste, and naked pool,
> The beacon crowning the lone eminence,
> The female and her garments vexed and tossed
> By the strong wind.

The host of shadowy things works changes here. The details are described twice, but no one can read the passage aloud without hearing the difference, the dreariness that invests itself over the ordinary sight, and a prose description of exactly how the language works to achieve the difference cannot do as well as the voice.

I did it, he says, or seems to say, by making the mind the main region of my song. But it also is the visionary dreariness that does the investing, some power to which he has yielded himself so that we are riveted not on Wordsworth's mind but on the objects, the pool, the beacon, and the girl. It is the that-there-ness of the objects that is so haunting, that keeps the experience fused with landscape, that insists we honor what happened and not trail along with inadequate explanations about how or why. In saying the guide-servant was lost, there is an overlay that implies the boy was found, right then, right there.

Still we are not done:

> When, in the blessed hours
> Of early love, the loved one at my side,
> I roamed, in the daily presence of this scene,
> Upon the naked pool and dreary crags,
> And on the melancholy beacon, fell
> A spirit of pleasure and youth's golden gleam;
> And think ye not with radiance more sublime
> For these remembrances, and for the power
> They had left behind?

This may not have happened to anyone else, before or since. Wordsworth does not take Mary back to enjoy the memory of a little childhood horror, and he insists that the pool, the beacon, and the crags are as they were, naked, dreary, melancholy. The scene has for him the unquestioned solidity, strength, and renovating virtue that elsewhere Wordsworth finds in Lucy, Margaret, and the leech-gatherer. Young love is given a sublime radiance because of the power the memories had left behind, or, to use the words of the stolen boat episode, high objects

> purifying thus
> The elements of feeling and of thought,
> And sanctifying, by such discipline,
> Both pain and fear, until we recognise
> A grandeur in the beatings of the heart.

Between the childhood terror and the return with Mary there had been a purifying, a discipline, a sanctification, all because he had yielded himself to the high objects that held him, because the scene was neither explained nor made symbolic.

The incidents themselves are not amazing; they are the stuff of realistic fiction rather than pastorals, or odes about retirement, or panegyrics to country places and country life. We all have done things like steal boats, flee from terrors, stand in wonderment at discharged soldiers, or make ourselves dizzy while ice skating. What happened to Wordsworth, though, during these experiences, was the process whereby his mind was "somehow" at once its own circumference and center. If we cannot say what it is for that to be true, we know it was true for this man, and if it can be said of others, it is those like Lucy and the leech-gatherer, who do not strike us as having had, as having needed, minds or consciousness at all. If, however, we find Wordsworth amazing, it can be said that he did too; he says, at the close of the incident of the murderer's name:

> I am lost, but see
> In simple childhood something of the base
> On which thy greatness stands; but this I feel,
> That from thyself it comes, that thou must give,
> Else never canst receive. The days gone by
> Return upon me almost from the dawn
> Of life; the hiding-places of man's power
> Open; I would approach them, but they close.
> I see by glimpses now; when age comes on,
> May scarcely see at all.

He had, just before this, risen to a full-plumaged utterance: "Oh! mystery of man, from what a depth Proceed thy honours." But rising, he fell, lost, contemplating the mystery. He recovers by trying to claim that childhoods like his were "simple"; he then slides off to his characteristic "something," and then addresses us: one must give oneself to the mystery to receive it. The hiding places of power open, begin to close, may be seen only in glimpses later on, or not at all, but what will remain are the basic ingredients: the transporting feeling, usually guilt or fear, and the riveting, unexplainable and unexplaining, details of the surrounding landscape.

Wordsworth had great difficulty when he came to inquiring into the ways his experience is like ours, the possibilities of moving from "I" to "we." On the brink of his great period of writing, in "Tintern Abbey," the problem arises almost without Wordsworth's seeming to know it; he is describing the "serene and blessed mood" in which he remembers, in the years after his first visit to the Wye Valley, his experience there, and its "tranquil restoration." He wants to generalize:

> that blessed mood,
> In which the burthen of the mystery,
> In which the heavy and the weary weight
> Of all this unintelligible world,
> Is lightened:—that serene and blessed mood,
> In which the affections gently lead *us* on,—
> Until, the breath of this corporeal frame
> And even the motion of *our* human blood
> Almost suspended, *we* are laid asleep
> In body, and become a living soul:
> While with an eye made quiet by the power
> Of harmony, and the deep power of joy,
> *We* see into the life of things.

This is Wordsworth working in the shards of allegory, the human being being led by affections, laid asleep, where harmony and joy come and enable—but there's the rub—Wordsworth? or all of us?—to see into the life of things.

Sensing the rub, Wordsworth pulls back from his claim: "If this Be but a vain belief." One might think he pulls back because he is uncertain if he can claim to see into the life of things, but the fact that he then moves on to the first-person singular and with great confidence shows that what really may be vain about his belief is the result of our not being like him, not able to see into the life of things, or as he does.

He was not ready to proclaim himself a writer of personal experience only, especially when contemplating a long poem. He opens *The Prelude* feeling that such a poem is within his power, blessed as he is by the gentle breeze that is his muse, but then he fumbles among the traditional stories to find a suitable subject, "some old Romantic tale by Milton left unsung." But the effort fails, because the past was past, its bearings lost, and epics and romances could not be written in a society unable to nurture them. Wordsworth then falls into the free association of memories that makes up his poem, his great poem, but one he can only call *The Prelude* because he continued to hope his really great poem would be philosophical rather than personal.

But he cannot let the matter rest there. In Book 3, about to leave the riches of his childhood to describe the flatter experiences of Cambridge, he again rises up to great claiming verse:

> O Heavens! how awful is the might of souls,
> And what they do within themselves while yet
> The yoke of earth is new to them, the world
> Nothing but a wide field where they were sown.
> This is, in truth, heroic argument,
> This genuine prowess, which I wished to touch
> With hand however weak, but in the main
> It lies far hidden from the reach of words.

Wordsworth takes up Milton's phrase, "heroic argument," and democratizes it by saying that the might of all our souls is heroic when young; he places the old heroic word "prowess" onto this might, though he has just said these souls were only seeds. So, as he often does when he is writing well, he tries to claim a great deal, but then backs off, insisting this prowess of ours must lie hidden from the reach of words.

No major writer before Wordsworth, of course, thought anything was hidden from the reach of words, since the universe was received and, children of Adam, our task was to name what we had been given. But Wordsworth knew that his universe had been given him mostly in the spots of time where something mighty happened within him while yet the yoke was new, and these spots could be hidden. Yet he is still going to try to insist on his "we":

> Points have we all of us within our souls
> Where all stand single; this I feel, and make
> Breathings for incommunicable powers;
> But is not each a memory to himself?—
> And, therefore, now that we must quit this theme,
> I am not heartless, for there's not a man
> That lives who hath not known his god-like hours,
> And feels not what an empire we inherit
> As natural beings in the strength of Nature.

That we all have points where we stand single no one ever doubted, but the next lines show Wordsworth is uncertain how to proceed. "This I feel, and make Breathings for incommunicable powers" has a strange grammar, since "make" is parallel to "feel" and so the breathings are only Wordsworth's, whereas he wants "make" to be an action in all our souls. Sensing this, perhaps, he comes back with an appeal—"is not each a memory to himself?"—which is too easy, since that truth cannot affirm the might of our souls when young. But, himself indeed not heartless, he leaves the matter dangling, and affirms we have all had godlike hours, we are all heirs to empires. Which is a statement some, but not many, could affirm along with him. Which is why Shelley and Keats knew that what is sublime in Wordsworth is egotistical and naive.

If the emphasis I am making about the specialness of Wordsworth's case and the strangeness of his use of language when exploring dark passages is right, it ought to identify those places where we can find his greatest achievement: *The Prelude,* "The Ruined Cottage" (*The Excursion,* Book 1), and the Lucy poems; as a prologue to these, "Tintern Abbey," and as epilogue, "Resolution and Independence." One might refine the list by deleting the showy mechanical climbing of Mount Snowden in Book 14 of *The Prelude* and put "Nutting" in its place. There are brilliant moments elsewhere, and, after the great period of 1797–1802 was over, he could still give some impressive performances, from the Intimations ode all the way down to "Written after the Death of Charles Lamb" in 1835, but the stress should fall on the spots of time and his encounters with Lucy, Margaret, and the leech-gatherer, those natural beings in the strength of Nature.

⫸⫸⫸⫸Friedrich Schiller's "Naive and Sentimental Poetry" of 1797 is the great gloss for the reader of Wordsworth, even more than the famous chapters in the *Biographia Literaria,* and a consideration of two of Schiller's passages can do a great deal to help us place Wordsworth in the history of traditions, passing on and coming later. First, a lovely straightforward meditation about our relation to the rest of nature:

> For, after all, is there anything specially charming in a flower of common appearance, in a spring, a moss-covered stone, the warbling of birds, or the buzzing of bees, etc.? What is it that can give these objects a claim to our love? It is not these objects in themselves; it is an idea represented by them that we love in them. We love in them life and its latent action, the effects produced by beings of themselves, existence under its proper laws, the inmost necessity of things, the eternal unity of their nature.
>
> These objects which captivate us *are* what we *were,* what we *must* be again some day. We were nature as they are; and culture, following the way of reason and of liberty, must bring us back to nature. Accordingly these objects are an image of our infancy irrevocably past—of our infancy which will remain eternally very dear to us; they are also our image of our highest perfection in the ideal world, whence they excite a sublime emotion in us.
>
> But the perfection of these objects is not a merit that belongs to them, because it is not the effect of their free choice. Accordingly, they procure quite a peculiar pleasure for us, by being our models without having anything humiliating for us. It is like a constant manifestation of the divinity sur-

rounding us, which refreshes without dazzling us. The very feature that constitutes their character is precisely what is lacking in ours to make it complete; and what distinguishes us from them is precisely what they lack to be divine. We are free and they are necessary; we change and they remain identical.

It is as though the Wanderer had turned philosopher. Here the "we" is secure—we all know what Schiller speaks of here, and differences among us would only be a matter of degree—in a way that shows us some of Wordsworth's specialness and torment. He could have applauded every word here, but he knew its truth not as an ordinary person but as one who had been possessed by a power expressed in nature. He is, actually, not a particularly good writer about natural objects because it was seldom the rocks, birds, and flowers that engaged him—a fact noted more than once by Dorothy Wordsworth in her journals—but the power and the memories of childhood that the thought of that power evoked. He was not the Wanderer.

On the other hand, lest the ease of Schiller's passage blind us to the fact, the "we" of whom he speaks, which includes us, and Wordsworth, as well as Schiller, would not have included, say, the Marvell of "The Garden" and "The Picture of Little T.C.," or the Shakespeare of *The Winter's Tale*, or the Herbert of "The Flower." Schiller's nature is unanalogical and unmediated; if the flower that captivates us *is* what we *were* and *must* be, we are not "but flowers that glide," Mopsa and Dorcas may have virgin branches on which their maidenheads are growing, but we never understood the matter that way. Schiller knows an ideal and a divinity, but these are vague, and we are cut off from them as we are from the rest of nature, and neither the divine nor the objects of nature are the materials for metaphors for ourselves. Nor were they for Wordsworth, and all he had left of the old feeling was that, at moments, at moments of childhood especially, he could be found, or seized, by a power in which he and the objects of nature could be forced into a unity whereby "an ordinary sight" could be invested with a "visionary dreariness." But by comparison with the earlier poets named above, Wordsworth, Schiller, and we ourselves are people in darkness, of the latter days.

Here, then, is Schiller contemplating this matter of the earlier and the later writer, those he calls the naive and the sentimental:

> Well, now let us take the idea of poetry, which is nothing else than *expressing humanity as completely as possible,* and let us apply this idea to these two states. We shall be brought to infer that on the one hand, in the state of natural simplicity, when all the faculties of man are exerted together, his being still manifests itself in a harmonious unity, where, consequently, the *totality* of his nature expresses itself in reality itself, the part of the *poet* is necessarily to imitate the real as completely as possible. In the state of civilization, on the contrary, when this harmonious completion of the whole of human nature is no longer anything but an idea, the part of the poet is necessarily to raise reality to the ideal, or, what amounts to the same thing, *to represent the ideal.* And, actually, these are the only two ways in which, in general, the poetic genius can manifest itself.

We can profitably employ this in two ways concerning Wordsworth.

We can say that those who are in a state of natural simplicity, when all the human faculties are exerted together, are Lucy, Margaret, the leech-gatherer, and, above all, the boy Wordsworth. None of these was a poet. Seen this way, Wordsworth the poet is sentimental, coming inevitably later, one for whom "this harmonious completion of the whole of human nature is no longer anything but an idea," so that the poet had to represent the ideal as loss, as elegy, as incompletion. The troubledness or doubt expressed in "My heart Leaps Up" and that has become almost formulaic in the Intimations ode shows how Wordsworth was sentimental, reflecting on the ideal naive.

But I have been trying, thus far, to show also how he comes as close as anyone after Chaucer to being a simple and naive poet. In his great dark passages, the totality of his nature expresses itself in reality itself, in his confidence that he does not, say, have to make anything of the crags, beacon, pool, and girl that surround his experience with the murderer's name, but need only name them and how he saw them. He is confident that during and after such experiences he has been disciplined, purified, and sanctified, and if the truly naive poet would not have to affirm this but would rather just exemplify it, nonetheless, Wordsworth accepts his experience, lets it take him whither it will, so that as poet all he must do is "to imitate the real as completely as possible." "Nutting" is a prime example of this naiveté. If a certain delicacy led Wordsworth to exclude this rape of a woodland scene from *The Prelude*, who else could have written it at all in its splendid simplicity? If one impulse *from* a vernal wood could teach more than all the poets, then one impulse *in* a vernal wood could lead to wanton, exultant destruction. The naive poet expresses what is true, the real, as it happened.

But I mentioned Chaucer a moment ago for a reason. By comparison with him, who strikes me as being truly simple or naive in Schiller's sense, Wordsworth is all cut off and longing, a writer afraid of being or becoming a sentimental, therefore elegiac, poet. The sequence in Book 2 of *Troilus and Criseyde,* in which Criseyde finishes her debate with herself about loving Troilus, listens to Antigone's song about the joys of love, goes to sleep listening to the song of the nightingale, and dreams of the eagle who silently takes her heart and replaces it with his own, is one of the most delicate passages in literature, because Chaucer gives full play to a variety of feelings and actions, swirls them around without ever giving less than full and equal weight to each one; by comparison, that later great valuer, and balancer, Herbert, is one we always see doing the balancing, whereas Chaucer just does it.

The end of Book 1 of *The Excursion* sets out Wordsworth's position perfectly. The Wanderer, *the* sentimental poet, finishes his tale of Margaret thus:

> "Yet still
> She loved this wretched spot, nor would for worlds
> Have parted hence; and still that length of road,
> And this rude bench, one torturing hope endeared,
> Fast rooted at her heart: and here, my Friend,—

In sickness she remained; and here she died;
Last human tenant of these ruined walls!"

Margaret is naive par excellence but no poet, enduring her last days nurtured by the hope her husband might return, making that torture endearing to her. Wordsworth rises, turning "aside in weakness," unable to thank the Wanderer for the tale, only able to review the tale, and the "plants, and weeds, and flowers, and silent overgrowings" that survived; this comforts him "While with a brother's love I blessed her in the impotence of grief." Feeling no such grief—"he could *afford* to suffer" Wordsworth says earlier—the Wanderer then delivers the homily:

"She sleeps in the calm earth, and peace is here.
I well remember that those very plumes,
Those weeds, and the high spear-grass on that wall,
By mist and silent rain-drops silvered o'er,
As once I passed, into my heart conveyed
So still an image of tranquility,
So calm and still, and looked so beautiful
Amid the uneasy thoughts which filled my mind,
That what we feel of sorrow and despair
From ruin and from change, and all the grief
The passing shows of Being leave behind,
Appeared an idle dream, that could maintain,
Nowhere, dominion o'er the enlightened spirit
Whose meditative sympathies repose
Upon the breast of Faith. I turned away,
And walked along my road in happiness."

So here is Margaret, the pathetic, and here still are the weeds and the spear-grass at her cottage; here is the Wanderer, wise, seeing the passing shows of grief unable to gain power over the breast of faith. The naive, and the sentimental seeing the ideal in the naive. But Wordsworth, who can affirm both, is neither:

He ceased. Ere long the sun declining shot
A slant and mellow radiance, which began
To fall upon us, while, beneath the trees,

> We sate on that low bench; and now we felt,
> Admonished thus, the sweet hour coming on.
> A linnet warbled from those lofty elms,
> A thrush sang loud, and other melodies,
> At distance heard, peopled the milder air.

In the fine flat tone, one he seldom used, Wordsworth refuses to locate himself as either still caught in the impotence of grief or able to walk along his road in happiness.

Perhaps the most striking instance of Wordsworth's way of placing himself so that the naive and the sentimental are both expressed is the greatest of the Lucy poems, and in this case, both are there simultaneously:

> A slumber did my spirit seal;
> I had no human fears;
> She seemed a thing that could not feel
> The touch of earthly years.

> No motion has she now, no force;
> She neither hears nor sees;
> Rolled round in earth's diurnal course,
> With rocks, and stones, and trees.

The second stanza can either be an intensification of the slumber, or a waking from it; "now" can continue the vision, or it can be a later time. If the second stanza describes the vision, "She" is triumphantly without motion or force, without need; unable to feel the touch of earthly years she rolls at one with earthly creation. If the second stanza breaks from the vision, and describes what happens after the slumber, then "She" *seemed* unable to feel the touch of earthly years, but she could and did; in the slumber she is immortal, but in life she was mortal. I see no way and no need to adjudicate between these two readings, though one has to read it aloud in two distinctly different ways to convey them. We can note, too, that the first reading corresponds to "Three years she grew in sun and shower," while the second corresponds to "She dwelt among untrodden ways." We are not, thus, dealing with some trick of language discovered by the clever critic at the expense of the impassioned but inadvertent poet, but with Wordsworth's two ways of placing himself in relation to Lucy, which is just what we have seen him do in relation to Margaret's story and the Wanderer's homily.

There lies the secret of Wordsworth's hauntedness. Lucy was, Lucy is; Lucy was, Lucy is no more, and O! the difference to him. What I had I have, and I embrace it triumphantly and naively; what I had I no longer have, and it can be embraced only as an ideal, sentimentally. In "A Slumber Did My Spirit Seal," he can take both positions at once; in the great moments of *The Prelude,* as in the shuffling for the right generalizations in the passages discussed above from Books 3 and 12, he teeters between the two; in *The Excursion,* Book 1, he balances himself between them. Knowing, haunted, fearing loss, darkness makes abode in the mystery of his greatest words.

››››To whom, then, is Wordsworth heir? The answer, it seems to me, is exactly what Wordsworth insisted it was: the child is father. But in a whole sequence of books Harold Bloom has kept insisting that the answer is Milton:

> *Tintern Abbey* is a Scene of Instruction in which the poet brings a Sublime response to a place or state of heightened demand, but the genius of the state counts for more than the genius of place, which means that Milton counts for more than nature does, both here and in *The Prelude.* It is Milton whose hidden presence in the poem makes the heightened demand that forces Wordsworth into the profoundly ambivalent defensive trope of memory. Renovation, or "tranquil restoration" as the text terms it, is only a mystification, a mask for the real concern of the poem. The Hermit is the synechdoche for Milton's hiddenness, and so for Milton's triumphant blindness towards anteriority. To see the writing or marking of nature is to see prophetically one's own absence or imaginative death. To see the "uncertain notice" of the Hermit's presence is to be disturbed into sublimity by way of repressing the mighty forces of remembering Milton's sublimity, particularly in the Creation of *Paradise Lost, Book VII,*

which haunts every Wordsworthian account of the subject-
and object-worlds approaching one another again.

This seems at once bizarre, impertinent, and obvious, but then it
is the function of antithetical readings, as Bloom calls them, to be
at least the first two of these. It is useful to have Bloom's way of
reading before us when trying to locate Wordsworth in the history of traditions I have been telling.

The major feeling of "Tintern Abbey" is gratitude. After the
disastrous breakdown of 1793, described in Books 10–11 of *The
Prelude*, Dorothy had rescued him, begun a long restoring of him,
and the visit to the Wye Valley in that year became an emblem of
that restoration. Five years later he returned, and it was still
there, green to the very door; in between there had been the
memory of his first visit, and Wordsworth is grateful for both the
new experience and the memory. But the poem keeps raising
problems for itself that it seems almost not to know are there. The
most obvious is the claim that in gaining a "sense of something
far more deeply interfused" he has found "abundant recompense," for a loss, presumably, but a loss that we, reading the
opening description, cannot locate. He once felt aching joys and
dizzying raptures, true, and no longer does, and he looks with
something like envy on his sister's wild eyes, but the strong pleasures of this second trip to Tintern seem to know no loss, no need
for recompense. No doubt Wordsworth felt some loss, but the
poem does not locate it.

But the reasons are not all that mysterious. The Wye Valley was
not home to him, was not his primary "scene of instruction." It is
notable that he misrepresents his childhood in "Tintern Abbey,"
not badly as in the Intimations ode, but *The Prelude* shows over
and over that "The coarser pleasures of my boyish days, / And
their glad animal movement" is not the point about the boy
Wordsworth. If "Tintern Abbey" is muffled it is because the
scene is not a scene of instruction, but a displaced one, and so in
this poem he could not encounter the child that was his true father, could not wrestle with questions of loss and recompense.
But he was shortly to return to the Lake District, and in *The Pre-*

lude there is of course no misreading, or swerving, and the unanswered questions are the magnificent heart of the spots of time.

One can hardly say that Wordsworth had no thought of Milton here; the reference to the "landscape to the blind man's eye," otherwise merely odd, may well indicate Wordsworth is thinking of Milton, but it is precisely the incidentalness of that reference that would lead one to believe that Milton's presence was mostly incidental for Wordsworth. As for the hermit who appears at the end of the opening description and who is not absorbed clearly into the poem, we find him so often in the poems of Wordsworth's next four years—as Lucy, the discharged soldier, the leech-gatherer, as the Wanderer even—that one need do no more here than note that he is not absorbed into "Tintern Abbey." Indeed, if Geoffrey Hartman and many others had not worked so diligently to offer what Bloom calls "canonical" readings in which every detail is calculated and knowingly fitted into the whole, there might have been no need for Bloom's "antithetical" reading. One can be admiring and critical of the poem without being antithetical to its stated aims.

No one denies that Wordsworth thought of Milton often, as anyone must have done around 1800 who was seeking a workable blank verse as the medium for a long poem. In "Wordsworth and the Tears of Adam," Neil Hertz shows how Milton's way of placing himself in relation to Michael and Adam in Book 11 of *Paradise Lost* may have shown Wordsworth how to place himself in relation to Margaret and the Wanderer in the scene in *The Excursion*, Book 1, discussed above. But this, if true, *is* an enabling, and Milton stands as no spectral blocking agent. We have seen that the problem Wordsworth faces is indigenous to his experience, and the aid Milton offers is one almost technical in nature, helping Wordsworth to this particular resolution of a hauntedness that would not disappear because he had found his resolution.

One hears Milton in much of Wordsworth's blank verse, and a good deal of the eighteenth-century Miltonic too; the wonder is that one does not hear it more often. But this is not what Bloom means by an influence, and Bloom really concedes a great deal when he says that "something richer and more mature in Wordsworth wins out over this spectral blocking agent [Milton] in *The Prelude*." When the scene is haunted in Wordsworth, it is fixed, in a landscape that needs no explaining; the heightened demand is made in a place of receiving, and the scene instructs only if it reveals—if by no more than glimpses—the hiding places of Wordsworth's power. To this central fact, all concern about Milton seems incidental. "Romantic tradition is consciously late," says Bloom, "and Romantic literary psychology is therefore a psychology of belatedness." Wordsworth was consciously late, later than his own past, and he therefore had to create a psychology of belatedness. But he was too busy, at least in the great years, to be a Romantic poet. What was to become a tradition in the next generation, what was much later still to be called Romantic, was begun in remarkable isolation, by a poet belated from himself. "Wordsworth, with that valuable self-confidence which could still plow its own way," says W. J. Bate, again not admitting how much he concedes as Wordsworth eludes *his* scheme about the burden of the past. Yes, Wordsworth plowed his own way. Fostered by fear, he then, in his great poems, faced and expressed that fear, and thereby gained the only triumph available over it. At which point, his valuable self-confidence began to seem like egotism, and, the wonderful relation between the naive and the sentimental in him lost, he began that long slide down into what Shelley called ultra-legitimate dulness in *Peter Bell the Third*.

⫸⫸⫸ For Shelley, and for Keats, it was all different.

Wordsworth, rather like Donne and Ben Jonson in this respect, had confidently brushed aside all he scorned in the poetry of the preceding generations—unable to ignore it, but able to absorb it easily into his own poetry—and, once he found his metier, could simply ignore Pope, Johnson, and Gray. But this book, which is about inheriting, always must gain its focus by seeing what happened next, after the strong poet, after Donne and Jonson, after Pope, after Wordsworth. Carew could compose Jonson and Donne, but Samuel Johnson could not compose Pope, though being unaware that he could not do so, paid his prices, diminished his scope, lived in darkness, and still had much composing and healthy inheriting to do. Keats and Shelley, however, knew from the outset that they came later.

They came later than Spenser, Shakespeare, and Milton, in Shelley's case later than Dante and the Greeks as well. But tradition for them had little in it of the living inheritance it had for most seventeenth-century writers. It was almost entirely a tradition of Great Authors, not of received modes and habits of thinking and feeling. Shelley was classically educated, Keats was self-taught, but both looked back and saw only mountain peaks. Wordsworth, as almost always when writing prose and working as a critic, was rooted in eighteenth-century common sense, so he could see the error of that way of thinking about the past. In his "Reply to 'Mathetes' " he sounds very much as one imagines Johnson might have, had he been similarly confronted:

> There are two errors, into which we easily slip when think-
> ing of past times. One lies in forgetting, in the excellence of
> what remains, the large overbalance of worthlessness that
> has been swept away. Ranging over the wide tracts of An-
> tiquity, the situation of the Mind may be likened to that
> of a Traveller, in some unpeopled part of America, who is
> attracted to the burial place of one of the primitive inhabi-
> tants. It is conspicuous upon an eminence, a "mount upon a
> mount!" He digs into it, and finds that it contains the bones
> of a Man of mighty stature: and he is tempted to give way to a
> belief, that as there were Giants in those days, so that all Men
> were Giants. But a second and wiser thought may suggest to
> him, that this tomb would never have forced itself upon his
> notice, if it had not contained a body that was distinguished
> from others, that of a Man who had been selected as a Chief-
> tan or Ruler for the very reason that he surpassed the rest of
> his Tribe in stature, and who now lies thus conspicuously in-
> humed upon the mountain-top, while the bones of his Fol-
> lowers are laid unobtrusively together in their burrows upon
> the Plain below. The second habitual error is, that in this
> comparison of the Ages we divide time merely into past and
> present, and place these in the balance to be weighed against
> each other, not considering that the present is in our estima-

tion not more than a period of thirty years, or half a century at most, and that the past is a mighty accumulation of many such periods, perhaps the whole of recorded time. . . .

Wordsworth, himself in darkness, heir only to his own childhood, maintained sense enough to see that others could easily fall into these nostalgic errors, could see the past not as tradition but as lonely mountain peaks. Thus, in Shelley's version of Wordsworth's Intimations ode, "The Triumph of Life":

> "Figures ever new
> Rise on the bubble, paint them as you may;
> We have but thrown, as those before us threw,
>
> "Our shadows on it as it past away.
> But mark how chained to the triumphal chair
> The mighty phantoms of an elder day;
>
> "All that is mortal of great Plato there
> Expiates the joy and woe his Master knew not; . . .

If Shelley does not make the first mistake Wordsworth mentions above, he nonetheless can see the past only as those chained to Life's triumphant chariot, phantoms, and a few looming figures, like Bacon and Rousseau.

One result of this way of seeing the past, sentimentally in Schiller's and in our more usual use of the word, was that Shelley and Keats could get trapped inside poetic forms enshrined by earlier giants, like the Spenserian stanza and the blank verse of Shakespeare and Milton. Neither poet had a clue to what *The Faerie Queene* is all about, and neither really could see the traditions informing the verse of Shakespeare and Milton. "They admired," William Empson writes of many nineteenth-century poets,

> the poetry of previous generations, very rightly, for the taste it left in the head, and failing to realise that the process of putting such a taste into a reader's head involves a great deal of work which does not feel like a taste in the head, attempting, therefore, to conceive a taste in the head and put it

straight on their paper, they produced tastes in the head which were in fact blurred, complacent, and unpleasing.

The "tastes in the head" produced by *Adonais* or *The Eve of St. Agnes* may be blurred and complacent, but they are not, alas, unpleasing; indeed, they pleased so much they riveted the attention of many Victorians. So too with the Shakespearizing of *The Cenci* and the Miltonizing of "Hyperion." These forms were no longer on their native ground and so were imitated—in our modern, "bad," sense—rather than inherited; the only reason for using the forms, really, was that they were impressive relics. Harold Bloom describes at length the anxieties and swervings one finds in the haunted halls of "Hyperion," but he might more easily have said that Keats did not know "the great deal of work which does not feel like a taste in the head" while it is being done that went into the making of a description in *Paradise Lost*. Milton was an enabled heir, and Keats was not.

This is said much too summarily for those interested in canonical readings, and I move quickly over this point because I want to get to something more central, Shelley's and Keats's relation to Wordsworth, the "dead" giant who outlived them both by a generation. I noted in my introduction that out of this relation, as something like a by-product, came the creation of possibilities for modern literary biography and, therefore, for modern literary history as well. That these possibilities were ignored, and picked up later only by those who did not see what Shelley and Keats had done, is only another sign that, in darkness, traditions get broken, the past gets distorted and ignored. But the achievement is there nonetheless; that it was something of a by-product, that it was ignored, shows us how twisted acts of inheritance had become.

Here was Wordsworth, in his late forties, Distributor of Stamps for Westmoreland, almost two decades after his last great spurt of poetry in the spring of 1802, a figure of "ultra-legitimate dulness." Shelley did not know when he wrote *Peter Bell the Third* that the Wordsworth poem that gave him his title was not an original poem of 1819 but a dusted-off and somewhat revised relic from much earlier. Nor did Shelley or Keats ever see *The Prelude,* which absorbed most of Wordsworth's best poetic energies after 1802. Their essential Wordsworth was the *Lyrical Ballads* of 1800, *Poems in Two Volumes* of 1807, and *The Excursion* of 1814.

Part of Shelley's response to the Wordsworth still alive was political, and rightly so, given, for instance, what we know of his response to the Peterloo Massacre in *The Mask of Anarchy* and what we can imagine Wordsworth's to have been. Part of Keats's response was the result of a series of meetings with Wordsworth late in 1817 and early in 1818, famous for Wordsworth's pronouncing Keats's "Hymn to Pan" a "very pretty piece of paganism," and for Mary Wordsworth's "Mr. Wordsworth is never interrupted." One result was Keats's letter to John Hamilton Reynolds of February 3, 1818:

> It may be said that we ought to read our Contemporaries—
> that Wordsworth &c. should have their due from us. But, for
> the sake of a few fine imaginative or domestic passages, are
> we to be bullied into a certain Philosophy engendered in the
> whims of an Egotist—Every man has his speculations, but
> every man does not brood and peacock over them till he
> makes a false coinage and deceives himself. . . . We hate
> poetry that has a palpable design on us—and if we do not
> agree, seems to put its hand in its breeches pocket.

We know that, unlike his friend Benjamin Haydon, Keats was not deeply wounded by Wordsworth's remark about his recitation from *Endymion,* but Wordsworth's deportment at their meetings clearly wearied him and diminished his sense of Wordsworth's achievement.

But both Shelley and Keats knew this was not the whole story. *Peter Bell the Third* gives us a fable, one out of which a full literary biography could be made, in which the strange sublime figure who was "at once circumference and centre / Of all he might feel or know" became the paid servant of devils and governments. In doing this he moves quite beyond the understanding of Johnson who, in *The Lives of the Poets,* creates a single and static conception of an author's character, and who makes that character express itself constantly over the course of a life. For Johnson, Milton,

Pope, and Savage were as they were; for Shelley, Wordsworth *became*. Johnson discusses Pope's works in chronological order, but as a convenience; after the juvenilia, the rest is just the works of Pope. He makes no inquiry into the relation of one work to another and little into the relation of the works to the life. Though he does not discuss a work of Wordsworth at all, Shelley makes possible a biography in which there is an active seeking relation among works and between works and the life. Faced as he was with the Wordsworth he knew still lived, and the Wordsworth he could imagine that had once been sublime, he tells a story, makes biography be more than a recitation of events, makes it in such a way that anyone can plug a great deal of Wordsworth's poetry into it so that the life explains the career and the poems help explain the life.

Keats never assembled his Wordsworth in this way, but in the letter to Reynolds of May 1818, concerning the Mansion of Many Apartments, he does something similar. After we spend some time in the Chamber of Maiden-Thought, the effect is of seeing

> into the heart and nature of Man of convincing one's nerves that the world is full of Misery and Heartbreak, Pain, Sickness, and oppression—whereby This Chamber of Maiden-Thought becomes gradually darken'd and at the same time on all sides of it many doors are set open—but all dark—all leading to dark passages—We see not the ballance of good and evil. We are in a Mist. *We* are now in that state—We feel the "burthen of the mystery." To this point was Wordsworth come, as far as I can conceive when he wrote "Tintern Abbey" and it seems to me that his Genius is explorative of those dark passages. . . . Here I must think Wordsworth is deeper than Milton.

Keats did not, so far as we know, trace the Wordsworth of "Tintern Abbey" through the Lucy poems and "Resolution and Independence" but it was toward this way of seeing a life and a career that he was groping. The apparently simple "To this point was Wordsworth come . . . when he wrote 'Tintern Abbey' " reveals possibilities for linking life and career of which Johnson was innocent. When Keats says, later in the same letter, that Milton's "philosophy, human and divine, may be tolerably understood by one not much advanced in years," he shows how cut off he was from earlier centuries, even its peaks. But Wordsworth he could understand, because all nineteenth-century poets were to be understood, and praised, as explorers of dark passages. Much as he deplored modern poets as little electors of small provinces, much though he knew Wordsworth could be a bully and a peacock, Keats could respond to and understand Wordsworth much better than earlier poets.

Much of what Shelley and Keats began to do when considering Wordsworth is like second nature to us now, so we may find it hard to know a time when these ways of thinking about writers and works were not instinctive habits of mind. Wordsworth had a life, a career, and in telling the story of it this poem had to come earlier, that one later. But it would not have mattered to Johnson's discussion of Shakespeare if *Two Gentlemen of Verona* were written after *Hamlet*, to that of Milton if *Paradise Lost* came before "Lycidas." We cannot imagine being ignorant of or indifferent to the way chronological order creates psychological order and historical order, growth, development, decline in people, styles, and institutions. But, so far as I know, Shelley's and Keats's responses to the Wordsworth that was thrust upon them were the first to see a need for such order and attendant storytelling. Carew had seen Jonson at his zenith, and knew his sun was setting, but for Carew that explained nothing because Jonson did not need explaining, just calming down, reminding. Wordsworth, though, had to be the kind of genius he was, the kind of person he was, in order for him to write the great poems he wrote and subsequently, in Shelley's terms, to be susceptible to the temptations of the devil. For Wordsworth was a weight for Shelley, and if Shelley did not have to write criticism or become a historian, he had to do something about the weight. All that Bloom finds central in the High Romantic tradition—the romance of trespass, the scene of instruction, the development of a psychology to respond to feeling belated—begins around 1820, with Shelley and Keats.

If *Peter Bell the Third* shows the bright, the enabled side of Shel-

ley's relation to Wordsworth, much of the other poetry shows a
darker, more debilitated side:

> The everlasting universe of things
> Flows through the mind, and rolls its rapid waves,
> Now dark—now glittering—now reflecting gloom—
> Now lending splendour, where from secret springs
> The source of human thought its tribute brings
> Of waters,—with a sound but half its own.

Shelley in Switzerland is Wordsworth five miles above Tintern
Abbey. Or:

> Spirit of BEAUTY, that dost consecrate
>   With thine own hues all thou dost shine upon
> Of human thought or form—where are thou gone?
> Why dost thou pass away and leave our state,
> This dim vast vale of tears, vacant and desolate?

Shelley's intellectual beauty is the clouds of glory of Wordsworth's Intimations ode, just as Shelley's Life in "The Triumph of
Life" is Wordsworth's light of common day.

In darkness, what one writer gives another is not a way of seeing the world we all share but a way of being oneself that is tied to
that individual self. To feel Wordsworth in the passages above is
to feel what Shelley does not want us to feel; when Shelley cannot
think and feel without doing it Wordsworth's way, he gags, as in
the climax of the "Ode to the West Wind":

>   If even
> I were as in my boyhood, and could be
>
> The Comrade of thy wanderings over Heaven,
> As then, when to outstrip thy skiey speed
> Scarce seemed a vision; I would ne'er have striven
>
> As thus with thee in prayer in my sore need.
> Oh, lift me as a wave, a leaf, a cloud!
> I fall upon the thorns of life! I bleed!
>
> A heavy weight of hours has chained and bowed
> One too like thee: tameless, and swift, and proud.

Wordsworth's boyhood and Wordsworth's prison house become Shelley's way of seeing his own boyhood and present life, and, especially in a poetry that seeks sincerity and inspiration, which cannot be composed, the effect is embarrassing. Wordsworth becomes Shelley's comrade in his wanderings, the one whose skiey speed Shelley wants to outrace, the one to whom he prays, and before whom he lies bleeding. That Shelley says here he "strives" with the wind indicates precisely that sense of competition that Shelley does *not* feel with the wind but *does* feel with Wordsworth. No wonder, then, that, unable to say this, Shelley feels resentful and self-pitying and resorts to the image of the chained martyr, "tameless, and swift, and proud," when the poem shows him to be these only as a sullen response to falling upon the thorns of life. Here the ostensible belatedness—that of Shelley from his boyhood—overlaps with his real belatedness—that of himself from Wordsworth—and unfaced bewilderment and resentment are the necessary results.

"Shelley grew up," writes George Santayana, "in the nursery among his young sisters, at school among rude boys, without any affectionate guidance, without imbibing any religious or social tradition." He did, of course, imbibe a huge amount of reading, but because it had no real sense of tradition behind it for Shelley, it could inspire, or weigh down, but could never enable or sustain. Shelley's history, being a history of the great, the dead giants, becomes, given Shelley's sense of Life, a history of defeated martyrs and a few untouchables. In the roll call of those who fell before, or who escaped, Life's triumphal car, we see the inevitable result, the sentimentalization of greatness; Stephen Spender's "I think continually on those who are truly great" is only a grosser version of what we find in "The Triumph of Life." It is a history that has no room for Donne, Jonson, Carew, Dryden, Pope, Johnson, Boswell, or Gibbon because it is so vague and so simplified.

Instead, Shelley finds a surrogate in Rousseau: "I Am one of those who have created, even if it be but a world of agony," and in Rousseau's account of his early years, we stumble, not unsurprisingly, once again on Wordsworth:

"And whether life had been before that sleep
The Heaven which I imagine, or a Hell

"Like this harsh world in which I wake to weep,
I know not. I arose, and for a space
The scene of woods and waters seemed to keep,

"Though it was not broad day, a gentle trace
Of light diviner than the common sun
Sheds on the common earth, and all the place

"Was filled with magic sounds woven into one
Oblivious melody, confusing sense
Amid the gliding waves and shadows dun; . . ."

What Shelley gives to Rousseau, so that Rousseau may then speak for Shelley, isn't anything but the mythologized version of Wordsworth's childhood offered in the "Ode."

I, for one, do not find "The Triumph of Life" embarrassing, as I do the fourth part of the "Ode to the West Wind"; the verse is accomplished enough, as it is in much of Shelley, but the effort to rise up to theme, to sound the notes of a lofty despair, is sustained only by a sentimental myth of history, that makes the poem a wearying lyric cry. Interestingly, "Julian and Maddalo," which covers some of the same ground, may work better, because the loose couplets do not demand the Dantean stance of the terza rima, and because Bryon's presence as Maddalo keeps Shelley away from Wordsworth without bringing him close enough to Byron to force Shelley to stumble on *him*.

Keats's situation was no different, but his responses to it were. We have seen that in 1818, during his meetings with Wordsworth, Keats had to struggle to reconcile himself to the great poet gone ultra-dull. As long as he thought of Wordsworth as Egotistical Sublime he was not in much trouble, since that way, so appealing to Shelley, was not Keats's. But Wordsworth as the explorer of dark passages was a different matter; that is an image of a modern poet that can make Keats happy to be one. But when, in the autumn of 1818, he began to write a poem in which some relation of the ancients to the moderns could be expressed, in which the past could be honored, lamented, and moved beyond, the result was "Hyperion," Miltonics, and not at all a poem exploratory of dark passages. In order to avoid the pitfalls into which Shelley fell, Keats had to avoid Wordsworth altogether, but the price was to ignore a good deal of himself. It was exhausting to write, and is exhausting to read.

The poems of 1819, especially the odes, "Lamia," and "The Fall of Hyperion," are all much better, poems of such lovely phrases and turns that one would never think to say a word against them had they not been so badly overrated. This might not have happened if Keats had not died at twenty-five and if the figure they offer of Keats were not so appealing:

> I see a schoolboy when I think of him,
> With face and nose pressed to a sweet-shop window,
> For certainly he sank into his grave
> His senses and his heart unsatisfied,
> And made—being poor, ailing, and ignorant,
> Shut off from all the luxury of the world,
> The coarse-bred son of a livery-stable keeper—
> Luxuriant song.

One need not see Keats as Yeats saw him in order to remember that we do make a figure of him, and most differ from Yeats's only in emphasis.

Since the poems show few direct Wordsworthian traces, there is no need for detailed treatment of them here. They are Romantic poems, and thereby poeticize and make available for later poets, Tennyson especially, the lulls and sighs and the mood of sweet melancholy that was to mark most poetry for the next two generations. Poetry is being taken to a special place, a place for "poetic feelings," Keats's face pressed to the sweet-shop window wishing life were as it is not, wishing that beauty were truth and truth beauty but knowing that only urns can offer such enticements.

My sense of their limitation is that they are not more than preliminarily explorative of the dark passages we know Keats was passing through. Wordsworth is not present in them, but, as I suggested above, it is as though the burden of the mystery could implore in them little more than the passing tribute of a sigh:

O brightest! though too late for antique vows,
  Too, too late for the fond believing lyre,
When holy were the haunted forest boughs,
  Holy the air, the water, and the fire;
Yet even in these days so far retir'd
  From happy pieties, thy lucent fans,
  Fluttering among the faint Olympians,
I see, and sing, by mine own eyes inspired.
So let me be thy choir, and make a moan
  Upon the midnight hours; . . .

Here is poetry of belatedness par excellence. Psyche appeals because she too is late—there is no other reason for her to be the "brightest"—and this keeps Keats from having to make up stories about her, as he tried to do with Apollo in "Hyperion." Lateness is a feeling only, and here it does not matter if the "believing lyre" belonged to Spenser, Shakespeare, Milton, or Wordsworth. In all the odes except "To Autumn," and in "Lamia" as well, Keats's major struggle is to avoid feeling sorry for himself, or for his surrogate Lycias. In the revised "Hyperion" lateness does achieve a momentary apotheosis in the image of Moneta, the priestess not just of Saturn and Thea but of the ruined Hyperion:

                  Then I saw a wan face,
  Not pined by human sorrows, but bright-blanch'd
  By an immortal sickness which kills not;
  It works a constant change, which happy death
  Can put no end to; deathwards progressing
  To no death was that visage; it had pass'd
  The lily and the snow; and beyond these
  I must not think now, though I saw that face.

"Beyond these," himself deathward progressing, Keats could not think.

The past was beautiful but gone, the possibilities for living were elsewhere. These were Keats's native feelings—he borrowed no childhood from Wordsworth—but they make for a very limited poetry, in which the language must always work against the sense that now more than ever were it rich to die, drawn as he was by its sweet sensuousness toward that richness. Wordsworth had his subject, and he too was both later than it, his childhood, or apart from it, Lucy, Margaret, the leech-gatherer. But he really had it for a subject and his poetry could explore its dark passages. By comparison, Keats only had the *situation* of being late; he hadn't lost his subject, but had only the circumstances of not having a sustaining one.

With both Shelley and Keats, though I know I value their poetry very differently from either Bloom or Bate, their sense of the situation of poetry seems quite right. For me, Bloom's oft-repeated reading of Browning's "Child Roland to the Dark Tower Came" as a triumphant wreckage of the palace of Shelley is his finest achievement, and Bate's attempt to claim all that can be claimed for "The Fall of Hyperion" is his. Surely, though, when poetic inheritance begins to resemble a psychic battlefield, a good deal must be lost. The demand to be original, to find one's own voice, is itself a cry of despair. Some poets we take to be major, like Eliot or Hopkins, end up writing relatively little, while others, like Tennyson, Shelley, Browning, Swinburne, and Pound, just write and write, ultra-legitimate dull, or just plain dull, following the example of the later Wordsworth. And when influence becomes an anxiety, the past a burden, poets of lesser gifts are uncomfortable with established traditions, and "minor poet" itself becomes a derogatory term. It may seem implausible to compare, say, the poetry of Matthew Arnold with that of the admittedly minor late sixteenth-century writer Samuel Daniel. Clearly, Arnold is the more impressive figure. Yet in his verse letters and especially in "Musophilus," Daniel is intelligent and impressive because he is so unbothered by being traditional, unoriginal, while Arnold wrote mostly bad poems because he was driven to make the gestures of a major poet without having anything like the necessary resources. When, finally, the word "traditional" itself becomes a term of at least some condescension, then the possibilities for poetry are very much reduced. It is not surprising that the most clearly and obviously "traditional" twentieth-century poet, Robert Frost, may also be the best; he assimilated the habits and manners of the Romantic lyric with little fuss, and was thereby free to write the best poems he could. Put Keats's "Ode to Psyche" and Pound's *Hugh Selwyn Mauberley* alongside Frost's "The Oven Bird" and you see which is the truest, most dignified, and most original response to belatedness.

But if the history of poetic tradition comes to seem too often a searching for ways to strike the father dead, that is hardly the end of the matter, of either literature or literary tradition. The great limitation of Bloom and most theorists and historians of our latter days is that they make ours a history of Romanticism when ours has been, ever since 1742 and the descent of darkness, the age of the novel. I have often felt that if it had not been for the special and extraordinary fact of Wordsworth this truth could have been more clearly seen all along. Wordsworth seemed to create new possibilities for poetry because he undoubtedly created a new kind of poetry. The difficulty was that you had to be Wordsworth in order to write it; the only excellent Wordsworthian poem I know not written by him is Coleridge's "Dejection." But while poetry began its long grappling with belatedness, the novel was allowed to be invented and to grow into a major art form almost without its being noticed. For long into this century, "criticism" meant, nine times out of ten, "criticism of poetry," most of it written by poets. Theories of criticism meant theories of poetry, traditions meant traditions of poetry. At the time when poetry on its own terms became anxious, self-conscious, and, often, self-restrictive, it was encouraged to do so by the way criticism turned history into the enshrinement of the great, and insisted that one must be great or else not count. The novel had almost a century before anyone wanted it to be a self-conscious "artistic" affair, another generation before it became that, and almost two centuries before one could be a great critic and write only about prose fiction.

Keats is a fascinating example of what was happening. He was, in Yeats's phrase, "poor, ailing, and ignorant," and, being that, he became heir to a tradition in which poetry was becoming a poetry of memory, dream, and withdrawal. Still, he assumed it was poetry he should write, and so he became "poetic." More than a century after he died, Leavis could write of the revised "Hyperion" that "It shows the interests of the letters realized—

become active—in technique: poet and letter-writer are at last one." Leavis betrays the same assumptions about Keats and poetry that Keats himself had. Leavis is sure that Keats's highest achievement had to lie in poetry, yet the letters themselves suggest otherwise. Granted, they may not be full of "technique," but they are astonishingly "active," much more so than the poems. From 1817 on, they are ahead of the poems, more expressive of Keats's present-tense interests and possibilities. The letter to Reynolds in May 1818 about Wordsworth and the Mansion of Many Apartments outstrips anything he had done in poetry to that date, and, as I have suggested, that in itself may have been responsible for the retreat into Miltonics in the original "Hyperion" that fall. As an achievement, the long rambling letter to George and Georgiana Keats written from February to May of 1819 may not seem comparable to "The Eve of St. Mark," "La Belle Dame Sans Merci," and "Ode to Psyche," written at the same time, but I doubt if I am the only one who would much rather reread the letter than the poems. The description of parish clergymen, and Keats's reasons for being sure he cannot like them, the dive into doubting the ability of humankind to be truly disinterested, the list of Coleridge's subjects for discourse one Sunday afternoon, then the delicious comment after copying out "La Belle Dame": "Why four kisses—you will say—why four because I wish to restrain the headlong impetuosity of my Muse— and would have fain said 'score' without hurting the rhyme—but we must temper the imagination as the Critics say with Judgement. I was obliged to choose an even number that both eyes might have fair play." All these show a range, a perkiness, an improvisation that make the poems seem written by a Johnny One Note. Furthermore, at the end of the letter is the account of the vale of Soul-making that, to my mind, is worth at least an ode or two:

> How then are Souls to be made? How then are these sparks which are God to have identity given them—so as ever to possess a bliss peculiar to each one's individual existence? How, but by the medium of a world like this? . . . An intelligence—without identity—and how is this identity to be

made? Through the medium of the heart? And how is the heart to become this medium but in a world of circumstances?

Keats's God is a century later than Pope's Maker, so in his vale we are all rather like Unitarians. But this passage helped later writers to think that Keats was moving away from the Miltonic and toward the Shakespearean, a thought that itself betrays the persistence of the assumption that poetry was the necessary medium. Surely, however, it is the novel that Keats approaches, *the* medium of our darkness, of "a world like this," "of Circumstances."

No need to say that had Keats lived he would have become a novelist. Say, rather, that at that time the novel was the medium that could have been adequate to the variousness we see in Keats's letters. He did not know this, nor did anyone around him; there was no Jane Austen, no novelist Scott, in Keats's world. But in the gap between his letters and his poems, we can see how limited poetry was becoming, and how beckoning were the prospects of the novel.

⟫⟫⟫⟫ In the next chapter I essay an account of the novel as it lived freely at the time poetry became bound. The nineteenth was Wordsworth's century, however, not just because he was its greatest poet, but because that poetry created a new means of inheriting, that of the adult as heir to the child. It is appropriate that the heirs to this means of bequeathing are not poets, but novelists, and, in fact, not so much novelists as the central characters of their fictions.

That childhood was to become one of the great fertile areas for literature could have been anticipated without Wordsworth, and can be, if necessary, described without reference to him. Further, Wordsworth's great poem of childhood was not published until the century was half over, too late to have any effect on the Brontës or much of Dickens in which the child is parent to the adult. Finally, one aspect that deeply absorbed the novelists—the *process* whereby the child grew—is the one where Wordsworth is least engaged, despite *The Prelude*'s subtitle.

Wordsworth opened the mine, however, and in so doing not only showed where rich ore lay but provided a means of understanding inheritance different from that known to earlier writers. In "My Heart Leaps Up . . ." he offered the essential formulation, and in "Tintern Abbey," the "Ode," and other famous poems we find variations on the essential theme. Perhaps most important, his way of rendering childhood experience became the novelists' way, a fidelity to experience, remembered or imagined, in the world reduced to the real. The false turn, taken by many poets, was to attempt to replace the old received universe with the poetic symbol. The decisive turn, taken by Wordsworth and the novelists, was toward realism, childhood experiences shaping the individual in carefully and hauntingly described settings.

In Wordsworth's own case, the fidelity is strictly to the remembered, actual experience. The hiding places of power lay open there, and could not be altered. The novelists may well have done this—Charlotte Brontë, like Jane Eyre, may have been locked in a Red Room, or Mary Ann Evans, like Maggie Tulliver, may have hacked at her hair—but what we tend to see them doing is transposing their characters into places they themselves knew little, if at all, as children. The aim, though, is the same: to render childhood experiences and feelings in places perfect for their occurrence.

Haworth Parsonage, thus, is not Wuthering Heights. George Eliot's St. Ogg's is not Nuneaton, Warwickshire, but Gainsborough, Lincolnshire. Hardy went to Fawley, Berkshire, a village vastly different from Puddletown, Dorset, in order to find a name and setting for Jude, the boy who, like Hardy, could not go to Oxford. And Dickens, master novelist of the child, transposes his actual experiences fascinatedly in order to let loose his childhood feelings in the "right" settings and situations, never giving a straight autobiographical rendering, never losing hold of the way the child is parent.

David Copperfield, clearly, comes closest to being Dickens's autobiographical novel, but its settings are only intermittently those of Dickens's childhood; the actual parents are displaced into the Micawbers so as to give David over to the Murdstones, make him more vulnerable, more a victim, more like what Dickens felt than like what actually happened to him. In *Nicholas Nickleby* he transposes his experiences at Wellington House Academy in London to the notorious Dotheboys Hall in Durham, which he never saw until he was a man. He makes Mrs. Pipchin in *Dombey and Son* out of Elizabeth Roylance, with whom he boarded before going to Wellington House, and has Paul Dombey board with her in Brighton, because Roylance had once kept school there, even though he barely knew Brighton. He had a wonderful knack of taking what he saw as an adult and putting his boyhood feelings into it, as though he himself had not only been raised by Mr. Murdstone, but had been taken into Bill Sikes's gang, swept the streets of Tom-All-Alone's, or been raised near the marshes of the Thames. In many of these instances, the child dies young, or barely arrives at manhood, so we are left only with pathos and indignation. But one reason *Great Expectations* is his supreme achievement is that he explores the child fathering the man in ways that hauntingly resemble *The Prelude*, a poem he never read. Very little in *Great Expectations* actually happened to Dickens, but so strong is his sense of the way the child creates the man he becomes that, though in one sense it is his most fantastic novel, in another, it is his most realistic.

In 1857–58 Dickens had toured with Ellen Ternan, an actress younger than his daughters, with his play *The Frozen Deep*. He fell in love with her and, at that time, she refused to become his mistress. Dickens and his wife then fought, messily, to a legal separation, Catherine believing Ternan was Dickens's mistress, Charles vehemently denying it—Ternan did consent later to being set up by Dickens, but that came after *Great Expectations*. When he began the novel, Ternan had made him feel, as the novel shows, helpless; he, almost thirty years older and the most famous writer in Europe, made her into an unreachable star, an Estella, and himself into a boy with coarse hands and thick boots.

I do not want here to offer anything like a full reading of *Great Expectations*, but rather want to look at one crucial instance of Pip's boyhood experience to show how that experience, more than his great expectations, more than his early or late encounters with Magwitch, shapes the man he becomes. In it the hiding places of power open, then close, and when they open again, Pip sees only by glimpses, since he is no poet, no heir to an empire. In chapter 8, Pip's first visit to Satis House, after Estella had humiliated him, Pip went out into the brewery lane, "and leaned my forehead on it and cried": "As I cried, I kicked the wall, and took a hard twist at my hair; so bitter were my feelings, and so sharp was the smart without a name, that needed counteraction." The voice of the older, storytelling Pip is often so calm in this novel, so sad and apparently knowing, that it can both make us concentrate on one thing and lull us into accepting many strange events, and many strange silences, that we might otherwise question. Pip says he suffered "the smart without a name," which seems right, since at the moment of anguish the feeling must be stronger than the feeling's name. Actually, though, he has already given us many right names—"I was so humiliated, hurt, spurned, offended, angry, sorry"—that we relax, knowing that the boy could not name the feelings but the man could.

We are, thus, set up to accept the astonishing paragraph that follows:

> My sister's bringing up had made me sensitive. In the little world in which children have their existence, whosoever brings them up, there is nothing so finely perceived and so finely felt as injustice. . . . I had known, from the time when I could speak, that my sister, in her capricious and violent coercion, was unjust to me. I had cherished a profound conviction that her bringing me up by hand gave her no right to bring me up by jerks. Through all my punishments, disgraces, fasts and vigils, and other penitential performances, I had nursed this assurance; and to my communing so much with it, in a solitary and unprotected way, I in great part refer the fact that I was morally timid and very sensitive.

The tone is slightly avuncular, but so sympathetic, and so clearly saying what we wish is true about Pip—we know of Mrs. Joe's injustice, and would not wish to think Pip himself does not know— that we can be led not to question the paragraph.

Pip says all children finely perceive and finely feel injustice. There is no trace of this perception and feeling in the first seven chapters, so we can only say that the experience here at Satis

House has made articulate a feeling that hitherto lay unspoken. The difficulty with that, however, is that Pip does not say that Estella has been unjust to him—that would seem to be the link between this paragraph and those preceding, yet it is not there. Indeed, Pip has accepted Estella's judgment by saying that, for the first time, his hands and boots seem to him "vulgar appendages"; he adds his wish that Joe had taught him to call jacks knaves, and had himself been more genteel. Pip has, in effect, shifted from suffering what he takes to be just accusations about his clothes and manners to thinking about suffering from the injustice of Mrs. Joe, thereby blurring the very distinction that he says is the most important one a child can make.

If the sweet reasonableness of the voice of the narrator Pip can keep us from asking about this strange shift and strange blurring, I think Wordsworth in *The Prelude* can show us how to question the passage without harming its effects. Wordsworth does not say why he fled from the stone carved with the murderer's name, nor why the experience of his father's death compelled him to remember the scene in which he waited to be taken home for the holidays. But, he insists, that is what happened. He asks us to acknowledge that he became who he did because of these spots of time, he shows us what happened, but does not inquire into the why. I think we can do the same thing here, and my sense of the way Dickens is heir to Wordsworth is embedded in our way of reading this scene. In Pip's conscious mind, Estella and Mrs. Joe are polarized, but here they are blended, and we can only say this happens because each has humiliated him. Pip cannot say this, because to do so would be to consider the possibility that Estella's accusations are unjust, and this he cannot manage; he is embarking, thus, on a life in which Estella's accusations are just and everything else is wrong or unimportant, and he begins this by a silent shift from Estella's accusations to Mrs. Joe's unjust bringing him up by jerks.

But the cry for fairness or justice is often the beginning of retaliation. Pip kicks the wall and tears his hair, and both responses, one directed outward and the other inward, are "natural." Since for much of the novel he continues to direct the hostility inward, to compensate for his coarse hands and thick boots, we may be inclined to ignore the kicking of the wall, the retaliation that first trains Pip's attention onto Mrs. Joe, though, whatever her meanness, she is not responsible for his hands and boots. For this smart without a name—and now we can recognize that for all Pip's naming, it is indeed nameless—someone must pay. I accept Estella's judgment, and tear my hair; I don't, I kick the wall, I accuse Mrs. Joe. Someone must pay.

In such a scene of heightened demand, where feelings are powerful, clear, and yet not clear, Wordsworth time and again embeds them in a landscape, dreamlike in its clarity and fixity. So too here:

> It was a deserted place, down to the pigeonhouse in the brewery-yard, which had been blown crooked on its pole by some high wind, and would have made the pigeons think themselves at sea, if there had been any pigeons there to be rocked by it. But, there were no pigeons in the dove-cot, no horses in the stable, no pigs in the sty, no malt in the storehouse, no smells of grain and beer in the copper or the vat. All the uses and scents of the brewery might have evaporated with its last reek of smoke. In a by-yard, there was a wilderness of empty casks, which had a certain sour remembrance of better days lingering about them; but it was too sour to be accepted as a sample of the beer that was gone— and in this respect I remember those recluses as being like most others.

Here is a first-rate instance of the world reduced to the real. It is so much like a description in a novel, especially a Dickens novel, that we can forget how little it shares in its working either with the Marvell or the Keats we looked at in the introduction. It is, rather, a Wordsworthian spot of time, the objects just are, and are made powerful by the presence of feelings with which they are associated only because it is in this scene that they are felt. The connection between person and landscape is not pastoral, not symbolic, but Wordsworthian. There is a pigeonhouse, a stable, a sty, a storehouse, a wilderness of beer casks—and someone, we remember, must pay.

It is Miss Havisham:

It was in this place, and at this moment, that a strange thing happened to my fancy. I thought it a strange thing then, and I thought it a stranger thing long afterwards. I turned my eyes—a little dimmed by looking up at the frosty light—towards a great wooden beam in a low nook of the building near me on my right hand, and I saw a figure hanging there by the neck. A figure all in yellow white, but with one shoe to the feet; and it hung so that I could see that the faded trimmings of the dress were like earthy paper, and the face was Miss Havisham's, with a movement going over the whole countenance as if she were trying to call to me.

Dickens is again at work to make us feel comfortably that we understand; "Pip revenges himself," writes Louis Crompton, "for his hurt feelings by imagining that Miss Havisham is suffering the indignity of a public hanging." True enough, but why Miss Havisham? She has not humiliated him, nor at this point has she hissed "Love her, love her" in his ear. Why is it not Estella hanging from the beam? Because it cannot be—she is the unattainable star. The hiding places of power lie open.

But the older Pip sees only by glimpses: "I thought it a stranger thing long afterwards," he says, without saying when, or what he then made of it. The narrative voice remains calm, so we may be lulled into thinking this is a novel about a boy who grew up to be a snob and then learned better. Other patterns emerge, however, if we read this as a Wordsworthian spot of time. Because the humiliation of Estella's mockery leads Pip to meditate on Mrs. Joe's injustices, the path that might have led to Pip's becoming like Joe Gargery, who understands why he accepts his wife's injustices, is closed to Pip forever. In refusing to retaliate against Estella, yet needing to retaliate, Pip finds Mrs. Joe, and then Miss Havisham. Not seeing that he does this, Pip forces the feelings underground. If we cannot see why this must happen, especially the hanging of Miss Havisham, we can accept, and say that it has happened.

For Wordsworth the child being father of the man is mostly a way of accounting for why he became a poet, and the particular poet he became. Power in the haunt and main region of his song was all that need concern him. For the novelist, however, the presence of such a childhood experience as Pip has here demands a story, an imagining of the character the childhood created as its heir. Dickens, in effect, must ask more questions than Wordsworth. Wordsworth's mind is powerful because it is being nurtured by another power, greater than anything the boy can imagine, variously given such names as "Wisdom and Spirit of the Universe," and "something far more deeply interfused." This happened, to me, to me *there*, and I was not alone, terrified though I was. The novelist can feel the same fidelity to the childhood experience, but Pip *is* alone, and so we must invent a psychology for him. When I write "Not seeing that he does this, Pip forces his feelings underground," I write in a way that would be impertinent to use in describing the boy Wordsworth, or, roughly speaking, any character in literature before him. This novel, and the nineteenth-century novel in general, achieved so much by creating a psychological realism based on characters where the adult is heir to the child, that it is no wonder that novel readers came to read older authors as if they too were novelists, living in darkness, reduced to the real. Thus, especially with Shakespeare: why does Hamlet delay? is Falstaff a coward? why does Iago hate Othello, or Leontes suspect Hermione? Having no childhood spots of time to explain these matters, nineteenth- and early twentieth-century critics were nonetheless driven to answer such questions by means of a psychological realism that the novelists were driven to invent to explain how the child is parent to the adult.

In the case of *Great Expectations*, the impulse to accept Estella's judgment absorbs most of Pip's conscious attention as he labors at the forge, as he interprets his great expectations as a validation of his desire for Estella, as he recoils from learning that Magwitch is his benefactor. The scene in the brewery yard, however, has other tales to tell, which involve retaliation and revenge, the invention of shadow figures like Orlick and Drummle to be the brutes and do the brutal deeds Pip cannot tell himself he wishes done, which include not just the assault on Mrs. Joe but the conquering of Estella. Dickens, in his great fidelity to the childhood scene in chapter 8, however, cannot be content until Pip is returned to the same scene. Wordsworth may be able to return to the scene of the gibbet mast and the murderer's name, and to find there "a radiance more sublime for these remembrances." But his was the extraordinary experience, the one that endowed so many commonplace events with such charged feeling; Pip may have extraordinary things happen to him, but he himself is ordinary, locked but not exultant in his exploration of his inheritance of his childhood experience.

Thus when, in chapter 49, he returns to Satis House for the last time, he can be as faithful to his first feelings there as Wordsworth could ever have been, but his way of being faithful is to complete the terrible punishment sought on his first visit there. Estella has said to him some chapters earlier that "you will get me out of your thoughts in a week," and Pip has protested, but in fact she is right, and Pip demonstrates her rightness by not thinking of her again until the last scene of the novel. She, however, was part of the judgment he always had accepted, and Miss Havisham is part of the desire to retaliate that went underground. Miss Havisham, by this point, is human wreckage, and for reasons Pip knows full well, but the grip of the need to destroy remains. After their last interview, in which he refuses her the forgiveness she seeks, he returns to the brewery yard, and once again hangs her from the beams.

So far as I know, one can find no such scene in literature before the nineteenth century; Wordsworth, having invented the spot of time, also invented the return to the place of the spot, and, able to find there "radiance more sublime for these remembrances," left it to his novelistic heirs to discover darker ways in which the child creates the adult experience. Though Miss Havisham never humiliated Pip, and though Pip has just told her he does not hold her responsible for what happened to him, he must hang her again nonetheless. And he must say, after he does so, that he must return to the house to "assure myself that Miss Havisham was as safe and well as I had left her." To accomplish this involves bringing in a whole alternative series of childhood spots of time, ones that did not involve hanging but fire: "Old Clem! Blow the fire, blow the fire—Old Clem!" The forge song had seemed mournful to Pip when he sang it at Satis House as a boy, but it is the fire of Pip the thief, the fire shared by the impossibly good Joe and the demonic Orlick, the fire in which Pip sees Estella's face at the forge, judging him. It now has been transposed, removed from the forge, and is roaring:

> I had a double-caped greatcoat on, and over my arm another thick coat. That I got them off, closed with her, threw her down, and got them over her; that I dragged the great cloth from the table for the same purpose and with it dragged down the heap of rottenness in the midst, and all the ugly things that sheltered there; that we were on the ground struggling like desperate enemies, and that the closer I covered her the more wildly she shrieked and tried to free herself; that this occurred I knew through the result, but not through anything I felt, or thought, or knew I did.

As with Wordsworth and the murderer's name, to say that one understands is to simplify. The grammar of Dickens's fabulous sentence makes sure we know what happened, and makes sure we do not know either. That Pip and Miss Havisham struggle like desperate enemies, that she thinks Pip wishes to kill her, yes, but for Pip to know what he is doing is to be other than who he is. The hiding places of power open for the last time, the pattern of Pip's first visit to Satis House completed in his last.

Great Expectations is a long look back taken by a Pip we understand to be older, sadder, and wiser than he once was, yet Pip never sees a thing, can say of nothing that happens: "This I understand." When the shadow of the past finally lifts, and Magwitch is dead and Pip is recovered from the delirium of his breakdown, Pip is a shell of a person, weak, decent, sad, his capacity to feel or know burnt out in the burning out of his childhood, the relic of one who has been gripped by Wordsworthian experiences but who is not Wordsworth himself. "All gone by, Biddy," he says of his old dreams, "All gone by." And with their passing, his own.

We cannot say that Dickens is heir to Wordsworth in any sense that we use to speak of Carew, or Johnson, or Shelley and Keats, as heirs. Yet we can say that *Great Expectations* is part of a tradition that has as its obvious source Wordsworth's childhood. It is neither a tradition of conscious inheriting from *auctores* nor a tangled inheriting of an anxious influence. It is a case of writers from Wordsworth to Lawrence sharing a sense of the shaping power of childhood; it may not begin to be a *conscious* sharing until George Eliot, or Hardy, and even when it becomes conscious it does not acknowledge Wordsworth as the founder or source. For much of the century, poetry was a self-conscious high art, while prose fiction was a stepchild, a popular medium, so it is difficult to see how, or why, the connection between Wordsworth and the novelists could be made, or was needed. It seems, rather, that a power was let loose, a power to imagine children, a power to imagine girls as powerful as boys when children; Wordsworth's role was not to let the power loose but to inaugurate the shaping in literary form. That, it seems to me, is his greatest legacy, and the fact that the heirs are novelists shows that it has only tangential relation with the history of Romanticism, itself a notion that came to be articulated in England very late in Wordsworth's century, after much of his legacy was spent. In the little bundle of shivers beginning to be afraid of it all in a marsh churchyard, in Jane Eyre's terror in the Red Room, in Heathcliff and Cathy on the Pennistone Crags, in Maggie Tulliver lashing at her hair, in Jude Fawley straining his eyes to see Christminster, in Paul Morel praying that his father will die, or not die, or stop drinking, we find spots of time that explore dark passages when yet the yoke of earth is new.

These characters were not possessed by the wisdom and spirit of the universe, and in these novels, therefore, there are no heroic arguments or godlike hours. Theirs is a secular inheritance, for that was what was possible. But these moments dot the century's fiction until they seem to begin to dominate it, and when they cease doing so in this century, we can then mark Wordsworth's passing as a decisive force. We should, though, in noting this, become aware that what it means to be precursor, what it means to be heir, is thus changing. If we find, in the instance of Henry James coming to London and seeing there the looming shadow of George Eliot, a classic case of anxious inheritance, we should not therefore continue to assume that that *kind* of inheriting was all that was left for latter-day writers to enact.

5 ∘ Henry James

⪢⪢⪢⪢ IN 1873 James left Quincy St., Cambridge, having in mind not just to leave his parents, his brother and sister, but to establish himself as a writer, in the old world preferably, and to be able to support himself. He spent each of the next four winters in one of the great cities: Rome in 1873, and out of that came his first novel, *Roderick Hudson*, as well as some stories and travel pieces; New York in 1874, and out of that came *Washington Square*; Paris in 1875, and out of that came *The American*. In the summer of 1876, he wrote to his brother William:

> Your remarks on my French tricks in my letters are doubtless most just, and shall be heeded. But it's an odd thing that such tricks should grow at a time when my last layers of resistance to a long-encroaching weariness and satiety with the French mind and its utterance has fallen from me like a garment. I have done with 'em, forever and am turning English all over. I desire only to feed on English life and the contact of English minds.

For a second goal had been created, especially after he left the United States in 1875: to be an established writer, free of financial ties to his family, and in London.

Writing in his notebook a few years later, he was unclear why he had not gone to London in the first place:

> I settled myself in Paris with the idea that I should spend several years there. This was not really what I wanted; what I

wanted was London—and Paris was only a stopgap. But London appeared to me then impossible. I believed that I might arrive there in the fullness of years, but there were all sorts of obstacles to my attempting to live there then. I wonder greatly now, in the light of my present knowledge of England, that these obstacles should have seemed so large, so overwhelming and depressing as they did at that time. When a year later I came really to look them in the face, they absolutely melted away.

But another reason for going to London when he did was that he had found Paris lacking. He had arranged with Whitelaw Reid to be Paris correspondent for the *New York Tribune,* but Reid had not cared for James's pieces, and broke off their agreement after nine months. James had as much as he wanted of Americans in Paris, but he didn't want Americans now, as he had when in Rome two years earlier. He had met and had come to adore Ivan Turgenev, he had met and had come at least to like and admire Flaubert, but the rest of the literary people bored him. He had gained no entrance to Parisian social life itself, as, in its way, *The American* reveals.

So he went, in December 1876, and took rooms at 3 Bolton Street, Piccadilly, where he was to live many years. "I take possession of the old world—I inhale it—I appropriate it!" he had triumphantly written a year earlier, while in London and on his way to Paris; "I take it as an artist and a bachelor; as one who had the passion for observation and whose business is the study of human life." He saw nothing contradictory in the idea that the conqueror conquers by observing, but we will need to ponder it, because to give equal weight to both terms, conqueror and observer, is to understand much about James and helps greatly in delineating a crucial moment in the history of the English novel.

James could be an observer anywhere. But he could not take possession of Paris or the French novel, and he did not want to take possession of Boston or New York or the American novel—he had done all the possessing of that kind that he felt he needed while in Rome, mastering Hawthorne's *The Marble Faun* in his *Roderick Hudson.* English society, he found, he could enter into

quite easily, and this occupies his letters, his later notebook recol-
lections, and, therefore, his most complete biographer, Leon
Edel. But it was to be some years before he felt he could conquer
not just London and country-house society, but the English
novel, the beast he really had in view, perhaps all along.

If it was the English novel James wanted to conquer, he had
given himself a large task indeed. In the forty years since the publication of *Pickwick Papers,* there had been Dickens, Thackeray,
and the Brontës, all now dead; George Eliot, Trollope, Collins,
and Meredith, all very much alive; Hardy, just beginning; a huge
mass of fiction, some of it quite impressive, ranging from *Wives
and Daughters* to *Alice in Wonderland,* from *Coningsby* to *Uncle Silas,*
from *The Cloister and the Hearth* to *Tom Brown's Schooldays.* James
may well have read it all. One of the difficulties in assessing
his reading is that he seldom speaks of spending much time at it,
and yet, for instance, when he came to write an essay on Trollope, a writer he refused to admire much, it turned out that he
had read a great deal of Trollope's huge output. But of this body
of fiction, James felt no need to take it all on, certainly. The one
obvious pervasive influence was Dickens, the one looming figure
was George Eliot, the one challenger was Hardy.

What England did not have was a Flaubert, or a Turgenev, a
master, a writer with an *idea* of fiction. As I have suggested earlier, this may well be a sign of its glory, its ability, while poetry
was giving the impression of being able to strangle itself in self-
conscious combat with looming predecessors, to invent freely
and to assimilate with ease. Jane Austen admired Richardson, as
did George Eliot, who also learned from Austen and from Charlotte Brontë; Thackeray admired Fielding and Smollett, and
shows traces of their work in his own, as does Trollope of Thackeray, as almost everyone after him does of Dickens. But there was
at work nothing like a tradition, no benchmarks had been created, and no one seems really an heir, enabled or disabled, of another, at least not until we begin to consider really minor writers.
No one, as a novelist or a critic of the novel, existed to set limits, to
indicate what could and could not be done.

The example of Trollope is very interesting in this respect. Trollope would have been puzzled to have been told that he had an

idea of fiction; he wrote to please an audience, nothing more. He wrote and wrote, his famous 2,500 words every morning. James had been surprised and a little enraged to find Trollope with him on board the *Bothnia* in 1875: "the season was unpropitious, the vessel overcrowded, the voyage detestable," James wrote. Trollope had the ship's carpenter fix him a rough writing desk, and "he drove his pen as steadily on the tumbling ocean as in Montague Square." For James, thus, the perfect image of a hack writer:

> As an artist he never took himself seriously; many people will say this was why he was so delightful. The people who take themselves seriously are prigs and bores; and Trollope, with his perpetual "story," which was the only thing he cared about, his strong good sense, hearty good nature, generous appreciation of life in all its varieties, responds in perfection to a certain English ideal. According to that ideal, it is rather dangerous to be explicitly or consciously an artist—to have a system, a doctrine, a form. Trollope, from the first, went in, as they say, for having as little form as possible; it is probably safe to say that he had no "views" whatever on the subject of novel writing.

One has no trouble reading this and knowing exactly what James thinks a novelist should do that Trollope did not. Yet doubtless James thought he was doing Trollope justice, and Leavis, writing two generations later, is content to judge Trollope in precisely the terms James did.

Yet, and it is no abuse of language to say so, Trollope was one of the great original novelists. Following in James's footsteps, Conrad and Ford attempted in the early years of the century to cut the stranglehold that "story" had on the novel, which for them often meant abjuring the "big scene" that triple-decker Victorian fiction seemed to love so much. Trollope could have shown them how to do it in at least one important way. In *The Way We Live Now*, is Augustus Melmotte a swindler? in *Orley Farm*, did Lady Mason forge her husband's will? Did Lizzie Eustace steal her own diamonds? In *Barchester Towers*, will Bertie Stanhope or Mr. Slope marry Eleanor Bold? In each case, Trollope plays along with the question for a while, even gathers his story as if toward a big scene in which the answer will be given, and then, in each case, before any such scene takes place, he will break in: of course Melmotte is a swindler; I hope my reader is in no doubt that Lady Mason was guilty; Lizzie stole her own diamonds—did you think this is a novel by Wilkie Collins; surely I would not give my lovely heroine away to the greasy Mr. Slope or the blandly irresponsible Bertie. That is, if Trollope, as James says, cares for nothing but his "story," he cares for it in a way that will not seduce him into straining his cleverness or our credulity, to offer art as some alternative to what we know of life.

In the first of the Palliser novels, *Can You Forgive Her?*, Trollope sets up three love triangles: Alice Vavasor, George Vavasor, John Grey; Glencora Palliser, Burgo Fitzgerald, Plantagenet Palliser; Mrs. Greenow, Lieutenant Bellfield, Mr. Cheesacre. In each the woman is tempted by the first named and "unsound" suitor to turn away from the known, solid, and landed suitor or husband. What Trollope then does with his carefully contrived parallels is to deny them, to release himself from the apparent implications of their artfulness. The tone and pace of each story is different, not for reasons of "pace" or "point," but because Glencora, being Glencora, must push her situation hard or not at all; the same pace used in Alice's story would insult her, and in Mrs. Greenow's it would be ludicrous. One reason "you" will find it hard to forgive Alice is that while Glencora is hastily running toward and then away from an elopement with Fitzgerald, Alice is still dithering, pushing the same counters of her life around the board again. The result is better than "a generous appreciation of life in all its varieties." It is the sense that each life demands different qualities of attentiveness from Trollope, so that while one life is approaching its only climax, another is looking back at one and ahead to another, while a third is never going to have a climax at all.

"Story" for Trollope is really different from both a Dickensian melodrama and a Jamesian "ado," and is really no tyrant over him. Not for him the invention of plots that will somehow gather everyone together, as Dickens does in the headlong chase in *Bleak House* where Inspector Bucket and Esther Summerson meet al-

most everyone in the novel on their way to the dead Lady Ded-
lock in Tom-All-Alone's. Nor for him the careful arrangement of
stories that manages to bring all the major characters of *Middlemarch* to the crises in their lives in a series of big scenes that take
place within a few days of each other. Not for him the cardboard
figures of Henrietta Stackpole, Mrs. Penniman, Maria Gostrey,
and Fanny Assingham, who exist only to set off the lives of others. Nor for him the single brooding tone of *Nostromo* that asks us
to imagine that all the people of Costaguana should be seen from
the same distance and in roughly the same way. All that, for Trollope, would be life-distorting and injurious to our sense of the individual lives of characters, and because it would be, he had to
discover stories that would never thus distort.

It would take much more careful treatment to do justice to Trollope's originality; I give it attention here because he is perhaps the
least original *seeming* master of the novel that had been so rich for
over a century. Needing to write in a given way, Trollope did not
worry if others had written similarly, or differently. "There is a
habit nowadays," Leavis wrote in 1958, "of suggesting that there
is a tradition of 'the English novel', and that all that can be said of
the tradition (that being its peculiarity) is that 'the English novel'
can be anything you like." Before James, at least, the English
novel *could* be anything the novelists wished it to be, but this does
not, in the sense we would use the term of the older culture, form
a tradition.

For one thing, in the older tradition there always were many
commentators, saying and re-saying in the present what had
been said in the past; it is a major way of keeping the past secure,
and alive. But in England, commentators on the novel are rare before 1850, and the first really important one is James. He was not
interested, though, in establishing or maintaining a tradition, in
keeping the past secure. He wanted to conquer, and long before
he made his permanent move to London, he had begun to down-
grade the previous and current occupants of the territory, and to
insist that what he could do was that which was most needed,
and that what he could not do was not worth doing: "*Our Mutual
Friend*, is, to our perception, the poorest of Dickens' works. And
it is poor with the poverty not of momentary embarrassment, but

of permanent exhaustion"; "*Middlemarch* is at once one of the strongest and one of the weakest of English novels . . . a treasure-house of detail, but . . . an indifferent whole"; "But by critics who prefer a grain of substance to a pound of shadow," *Far From the Madding Crowd* "will, we think, be pronounced a decidedly delusive performance; it has a fatal lack of magic."

Even in these sporadic forays, James is also beginning to insist on the kind of novel and novelist that England really needs: "[*Middlemarch*] sets a limit, we think, to the development of the old-fashioned English novel. Its diffuseness, on which we have touched, makes it too copious a dose of pure fiction. If we write novels so, how shall we write History?" James the pruner, James the writer of difficult ados, is making his way onto the stage. Having pronounced that Hardy "reminds us of a person fishing with an enormous net, of which the meshes should be thrice too wide," he proposes his solution:

> We are happily not subject, in this (as to minor matters) much-emancipated land, to the tyranny of the three volumes; but we confess that we are nevertheless being rapidly urged to a conviction that (since it is the nature of fashions to revolve and recur) the day has come round again for some of the antique restrictions as to literary form. The three unities, in Aristotle's day, were inexorably imposed on Greek tragedy: why shouldn't we have something of the same sort for English fiction in the day of Mr. Hardy?

Fiction needed to stop being old-fashioned, it needed restrictions, it needed a master novelist who would also be a literary dictator, and James was booking his berth on the next boat.

Needless to say, *Our Mutual Friend* is far from being the poorest of Dickens's works, *Middlemarch* is not an indifferent whole, *Far From the Madding Crowd* is quite a magical novel indeed. But James had to think otherwise in order to begin his conquest. Halfway through his career, and the strenuous part of his conquering done, he still felt he needed amiably to patronize Trollope, and, as late as 1907, in the preface to *The Portrait of a Lady*, he is still delightedly holding up his distorting glass and calling its images truth:

George Eliot has admirably noted it—"in these frail vessels is borne onward through the ages the treasure of human affection." In "Romeo and Juliet" Juliet has to be important, just as, in "Adam Bede" and "The Mill on the Floss" and "Middlemarch" and "Daniel Deronda," Hetty Sorel and Maggie Tulliver and Rosamond Vincy and Gwendolen Harleth have to be; with that much of firm ground, that much of bracing air, at the disposal all the while of their feet and their lungs. They are typical, nonetheless, of a class difficult, in the individual case, to make a centre of interest; so difficult in fact that many an expert painter, as for instance Dickens and Walter Scott, as for instance even in the main so subtle a hand as that of R. L. Stevenson, has preferred to leave the task unattempted. There are in fact writers as to whom we make out that their refuge from this is to assume it to be not worth their attempting; by which pusillanimity in truth their honour is scantly saved. It is never an attestation of a value, or even of our imperfect sense of one, it is never a tribute to any truth at all, that we shall represent that value badly. It never makes up, artistically, for an artist's dim feeling about a thing that he shall "do" the thing as ill as possible.

George Eliot's statement about frail vessels concerns the treasure of human affection, but within a sentence or two James is only concerning himself with the difficulties in making women the center of interest in a tale, as a way of congratulating himself for having attempted it so often.

One would think, reading this passage, that except for George Eliot, English fiction has no women as central characters. In fact it is the first art form in which women counted as much as men. *Pace* James, Dickens has his Esther Summerson, Scott his estimable Jeanie Deans. Indeed, except for Smollett, all first- and second-rate English novelists had made women their central characters: Pamela, Clarissa, Amelia, the heroines of Jane Austen and Anne Radcliffe, Becky Sharp, Jane Eyre, Catherine Earnshaw, Lucy Snow, Dorrit, Bathsheba Everdene, Diana Marion, George Eliot's array, Marian Halcombe, Monica Knollys, the Alice of Wonderland, and, in Trollope, as many as half of the interesting women characters written by a man: Mrs. Proudie, Madeline Vesey Neroni, Laura Kennedy, Violet Effingham, Glencora Palliser, Alice Vavasor, Lizzie Eustace, Miss Boncassen, Lady Mabel Grex, Mrs. Hurtle, an array that manages, furthermore, to make James's many heroines begin to seem somewhat like interchangeable parts. The "thing," we may say, had been done, and done profusely and well.

Just as he was not going to see what writers had done in creating women characters, so he was not going to see women novelists:

> Jane Austen, with all her light felicity, leaves us hardly more curious of her process, or of the experiences in her that fed it, than the brown thrush who tells his story from the garden bough. . . . The key to Jane Austen's fortune with posterity has been in part the extraordinary grace of her facility, in fact of her unconsciousness: as if, at the most, for difficulty, for embarrassment, she sometimes, over her work basket, her tapestry flowers, in the spare cool drawing-room of other days, fell a-musing, lapsed too metaphorically, as one may say, into wool gathering, and her dropped stitches, of these pardonable, of these precious moments, were afterwards picked up as little touches of human truth, little glimpses of steady vision, little masterstrokes of imagination.

With the Brontës he is even more simply dismissive:

> Literature is an objective, a projected result; it is life that is the unconscious, the agitated, the struggling, floundering cause. But the fashion has been, in looking at the Brontës, so to confound the cause with the result that we cease to know, in the presence of such ecstasies, what we have hold of or what we are talking about. They represent the high-water mark of sentimental judgment.

Given these patronizing tones, we should not be surprised to discover, as we will when we come to *The Portrait of a Lady*, that James is not so much interested in women as in the processes required for him to look at them.

But the one English writer of either sex that James could not dismiss so easily was George Eliot. He tried, in many things he wrote about her, to place her with some patronizing, but with her, clearly, his tone is as much the result of his being so admiring and in awe of her as of any genuine sense of his superiority to her. Furthermore, she had, in *Daniel Deronda*, the novel that was appearing as he was leaving Paris for London, written her first contemporary novel of high life, the kind of novel that James wanted to write. There would be no rural carpenters, weavers, evangelical preachers, or country parsons in his works, and of course no Mordecai Cohens and Mirah Lapidoths, but, in making his conquest of London and England, there would be, as if there had to be, Gwendolen Harleth, Henleigh Grandcourt, and a version of Daniel Deronda. After his arrival in London, it would be five years, and he would write three novels and a number of tales in the meantime, before he took on George Eliot, in what he called his "big novel," *The Portrait of a Lady*, about which he said before he began: "It is from that that I myself shall pretend to date—on that I shall take my stand."

▷▷▷▷Though I want the emphasis to fall on the relation of James to George Eliot, I can state that relation best by saying she was not his first master, but something like his fourth or fifth: Henry James, Sr., Hawthorne, Turgenev, and Balzac all loom large for James in the fifteen years before *The Portrait of a Lady*. James's capacity for love and admiration was very great, but he could feel most warmly when he was not forced by a feeling of competitiveness into effusions that seem only a mask for aggressiveness, and with all his masters he sought a love that resulted from his having triumphed over them.

By the time James was an adult, his father was a background figure for him, and the tone of Henry's letters to him is always somewhat patronizing, though this seems not a matter of an actual attitude so much as a relaxation attendant upon the son's sense that he can control the situation. His tone toward his brother William, by comparison, is always tense, edgy, competitive. William could, and did, criticize Henry's work, often very

acutely; their mother could criticize Henry's record as a correspondent or a manager of finances; Henry James, Sr., though,
was content to be the benign, aged, and slightly irrelevant patri-
arch of Quincy St. Whatever struggles James may have had with
him earlier in life, by the time he got to Europe he could be a free
heir, a subtle adapter and molder of his father's ideas and out-
looks.

James's relation to Hawthorne is similar. Hawthorne influ-
ences James because James freely lets that happen. He set himself
up as an apprentice in Hawthorne's shop, so that Hawthorne is
the only writer from whom one might quote passages that could
be mistaken for something by James. But this, because James
chose it, James could control. He was sure that in *Roderick Hudson*
he had written the novel about Americans in Rome that Hawthorne had written imperfectly in *The Marble Faun*. In his excellent
little book on Hawthorne, we find the same mixture of love, admiration, and condescension that we see in James's letters to his
father. Still, the matter was more complicated than that, and in
the complications we find hints of what we will find in his relation
to George Eliot.

In his *Hawthorne*, James comes down hard on allegory as a
mode, on Spenser, and Bunyan, and on Hawthorne's use of
them. Hawthorne began with abstractions, and the result, James
says, is a shadowiness in Hawthorne's creations; he himself began with a person, perhaps a person in a suggestive situation
or scene, and he was pleased when Turgenev told him he too
worked that way. He similarly criticized Hawthorne's idea of "romance" as opposed to "novel" (though he was willing enough to
steal that idea in his preface to *The American*), and to hint that
Hawthorne wrote allegorical romances because his world was
thin in social tones and institutions.

All of which may be true, but it is characteristic of James that
in the one respect where Hawthorne is clearly his superior, he
wanted to say it doesn't matter. The Hawthorne of "The Celestial
Railroad," "Ethan Brand," or "The Birthmark" may well be described as a writer of inferior allegory, but the Hawthorne who in-
vents the scarlet letter, Pearl, their relation to each other and to
Hester Prynne is a different matter entirely. Hawthorne there

embraces his symbols and is then free to work within them with excellent moment-to-moment inventiveness so that one feels the point is not the symbols but the inventiveness. In the brilliant fifth and sixth chapters, "Hester at Her Needle," and "Pearl," Hester embraces her letter so as to equivocate but not deny her shame, and Pearl is antagonistic toward both Hester and the scarlet A. Pearl then gathers handsful of flowers and throws them at the letter:

> "Child, what art thou?" cried the mother.
>
> "Oh, I am your little Pearl!" answered the child.
>
> But while she said it, Pearl laughed, and began to dance up and down, with the humorsome gesticulation of a little imp, whose next freak might be to fly up the chimney.
>
> "Art thou my child, in very truth?" asked Hester.
>
> Nor did she put the question altogether idly, but, for the moment, with a portion of genuine earnestness; for such was Pearl's wonderful intelligence, that her mother half doubted whether she were not acquainted with the secret spell of her existence, and might not now reveal herself.
>
> "Yes, I am little Pearl," repeated the child, continuing her antics.
>
> "Thou art not my child! Thou art no Pearl of mine," said the mother, half playfully; for it was often the case that a sportive impulse came over her, in the midst of her deepest suffering. "Tell me, then, what thou art, and who sent thee hither."
>
> "Tell me, mother!" said the child seriously, coming up to Hester, and pressing herself close to her knees. "Do thou tell me!"
>
> "Thy Heavenly Father sent thee!" answered Hester Prynne.
>
> But she said it with a hesitation that did not escape the acuteness of the child. Whether moved only by her ordinary freakishness, or because an evil spirit prompted her, she put up her small forefinger, and touched the scarlet letter.
>
> "He did not send me!" cried she, positively. "I have no Heavenly Father."

"Hush, Pearl, hush! Thou must not talk so!" answered the
mother, suppressing a groan. "He sent us all into this world,
He even sent me, thy mother. Then, much more, thee! Or, if
not, thou strange and elfish child, whence did thou come?"

"Tell me! Tell me!" repeated Pearl, no longer seriously,
but laughing, and capering about the floor. "It is thou that
must tell me!"

Hawthorne can write thus because he is working in what began
as an allegorical mode.

The result is a wonderful liquidity. Hester's playful "Thou art
no Pearl of mine" is like her luxurious design for the letter; she
toys with an idea that in another mood she takes very seriously:
who is this child? whence did she come? Likewise, Pearl can say
"Do thou tell me!" as in a catechism, receive a catechismal answer, and, catching Hester's hesitation in the answer, touch the
letter and dart away, powerful in the number of ways she can
probe. Powerful herself but vulnerable, Hester is cast into "a dis-
mal labyrinth of doubt" when Pearl taunts her. In the midst of it
all, Hawthorne can slip in his "whether moved only by her ordinary freakishness, or because an evil spirit prompted her," confident that by now "ordinary freakishness" will seem a plausible
way to describe the child of the letter, the daughter of the mer-
curial Hester, both trapped and both free.

Intellectually, James understands this aspect of Hawthorne
very well:

> Nothing is more curious and interesting than this almost
> exclusively *imported* character of the sense of sin in Haw-
> thorne's mind; it seems to exist there merely for an artistic or
> literary purpose. He had ample cognizance of the Puritan
> conscience; it was his natural heritage; it was reproduced in
> him; looking into his soul, he found it there. But his relation
> to it was only, as one may say, intellectual; it was not moral
> and theological. He played with it, and used it as a pigment;
> he treated it, as the metaphysicians say, objectively.

But Hawthorne's playing with Hester Prynne's sense of sin is
wanton, and one knows that James wanted to prune such pas-

sages, perhaps as much frightened as embarrassed by them.

The Marble Faun, James's immediate object of attention when he began his novelistic career, is rife with wanton passages, none perhaps as good as the best in *The Scarlet Letter*. James could rightly feel that when he reworked that novel into *Roderick Hudson*, he could do much just by pruning, by not loading his fiction with travelogue, by skirting the supernatural that Hawthorne loved to dabble in, by never writing scenes like the following in "A Moonlight Ramble," when the four central characters come upon Trajan's Column and Miriam and Hilda take turns offering moral and artistic epithets:

> Their moralizing strain was interrupted by a demonstration from the rest of the party, who, after talking and laughing together, suddenly joined their voices and shouted at full pitch—
>
> "Trajan! Trajan!"
>
> "Why do you deafen us with such an uproar?" inquired Miriam.
>
> In truth, the whole piazza had been filled with their idle vociferation; the echoes from the surrounding houses reverberating the cry of "Trajan," on all sides; as if there was a great search for that imperial personage, and not so much as a handfull of his ashes to be found.

Here Hawthorne is setting us up for a murder, yet always sufficiently liquid as to be able to let such outbursts fill his pages.

No one is going to shout "Trajan! Trajan!" in *Roderick Hudson*, which is to suggest that James may have pruned Hawthorne's luxuriousness too heavily. Roderick, the sculptor, is not even going to talk much about sculpture, almost because his predecessor, Kenyon, talks too much about it in *The Marble Faun*, which is to suggest that James may not have known how to stop pruning once he started. "I feel his principle was wrong," James told Julian Hawthorne, "Imagination is out of place; only the strictest realism can be right." But the relation of imagination to realism cannot be strict, and one might say that, odd as they are, the scenes between Hester and Pearl, and even the one by Trajan's Column, are as "real" or "realistic" as most of those in *Roderick*

Hudson or *The American,* where the characters seem to be floating a foot above the floor and speaking a language created specially for such conditions. Of course James was a greater writer than Hawthorne, but in his impulse to prune and control when he redoes Hawthorne, we can note a potential difficulty for James, a resultant thinness of air, a sameness of effect. *Roderick Hudson* is better than *The Marble Faun* in the way Shakespeare's *Titus Andronicus* is greater than Kyd's *The Spanish Tragedy;* the young writer at the beginning of a career is more coolly controlled than his mature predecessor. Yet I would sooner reread the clumsier works than the more accomplished ones.

James's relation with Turgenev shows no such wrinkles. Never having been an apprentice in Turgenev's shop, never having imagined he wanted to write a Russian or a French novel, James could place Turgenev into the empyrean. He was useful to expose the provinciality or blockheadedness of those who did not know or admire him—especially useful in the years before Turgenev was translated into English—and he was useful in showing up the limitations of Flaubert and his circle, or Tolstoi, or Hawthorne. He was the first great writer who was nice to James, who flattered him by taking him in, returning invitations, talking about writing, and James seems not to have minded much when he discovered Turgenev never read him. James had conquering to do, as Turgenev did not, and it helped that he would not need to conquer Turgenev. He would also be more of a moralist, more didactic, than Turgenev would have thought polite, but since James too was an observer, he could feel buoyed by the example of Turgenev, and feel that showed he was on the right track.

By comparison, James's admiration of Balzac always seems somewhat forced, because it was not instinctive and not truly literary. Balzac impressed James as Trollope might have done, for his dedication to being a novelist, for his huge productivity, for his saturation with the task of making France into *La Comédie Humaine.* Balzac had no shapely ideal of a novel, and none of Turgenev's delicacy, but he got the job done. So, using him as a standard, Hawthorne can be pronounced thin, Austen and the Brontës can be set down as unconscious, Flaubert and the younger French can be said to be interested in the wrong things, George

Sand can be called "too romantic." Then, as the shelf of James's works grew almost to the size of Balzac's, the lesson of Balzac can implicitly stand as an introduction to the lesson of Henry James.

Never having felt competitive with Balzac, James did not write *Washington Square* to conquer Balzac and *Eugénie Grandet;* it seems more like a calisthenic done before taking on *Daniel Deronda* in *The Portrait of a Lady*. James could say he got this novel from a tale told him by Fanny Kemble, but he must have known how much Kemble's story resembled Balzac's, since everyone else is instantly aware of it. Nor was it hard for James to see how to improve on what is still considered one of Balzac's best books. Grandet is its outstanding figure, a caricature because his miserliness makes him into one, so that his crudeness, and our inability ever quite to believe him possible, are the sources of his strength as a person and as a creation. James takes Grandet and scrubs him up, transforming his miserliness into Dr. Sloper's assurance that he is right about Morris Townsend. This makes him anything but a caricature, only an intelligent man, since he *is* right about Townsend, and, for half the novel, right enough about his daughter Catherine. She is, as he says, not particularly intelligent, sheltered, and an easy mark for a fortune hunter.

James's superiority to Balzac lies not just in his ability to bring a provincial caricature into an urban setting, or in his much more polished wit, but in his ability to conceive of father and daughter interestingly as a relation. Eugénie and Grandet barely have a relation, since Grandet never looks at Eugénie, and since they are conceived in two different modes. What James uncovers as *Washington Square* unfolds is the way Catherine is her father's daughter, not intelligent, not the least ironic, but clear-eyed, iron-willed, and quite beautiful in her strength:

> "We must ask no favours of him—we must ask nothing more. He won't relent, and nothing good will come of it. I know it now—I have a very good reason."
>
> "And pray what is your reason?"
>
> She hesitated to bring it out, but at last it came. "He is not very fond of me."
>
> "Oh, bother!" cried Morris, angrily.

"I wouldn't say such a thing without being sure. I saw it, I felt it, in England, just before he came away. He talked to me one night—the last night—and then it came over me. You can tell when a person feels that way. I wouldn't accuse him if he hadn't made me feel that way. I don't accuse him; I just tell you that that's how it is. He can't help it; we can't govern our affections. Do I govern mine? . . . Of course it isn't my fault; but neither is it his fault. All I mean is, it's true; and it's a stronger reason for his never being reconciled than simply his dislike for you."

Catherine has discovered what Dr. Sloper has not, and because she has, he loses control over her and, eventually, over himself, his will becoming tyrannical as Catherine's becomes serene. Catherine grows before our eyes, which is what Eugénie Grandet cannot do. James seems to have had little personal stake in his material in this novel, but that may be a source of its strength. For all that James called it "a poorish story" and did not include it in the New York edition of 1907, *Washington Square* is one of his finest works, far more than a subtle placing of Balzac, however much it may have been launched as that.

One reason James spoke slightingly of *Washington Square*, and of the also excellent *The Europeans* and *Hawthorne* done at the same time, is that for him all these things were preliminary to his "big novel," his attempt to conquer George Eliot. She had been on his mind longer than any of the others; in 1866, the year he first read Hawthorne's novels, he also published his first extended work of criticism, "The Novels of George Eliot." He met her in 1868 and, in a telling symbolic gesture, fell down at her feet, on the floor with Thornie Lewes, who was suffering painfully from tuberculosis of the spine; James makes his gesture even more telling when he imagines, in *The Middle Years*, that young Lewes had been gored by a bull. He reviewed *Middlemarch*, *The Spanish Gypsy*, *The Legend of Jubal*, and *Daniel Deronda* as they appeared, and followed this last with "*Daniel Deronda*: A Conversation." Always he was admiring, disappointed, and muddled about George Eliot. In his first look at her, he praises her most for what he calls her touches—which means the rustic detail of *Adam Bede* and *Silas Marner*—but adds that, as of 1866, *Romola* is her best book, though it is poor in touches. Then, *Middlemarch* is one of the best and worst of novels. After that, *Daniel Deronda* is her greatest work, but disappointing.

He really makes a spectacle of himself as he tries to get her into clear focus:

> We have a feeling that, both intellectually and morally, her genius is essentially of a simpler order than most of her recent manifestations of it. Intellectually, it has run to epigram and polished cleverness, and morally to a sort of conscious and ambitious scepticism, with which it only half commingles. The interesting thing would be to trace the moral divergence from the characteristic type. At bottom, according to this notion, the author of *Romola* and *Middlemarch* has an ardent desire for positive, active, constructive belief of the old-fashioned kind, but she has fallen upon a critical age and felt its contagion and dominion. If, with her magnificent gifts, she had been borne by the mighty general current in the direction of passionate faith, we often think she would have achieved something incalculably great.

The focus is unclear, or, if it is clear, it is ridiculous, since it implies that George Eliot's magnificent gifts are intellectually and morally simple—to be more easily found in *Adam Bede* than in *Middlemarch,* presumably—and that if, whatever those gifts, she had been "borne by the mighty general current in the direction of passionate faith," she could have become "incalculably great," when she would have become Dame Juliana of Norwich, maybe, or, more likely, Dinah Morris, who also may be said to be magnificently gifted but who is no novelist.

Is James asking that a woman be more like a woman? I think that strain is evident in all James says and writes about George Eliot, but it is hardly all he means, or says. "*Daniel Deronda*: A Conversation" shows him awash in patronizing love; Constantius says in one speech, "Speaking brutally, I consider *Daniel Deronda* the weakest of her books," and in the next, "The intellectual brilliancy of *Daniel Deronda* strikes me as very great, in excess of anything the author has done." This can mean: George Eliot's intellect is not very great; a version of George Eliot's own comment on Sir James Chettam: "a man's mind—what there is of it—has always the advantage of being masculine—as the smallest birch tree is of a higher kind than the most soaring palm"; intellect in fiction is a detriment to the achievement of great novels; Constantius can say anything because Theodora and Pulcheria will never catch him out. James clearly did not believe George Eliot's intellect was not great, but he betrays a belief in each of these last three possibilities.

It was her mind that he kept returning to, as though never able to take in the fact that a woman could be so smart, and as though, more legitimately perhaps, he was unsure what the use of such an intelligence was in the creation of novels. In his troubled review of *Middlemarch*, he says that "the constant presence of thought, of generalizing instinct, of *brain*, in a word, behind her observation, gives the latter its great value and her whole manner its high superiority." In his review of Cross's *Life* a dozen years later, he echoes this: "All the elements of an eventual happy fortune met in her constitution. The great foundation, to begin with —the magnificent mind, vigorous, luminous, and eminently sane." Each time James follows with a disclaimer, but not in an undercutting way. And there is certainly no irony or condescension in this passage from a letter to Alice James:

> I paid John Cross a longish visit some little time since and sat in his poor wife's empty chair, in the beautiful little study they had just made perfect, while he told me, very frankly, many interesting things about her. She was surely an extraordinary woman—her intellectual force and activity have, I suspect, never been equalled in any woman. If, with these powers, she had only been able to see and know more of life, she would have done greater things. As for the head itself, it was evidently of the first order—capable of almost any responsibilities. She led a wonderfully *large* intellectual life— and Cross said that her memory and her absolute exemption from the sense of fatigue, were more amazing the more he knew her. He, poor fellow, is left very much lamenting; but my private impression is that, if she had not died, she would

have killed him. He couldn't keep up the intellectual pace—
all Dante and Goethe, Cervantes and the Greek tragedies.
As he said himself, it was a cart-house married to a racer. . . .

Since this was written in January 1881, when James was about
halfway through *The Portrait of a Lady*, bringing Isabel Archer to
the point where she most resembles Gwendolen Harleth, we can
perhaps pause and try to assess James's feelings about his great
predecessor.

First, there was no one, with the exception of his brother William, about whom James was so unable to settle his attitudes.
Normally he could decide confidently how he felt about a person
or a book rather quickly, but every time he tried to do that with
her, he got tangled. Nowhere is this more in evidence than in his
letters and reviews about *Daniel Deronda*, which almost by itself
seemed to lure James to England after he had wearied of the
French, and which he kept praising and deploring. Second, we
can note that the younger man of twenty-five who hurled himself
at Thornie Lewes's side and George Eliot's feet had become, thir-
teen years later, someone who sat in George Eliot's chair in her
"beautiful little study." *Deronda* had offered the perfect challenge, and he clearly felt he had met it successfully. George Eliot
had given him, in Gwendolen and Grandcourt, characters he
could work with, coming as they do from the segment of society
James knew. She had also juxtaposed the static and isolated Wessex high life with a story that finds a source and direction for energies more vital and purposeful, Daniel's absorption into the lives
of Mirah and Mordecai and his taking on the mantle of a new Jewish leader. What James offered to do was to find, in Isabel Archer
and within the established Anglo-American society, that same alternative source of energy, so that within a single story he could
gain the tragedy of Gwendolen and the equivalent of the political
and ethnic energies of Deronda. He would do as he had done
with Hawthorne, namely do what the predecessor had done, but
do it more carefully, less mistakenly, gaining concentration
where the predecessor had been diffuse or uncontrolled. *That*
would earn the right to sit in George Eliot's chair.

Back in 1876, James had been delighted to report to William

that F. T. Palgrave had told him "G. Eliot's picture of English country-house life in *Daniel Deronda* might have been written by a house-maid!" Though in fact James soon learned more of English country-house life than George Eliot ever knew or wanted to know, he was not going to compete with her this way; he might want to outdo George Eliot, but he was not at this juncture going to try to out-English the English. She did not need any more knowledge of that life than a housemaid might tell her; she did no more to prepare herself for writing that part of her novel than take a brief trip through the west country. Her concerns not being satiric, she had only to be certain of a few things concerning country high life: its world had to be sufficiently vulnerable to outside money matters so that the failure of the house of Grapnell & Co. can blast the Reverend Mr. Gascoigne and totally alter the prospects of Gwendolen and Mrs. Davilow; it had to be sufficiently shallow to accept the spoiled child Gwendolen as a person to be reckoned with and to make Herr Klesmer seem like a giant in its drawing rooms; it had to be sufficiently inert and incurious so that Sir Hugo Mallinger can know next to nothing about his heir so that Gwendolen can be the first person within its boundaries to learn what a monster Grandcourt is. A housemaid could know that much.

James, however, was not going to compete by claiming to know more, but by insisting that such knowledge did not matter. His Gardencourt is someplace—on the Thames, actually, but that is unimportant—and Lord Warburton lives nearby, and he has sisters, and that is about it. James's way of conquering is to prune and thin, and that is his strength, his deflection, and his grave limitation. Perhaps the strongest case that has been put for the way this pruning and thinning led to strength is made by Quentin Anderson in his *The American Henry James*. It is an interesting book, and concerns itself with James as heir, so a brief account of its argument is in order here.

"Those critics," Anderson begins,

> whose preferences among the novels lie with *The Bostonians*, *The Europeans*, *Washington Square*, *What Maisie Knew*, and *The Awkward Age* are in my eyes ducking the problem of tradition

> as it affects James, since they are occupied with those of his
> works which are . . . open, depending as they do on a spec-
> trum of moral judgments and presumptions about the social
> scene which the reader possesses before he begins to read.

Since the central concern of this book is tradition, inheriting and
passing on, the last thing I want to do is to duck "the problem of
tradition as it affects James." Yet my preference among the novels
is, by and large, for those Anderson mentions, which is why he is
so helpful to me as he seeks to establish one sense of James as heir
and I seek to establish another.

On Anderson's terms, *The Portrait of a Lady* is a closed book in
which the reader is effectively sealed off from "moral judgments
and presumptions about the social scene." Density of description
about a social scene shared by author and reader is what George
Eliot seeks, and what James avoids on the grounds that, to use
one of Henry James, Sr.'s, favorite words, it would only "distract." James gives us only enough detail to show us Isabel Archer's possibilities: the American comes to Europe to discover
and confront the greatness of an other, and if the American tries
to appropriate Europe, by being only a tourist or by making it pic-
turesque, then the confrontation is avoided and the possibilities
diminish:

> At Gardencourt, Isabel wonders whether after a childhood
> so generally pleasant she does not require a certain amount
> of education through suffering. James reveals in a number of
> places Isabel's desire to *see* life, without either judging or suf-
> fering. This same impulse is seen many times in the desire
> for the picturesque in James's American travelers—and of
> course this guilt is common to us all. It is through this delight
> that terror comes; that we perceive the need for transcending
> our selfish self and our social self, and arriving at the particu-
> lar style which frees us from selfhood.

Some of these terms are derived from Henry James, Sr., the ancestor Anderson sees as most important for James, and have the
ring of jargon, but it is clear what Anderson intends.

It is a view of Isabel innocently imagining that she may feel the need to suffer but who wants something shallower, and more selfish:

> This emphasis on Isabel's greed runs quite contrary to our image of her as "spreading her wings," as holding high the torch of possibility, of readiness for moral adventure. . . . It is a way of summing up his technical problem in *The Portrait* to say that he must at one and the same time give us this sense of Isabel, which is Ralph's and her own, and also make us aware that her frozen desires must find a frozen complement —that the aim of being "exquisite" which the black Osmond quite honestly proffers is completely congruent with Isabel's own aim as a young woman. The point is that only the self-absorbed person can be trapped by the self-absorbed person; and the imagination of greatness can never be the imagination of one's own greatness. Isabel makes a disastrous marriage because she fails to discover "Europe." . . . Isabel evades that relation with something quite "other" which makes for real adventure.

Rejecting Warburton and Goodwood is rejecting adventure; accepting Osmond is keeping her "portrait" intact.

The Portrait of a Lady yields much to Anderson's reading; it is one James himself might have been willing to embrace. If he thinks, however, that James has cleared the clutter and debris of daily life the better to expose the tragic tale of a woman who learns she has tried to make her surroundings into a portrait of herself, it might be replied that in such a closed tale there is nothing for anyone to think or talk about but each other. The result often must seem like an extended stay on the moon, where everyone wants to "see" life, everyone is self-absorbed, in portraits of themselves or others. What Anderson says of Isabel and Osmond could as easily be said of Ralph Touchett, and, by implication, of Henry James.

But rather than argue against Anderson, I would like now to compare some passages from *Daniel Deronda* and *The Portrait of a Lady*, trying to show what James does when he prunes, when he works toward Anderson's "closed novel," and what price he pays for doing so. At the end of the fourth chapter of each novel

are descriptions of the present and future of Gwendolen and
Isabel:

> Always she was the princess in exile, who in time of famine
> was to have her breakfast-roll made of the finest-bolted flour
> from the seven thin ears of wheat, and in a general decamp-
> ment was to have her silver fork kept out of the baggage.
> How was this to be accounted for? The answer may seem to
> lie quite on the surface; in her beauty, in a certain unusual-
> ness about her, a decision of will which made itself felt in her
> graceful movements and clear unhesitating tones, so that if
> she came into the room on a rainy day when everyone else
> was flaccid and the use of things in general was not apparent
> to them, there seemed to be a sudden, sufficient reason for
> keeping up the forms of life; and even the waiters at hotels
> showed the more alacrity in doing away with crumbs and
> creases and dregs with struggling flies in them. This potent
> charm, added to the fact that she was the eldest daughter, to-
> ward whom her mamma had always been in an apologetic
> state of mind for the evils brought on her by her stepfather,
> may seem so full a reason for Gwendolen's domestic empire,
> that to look for any other would be to ask the reason of day-
> light when the sun is shining.

The passage continues brilliantly but it is best to bring James in
here to keep the quotations from being unmanageably long:

> Her reputation of reading a great deal hung about her like the
> cloudy envelope of a goddess in an epic; it was supposed to
> engender difficult questions, and to keep the conversation at
> a low temperature. The poor girl liked to be thought clever,
> but she hated to be thought bookish, she used to read in se-
> cret, and, though her memory was excellent, to abstain from
> quotation. She had a great desire for knowledge, but she
> really preferred almost any source of information to the
> printed page; she had an immense curiosity about life, and
> was constantly staring and wondering. She carried within
> herself a great fund of life, and her deepest enjoyment was to
> feel the continuity between the movements of her own heart

and the agitations of the world. For this reason she was fond of seeing great crowds and large stretches of country, or reading about revolutions and wars, of looking at historical pictures—a class of efforts to which she had often gone so far as to forgive much bad painting for the sake of the subject.

Both passages are characteristic, and both sufficiently attempt the same thing as to make comparison possible.

One stands alongside George Eliot and looks out into the world. One sees James standing on a raised platform and watches him examine and carefully explain something he might be holding in his hands, but which we cannot see ourselves. George Eliot suggests Gwendolen is like Joseph in Egypt—as the passage continues she will include spoiled sons and Macbeth in her comparing—and one knows James would never compare Isabel to anything male or masculine for fear of marring his effect. The rainy day, the waiters cleaning up crumbs, Mrs. Davilow's awareness of her bad second marriage, all appear in George Eliot's landscape, items gathered from near and far, but all familiar to us. James is like Isabel; though his memory is excellent, he abstains from quotation, and the reference to the goddess in an epic is only decorative. He is absorbed in his "difficulty," the mystery not just of Isabel, but of how much he can say about her, and when.

"She carried within her a great fund of life, and her deepest enjoyment was to feel the continuity between the movements of her own heart and the agitations of the world." Such a sentence may seem eager to reveal, but is very enigmatic. Is "a great fund of life" connected to "she had an immense curiosity about life" in the previous sentence, and, if so, how? The relation of the "great fund" to the rest of the sentence is unclear, and we do not know how much weight, and of what kind, James is putting on that phrase about Isabel's deepest enjoyment. Is she naive, sentimental, in wanting the world to be a mirror of herself? Is her great curiosity about life thus rendered bogus? Is the appetite for crowds and historical pictures an inheritance of a meagre America or a telling assessment of her personal fantasizing? Is she, does she wish to be, a pastoral hero able to express the world in expressing herself? Is it not the case that in this passage we are

not so much finding out about Isabel Archer as watching James
suggest terms under which she might be understood when we do
see her, and the terms are sufficiently elusive as to draw attention
away from Isabel and toward James as narrator?

Having gotten us to seeing how Gwendolen's beauty and
charm may account for her power, George Eliot continues:

> But beware of arriving at conclusions without comparison.
> I remember having seen the same assiduous, apologetic at-
> tention awarded to persons who were not at all unusual,
> whose firmness showed itself in no very graceful or eupho-
> nious way, and who were not eldest daughters with a ten-
> der, timid mother, compunctious at having subjected them
> to inconveniences. Some of them were a very common sort
> of men. And the only point of resemblance among them all
> was a strong determination to have what was pleasant, with
> a total fearlessness in making themselves disagreeable or
> dangerous when they did not get it. Who is so much cajoled
> and served with trembling by the weak females of a house-
> hold as the unscrupulous male—capable, if he has not free
> way at home, of going and doing worse elsewhere?

This is the George Eliot magic. Having insisted the princess in
exile need not be beautiful or graceful in order to have her fork
kept out of the baggage in a general decampment, she taxono-
mizes. Exiled princesses are a subtype of the larger class of people
—those determined to have their own way—a class mostly made
up of men, who do not have to be graceful or euphonious, and
who can be frightening and dangerous. The novel, without saying so, looms before us; two men who can do what Gwendolen
cannot, Grandcourt going and doing worse elsewhere, Daniel
not doing so but free to explore and to imagine that his fearless-
ness can become courage rather than disagreeable or dangerous.

But George Eliot is not yet finished, since the point about creating the larger class of people is to return us enlightened to
Gwendolen:

> Hence I am forced to doubt whether even without her potent
> charm and peculiar filial position Gwendolen might not still

have played the queen in exile, if only she had kept her in-born energy of egoistic desire, and her power of inspiring fear as to what she might say or do. However, she had the charm, and those who feared her were also fond of her; the fear and the fondness being perhaps both heightened by what may be called the iridescence of her character—the play of various, nay, contrary tendencies. For Macbeth's rhetoric about the impossibility of being many opposite things in the same moment, referred to the clumsy necessi-ties of action and not to the subtler possibilities of feeling. We cannot speak a loyal word and be meanly silent; we cannot kill and not kill in the same moment; but a moment is room wide enough for the loyal and mean desire, for the outlash of a murderous thought and the sharp backward stroke of re-pentance.

Here is brain, here is the result of a large intellectual life. We know, reading it, that George Eliot is giving us more than the current situation seems to warrant, and is asking us to load our circuits, to remember the passage's terms as we later see Gwen-dolen's life with Grandcourt expressed in its loyal and mean de-sires, its murderous thoughts and backward strokes of repen-tance. But that, like the suggestion that Gwendolen will lose "her inborn energy of egoistic desire," is for later. For now, the un-scrupulous male and Macbeth refer us primarily to "the clumsy necessities of action." Since men are free to act, they will act, think acting is all important, become clumsy, and lose sight of the refinements of their feeling.

Women, though, more restricted as to their actions, are there-fore more able to be subtle and complicated in feeling. Gwendo-len says later, while Grandcourt is wooing: "We must stay where we grow, or where the gardeners like to transplant us." George Eliot has said earlier, concerning women and flowers: "It was a poor eight months since she had come to Offendene, and some inclinations became manifest slowly, like the sunward creeping of plants." And Gwendolen goes on with her own statement: "We are brought up like the flowers, to look as pretty as we can, and be dull without complaining. That is my notion about the plants; they are often bored, and that is the reason why some of them have got poisonous." She is lightly whipping a rhododendron as she says this, being as she is a plant creeping toward the sun and bored and liable to go poisonous. All this reaches its first climax when Gwendolen listens to Lydia Glasher's revelation about her life with Grandcourt and "it was as if some ghastly vision had come to her in a dream and said: 'I am a woman's life.' "

To learn of a spoiled child is to learn about unscrupulous men is to learn about confined women, murdering and repenting, seeking sunlight and going poisonous, recognizing with compassion and horror the lot shared by courted maidens and kept mistresses. One could then turn to the range of metaphors concerning, on the one hand, astronomy and climate, and, on the other, reptiles, insects, and crustaceans, all put to work to describe Grandcourt; these reach their climax with this: "And she had found [in him] a will like that of a crab or a boa-constrictor, which goes on pinching or crushing without alarm at thunder."

Of all writers after Pope, George Eliot at her best is the one most able to achieve the density and precision of reference for which the great Renaissance writers are remarkable. Though it took immense work to achieve it, the past and present were really *available* to her as enabling resource as it was for so few after the onset of darkness. At one point Grandcourt is described as being "neutral as an alligator," and the wit and daring of the metaphor derive from its great precision, as is so often the case with the metaphors of Shakespeare, or Donne. Her flowers may seem Linnaean by comparison with the pastoral flowers of Perdita, T. C., or Eve, and she always had to work to gain what earlier writers seemed to create with ease. But her language at its richest seems both natural and daring and she can make us thereby feel larger citizens of a larger world. Nowhere is this more true than in the Gwendolen-Grandcourt half of *Daniel Deronda*, where she is "vigorous, luminous, and eminently sane."

James knew all this, of course, but would not compete with Eliot on these grounds. He had, instead, to insist on the virtues of closing the window on the large world, on intently observing and meditating. To go back to another description of Isabel Archer, and especially to see what happens when James makes an Eliotic appeal to our sense of common experience:

> It was wrong to be mean, to be jealous, to be false, to be cruel; she had seen very little of the evil of the world, but she had seen women who lied and tried to hurt each other. Seeing such things had quickened her high spirit; it seemed right to scorn them. Of course the danger of a high spirit is the danger of inconsistency—the danger of keeping up the flag after the place has surrendered; a sort of behaviour so anomalous as to be almost a dishonour to the flag.

"Of course the danger of a high spirit is the danger of inconsistency"—that is the George Eliot manner when she is widening or shifting her focus, or forestalling an easy judgment. James does something quite different with it. A high spirit sees someone lie, or hurt someone else, and is scornful, and "high" describes a spirit that might not be compassionate, or eager to help the injured party, and that is its innocence. If so, it is hardly "of course" that the danger of such a spirit is inconsistency; one might think the danger is the opposite, an inflexible assurance, and, indeed, after the dash James describes the danger of inconsistency as "the danger of keeping up the flag after the place has surrendered." The two dangers don't seem compatible, and Isabel's spirit is really clearer to us before that sentence than after; "inconsistency" ends up seeming to refer to a moral spirit that does less than justice to itself or morality because it is so "high," but I'm not clear we can pin it down any more than that.

Characteristically, James does not then try to clarify the enigma he has created: "But Isabel, who knew little of the sorts of artillery to which young ladies are exposed, flattered herself that such contradictions would never be observed in her own conduct." The contradictions we can note do not refer to anything Isabel *can* be aware of—we left her, as it were, in a high spirit, scorning A, who injures B: "Her life should always be in harmony with the most pleasing impression she should produce; she would be what she appeared, and she would appear what she was. Sometimes she went so far as to wish that she should find herself someday in a difficult position, so that she might have the pleasure of being so heroic as the occasion demanded." The military metaphor keeps shifting. The one who keeps up the flag of scorn after the place has surrendered is the assailant, while the one who does not know about the artillery of others is the one assailed, while the one who wishes herself in a difficult position could be either one. The besieger and the besieged may both be innocent, but cannot be in the same way. James takes our knowledge of military attack and defense and then clouds it over; we are asked to think of Isabel in two different ways, but are not told how to do so, which makes our apparently relevant knowledge useless. Nor does it help when James proceeds to list more shortcomings of Isabel, and then ends: "She would be an easy victim of scientific criticism, if she were not intended to awaken on the reader's part an impulse more tender and more purely expectant."

Again, I know about tender and expectant impulses, but I am not clear why James invokes their use to conclude a passage in which he has apparently sought to invoke other, very different, impulses. Or, rather, I am clear, but am not clear about Isabel so much as about what James is doing, asking of his reader. Again, he stands on his raised platform, seems to be showing an Isabel we can see, but then beclouds such seeing, and even says that the matter is too delicate for what he has been apparently seeking, namely, "scientific criticism." This, presumably, is what Quentin Anderson means by calling *The Portrait of a Lady* a closed book; one is given referents whereby we might say we "see" Isabel, but James then, in effect, directs us not to look. James deflects from George Eliot here, and throughout the first half of the novel, by seeming to invite us to share his view of Isabel and then by frustrating us, by denying the invitation was ever given, if one likes, or by insisting the matter is too difficult to allow for the vulgarities of a public viewing. His sentences invite close examination, then, as if deliberately, they shrivel up and disappear in the face of such examination, such mere "scientific criticism." The impulses George Eliot can deeply satisfy are precisely those James wants to say he is somehow above satisfying.

The conqueror is an observer—we can return to that now with some fuller sense of what it might entail. In his preface to *The Por-*

trait of a Lady, James writes, as if to show that it is the observer, not the thing observed, that is important: "The spreading field, the human scene, is the 'choice of subject'; the pierced aperture, either broad or balconied or slitlike and low-browed, is the 'literary form'; but they are, singly or together, as nothing without the presence of the watcher—without, in other words, the consciousness of the artist." Though James might be proud of having made an innocent woman as his choice of subject in the spreading field, he here makes clear how little she matters—George Eliot makes her matter, as it were, and he, challenging but deflecting or retreating, will not—compared to the chooser, the watcher, James himself. To conquer George Eliot he must conquer us, and to do that, he must keep drawing attention to himself, and to paint himself, as observer, in heroic colors. What he proclaims in his preface, he enacts in many passages in the novel.

To be such a conqueror, he had to make the consciousness of the artist crucial; that was the whole point of his remaining privately not just single but celibate. In *Roderick Hudson* is a very odd, revealing passage in which James, describing himself in Rowland Mallet, responds to the news that an attractive woman of his acquaintance is going to be married:

> He had half an hour's talk with her; a farewell talk, as it seemed to him—a farewell not to a real illusion, but to the idea that for him, in the matter of committing himself for life, grim thought, there could ever be a motive that wouldn't ache like a wound. Such a pressure would resemble that of the button of an electric bell kept down by the thumb—prescribing definite action to stop the merciless ring.

"A motive that would ache like a wound"—such a striking phrase, one feels it says precisely what it means. Mallet, and James, might have entertained the idea that committing oneself to another for life would not entail the presence of such a motive, or of a mercilessly ringing bell, but it really takes only a brief conversation to banish it forever. To remain unwounded, one must be uncommitted, an observer; one must be, if one is James, an artist.

George Eliot's genius is for committing herself to her characters, and, thereby, for exposing herself to motives that might ache like wounds. We can see this most directly in scenes like Maggie Tulliver cutting her hair, or Dorothea Brooke crying in Rome, or Gwendolen receiving the diamonds Lydia Glasher sends her, places where a defenseless self needs sympathy but receives, instead, an aching sympathy that derives from our knowledge that something terrible has happened and that the victim has helped bring it about. We see it, also, though, when we contemplate Fred Vincy and Mary Garth from the angle of Camden Farebrother, or Gwendolen and her mother after all other relations fail or disappear, places where helplessness is made the partner of dignity. In many ways George Eliot plays God the creator, working as narrator, God the Sacrificed Son, as she insists the lots she creates for her characters demand from her a response similar to "Lord forgive them, for they know not what they do," and God the Holy Spirit, working to bring us into her community, suffering, helpless, dignified.

James could do none of this, and perhaps his deepest knowledge of himself was that he could not. He had to say farewell to motives that could ache like wounds, he had to insist he was triumphant in so doing. He could say that George Eliot's novels were indifferent wholes, and be right to the extent that it is always the potential defect of her genius that the multitudinousness of her impulses would not always be controlled. He would prune that multitudinousness, control the impulses, create his raised platform, his aperture or balcony, and in effect always draw attention away from his characters and back toward himself, his difficulties.

On the face of it, anyone reading *Daniel Deronda* and *The Portrait of a Lady* consecutively might say that James's is the superior novel; it is not without reason that her novel remained out of print for two generations without anyone's protesting while his has always been one of the novels everyone should read. James would never have made the blunder George Eliot does in the Jewish sections of *Daniel Deronda*. There, we may say, George Eliot's motives ache like a wound, but without any ability to enliven or embody the impulse successfully. The writing is slack, and George Eliot cannot really afford to ask us to be alert as readers. Her genius lies in the range of her referents and the depth of her absorption, and with Mirah Lapidoth and Mordecai she simply does not know enough. Even the great scenes with Daniel's mother, the Alchirisi, are badly compromised by the role they play in the plot. The point about her, one feels while reading, is that she is neither Lydia Glasher nor Gwendolen Grandcourt, and that her way of saying "I am a woman's life" should stand as a bitterly achieved but triumphant alternative to theirs, much as Herr Klesmer's life stands as an alternative to those of the other men in the Wessex world. But George Eliot twists this, has the Alchirisi insist she did not want to be a Jew, which enables Daniel to ally himself in spirit with her father, his grandfather; George Eliot becomes a party to that alliance and an implicit repudiator of the great woman with great talents who could not love her child.

Still, badly flawed though it is, *Daniel Deronda* does achieve, as a whole, much of what George Eliot seeks for it. In the Gwendolen-Grandcourt half there is no blemish such as one finds in the creation of Arthur Donnithorne or Will Ladislaw. Everything slightly faked in the handling of Dorothea Brooke's acceptance of Casaubon is expunged in the superb scenes in which Gwendolen is drawn into her acceptance of Grandcourt. And, as one returns to this half from the other, one increasingly feels the smallness of Gwendolen's world, not just confining because she is a trapped woman, but ghastly because no one in that world can entertain any thoughts about a world outside its confines. Cynthia Chase notes that Daniel's not knowing he is a Jew means he did not know he was circumcised—he never looked down, she says. He might well have looked, however, and not have known what he was seeing, and his guardian, Sir Hugo Mallinger, in his amiable clumsy insensitivity, might well have not known how to tell him or seen any reason to do so; it is not the kind of problem George Eliot could easily raise, but at least she has created an England sufficiently dead as to provide ample explanation for Daniel's ignorance. What she wanted was an alternative to this England, and this, as embodied in Zionism, she did not really know about, and so, whatever apologies one makes, her novel *is* an indifferent whole.

James knew that in Isabel Archer he had an alternative source of energy, and one that could live and move inside the Anglo-European society he wanted to create. No need for his book, therefore, to flop into two halves, no need for elaborately contrived and imperfectly achieved parallel lines of action. And in that sense *The Portrait of a Lady is* a better novel than *Daniel Deronda*. But when one is put, as a reader, in the position James creates for us, one is not able, as one can do with George Eliot, constantly to assent, or demur, or modify; one either accepts or rebels against the whole enterprise, and I can say for myself that over the years with each rereading what once had been acceptance is now rebellion.

One point on which even many admiring readers have found themselves trying to escape the clutches of James's mastery and to assert their own points of view concerns the central event of the book, Isabel's acceptance of Osmond as husband. James works hard to provide ways to understand this, especially after Isabel is rich, Madame Merle appears, and Isabel and Mrs. Touchett go to Florence. Quentin Anderson's answer, that only a self-absorbed person can be trapped by another self-absorbed person, seems true enough, but not really more helpful than Leavis's statement that James must have her marry Osmond so her fate can resemble Gwendolen Harleth's. There are other answers: Isabel is frightened of sex: she is afraid when Lord Warburton makes his first advances; she cries every time the aggressively masculine Caspar Goodwood gets near her; Osmond, by comparison, makes her feel admired. Or: Isabel could only be encircled within completed systems were she to accept Warburton or Goodwood, while with Osmond she has a chance to do something "exquisite." Or: since James wants our attitude toward Isabel to be "purely expectant," she never learns the worst about Osmond until after they are married, and her innocence is thereby quite understandable. There is ample evidence for all these answers, but those that seem closest to a rich understanding of Isabel are precisely those that also have to be secured against the grain and demands of James's manner. We can say we understand, but he will not say so; he gives us frames of reference that seem to lead us to an understanding or a judgment, and then patronizes us by denying their validity or our ability to make any reading decisive.

Isabel comes to Osmond's villa in chapter 24 and he proposes to her in chapter 29; it is a matter of forty pages, within which the two have three or four brief conversations, none by themselves of more than small consequence. James makes little effort to have Osmond seem interesting or attractive, as though such efforts should be expended on the Warburtons or Goodwoods. There is a long passage in the middle of their first meeting at Osmond's which is perfectly characteristic, James hovering, seeking the enigmatic. Osmond, Pansy, Madame Merle, Countess Gemini, and Isabel all chat briefly, then Madame Merle draws the countess off and Pansy retires. Osmond asks Isabel what she thinks of the countess, and proceeds to make a speech about his sister. Then:

> He resembled no one she had ever seen; most of the people she knew might be divided into groups of half a dozen specimens. There were one or two exceptions to this; she could think, for instance, of no group that would contain her aunt Lydia. There were other people who were, relatively speaking, original—original, as one might say, by courtesy—such as Mr. Goodwood, as her cousin Ralph, as Henrietta Stackpole, as Lord Warburton, as Madame Merle. But in essentials, when one came to look at them, these individuals belonged to types which were already present to her mind. Her mind contained no class which offered a natural place to Mr. Osmond—he was a specimen apart. . . . It was not so much what he said and did, but rather what he withheld, that distinguished him; he indulged in no striking deflections from common usage; he was an original without being an eccentric.

It seems to me, as I suspect it does to most readers of this novel, that if one can find the types to which Mrs. Touchett and Ralph and Madame Merle belong, one is not going to have much difficulty finding that Osmond is at most a subset of the same type,

Americans in Europe, settled in that role even when peripatetic, neither idle nor well employed.

To say that, though, one must work against James's gestures, all of which work us away from imagining we know these characters. Here, especially, he is saying we do not know Osmond—we, after all, only see what he says and does, and his originality lies in what he withholds—and he is asking us to imagine an original whose originality we cannot quite place or specify. High on his platform, peering intently but not saying, James insists we must be careful; Osmond "indulged in no striking deflections from the common usage," is no eccentric; weaving his way through a long insistence that Osmond is like Ralph but is not Ralph, shy but in a good way, James ends this meditation: "His suddenly asking her what she thought of the Countess Gemini— that was doubtless a proof that he was interested in her feelings; it could scarcely be as a help to his knowledge of his own sister. That he should be so interested showed an inquiring mind; but it was a little singular that he should sacrifice his fraternal feeling to his curiosity. This was the most eccentric thing he had done." Not an eccentric, yet the most eccentric thing he does is almost the only thing he has done to this point. If there is an aperture through which James sees, James puts his hand over it whenever we try to see for ourselves.

If we take all this to be Isabel's view of Osmond rather than James's, we can then attribute the tissue of blindnesses and self-contradictions as a matter of innocence rather than coy mastery, but it will help little because we are given little sense of why Isabel should respond this way since, in any event, we still do not know what there is in Osmond to be interested in or attracted to. With the delusions of Dorothea Brooke about Casaubon, or of Catherine Sloper about Morris Townsend, we at least know what in them leads to such blindness, but James here will not even let us be that clear about Isabel. Instead, he keeps fencing us off, insisting that clarity about Osmond is itself deflective:

> Mrs. Touchett easily remembered that the girl had refused an English peer; and that a young lady for whom Lord Warburton had not been up to the mark should content herself

with an obscure American dilettante, a middle-aged wid-
ower with an overgrown daughter and an income of nothing
—this answered to nothing in Mrs. Touchett's conception of
success. She took, it will be observed, not the sentimental,
but the political, view of matrimony, a view which has always had much to recommend it.

Who would say that, whatever his "originality," Gilbert Osmond
is an obscure American dilettante? Mrs. Touchett, Ralph Touchett, all readers, and James himself. But such typing, James insists, is to take a political view of marriage, and Isabel has no reason to settle for political views of matrimony. Which once again
blocks us out without showing us Isabel's way or James's sense of
why that is her way.

Finally, the acceptance of Osmond is never described. He
makes his offer, Isabel travels for a year with Madame Merle, and
suddenly we are told she is engaged. We have known all along
that she will accept him, but only because novel readers can feel
which way the wind is blowing. In fact, for most of these crucial
chapters James has absented himself from any accounting for Isabel, so we are thrown back on saying, either sympathetically or
critically, that Isabel accepts Osmond because he is different from
Warburton and Goodwood. Which is a statement so crude that it
has taken every subtlety James can command to keep us from
making it, since we have known all along that Warburton and
Goodwood exist in the novel to be rejected, for whatever reasons
we may wish to name.

It never was Isabel that James was interested in; genuinely
committing himself to her, to an exploration of her, would have
been having a motive that aches like a wound. She is only the
specimen, the alternative source of energy, and whenever anyone tries to say who Isabel Archer is, James will move to show
them limited, mistaken, vulgar, or guilty of trying to possess another. Even Ralph Touchett can be shown to be guilty of, to use
William Gass's excellent phrase for him, the high brutality of
good intentions. In the conversation between Ralph and his father—one of the finest scenes in the book—Ralph talks the old
man into leaving his money to Isabel, and Mr. Touchett tells him

he is using Isabel for his entertainment. Ralph does not deny this, cannot do so. But he is not wrong about Isabel, wrong only in his desire to create in her someone who can do as she likes for his, Ralph's, pleasure. Yet James will insist that Ralph is mistaken about Isabel, since he could not anticipate Isabel's acceptance of Osmond. But that wrongness is not a failure in intelligence, since he sees what we see; it only serves to emphasize the element of perverseness we must ascribe to Isabel if we are to accept her marriage to Osmond as a choice James had truly given her. "Perverseness," furthermore, is a word we might use when frustrated, but not one we can really give to Isabel herself.

The first half of *The Portrait of a Lady* is the crucial half, the place where James would enact his triumph over George Eliot. James here limits and stylizes his art in ways that make him insistently evasive; George Eliot's implicit presence makes him both different and less than he was, or need have been. And the moment Isabel accepts Osmond she becomes Gwendolen Harleth and Osmond loses all trace of his model in James's life, Frank Boutt, and emerges as a variation of Grandcourt. When this happens, James relaxes, and the second half, much less "original," if one likes, is also much better, the triumph and the need to triumph over George Eliot passed. The scale is reduced, so that small domestic matters, like Osmond's desire to have Lord Warburton as his son-in-law, or even Ralph's presence in Rome, can generate a good deal of the action. Madame Merle, who suffers from having to be "the round world itself," in the first half of the book, almost disappears. The scene near the end, Ralph dying in Isabel's arms, is soft, but probably should be, since nothing said there can alter the fact that Ralph must die and Isabel must return to Rome and her husband. Let Ralph say "You wanted to look at life for yourself . . . and you were punished for your wish," and if that distorts the story we have been given, at least by now we have been given enough of a story to say so.

The very end of the novel is something else again, however, and I would like to discuss it briefly in order to suggest something about the later, post–George Eliot phase of James's career. He had been able to scorn those who wanted Christopher Newman in *The American* to end up married to Claire de Cintré; he had written everything in the second half of *The Portrait of a Lady* so that Isabel can accept as well as discover her folly and the ghastly life she chose. So she must bury Ralph and return to Rome. But James does not leave it at that; he comes up with a last scene with Caspar Goodwood, he who Isabel has rejected even before the action of the novel begins. He is really a comic figure, unable to want to understand Isabel, unable to listen to her except to complain or pout. When he says at the end, "The world is all before us—and the world is very large," he is only saying what he said from the beginning. To accept Goodwood would be like dying, so Isabel must say: "As you love me, as you pity me, leave me alone."

The difficulty is that the dying that acceptance of Goodwood resembles is sexual: "but she believed that to let him take her in his arms would be the next best thing to dying. This belief, for a moment, was a kind of rapture, in which she felt herself sinking and sinking." So that to reject him is to reject sex. In his 1907 revision James underscores this, so that when she senses that Goodwood loves her it "was the hot wind of the desert, at the approach of which the others dropped dead, like mere sweet airs of the garden. It wrapped her about; it lifted her off her feet, while the very taste of it, as of something potent, acrid and strange forced open her set teeth." Goodwood's kiss, which is, in 1881, a "flash of lightning," is this in 1907:

> His kiss was like white lightning, a flash that spread, and spread again, and stayed; and it was extraordinary as if, while she took it, she felt each thing in his hard manhood that had least pleased her, each aggressive fact of his face, his figure, his presence, justified of intense identity and made one with this act of possession. So she had heard of those wrecked and under water following a train of images before they sink.

This may reveal that James learned more about how he wanted to write about sex in the intervening years, but it shows a nervousness about the way he has handled Isabel all along and a shocking callousness in his response to that nervousness.

It does no good to insist, and to insist even more strenuously in his revision, that rejecting Goodwood is a sexual failure in Isabel Archer. That her fear of Goodwood all along includes a fear of his aggressive sexuality—that her acceptance of the sterile dilettante includes a desire not to have something "potent, acrid and strange" force "open her set teeth"—that is part of the novel we have read, though never so much so that this final insistence seems the best way to end. Isabel is not noble to return to Rome, but she must go back to live those definitions of herself she helped create, and James does no good by saying she is a sexual coward as she goes back.

George Eliot handles Gwendolen much better at the end of *Daniel Deronda*. Gwendolen's passion has been the desire to murder Grandcourt, and if Shakespeare in *Macbeth* is more brilliant in articulating such a passion, not he or anyone else is as careful as George Eliot in showing how that passion is born, grows, is treasured, and recoiled from even as its potential victim seems to invite it and to exult in the invitation. Having had that passion and having been deeply etched by it, Gwendolen pathetically wants to fall in love with Deronda, but George Eliot will not sentimentalize or overvalue that desire:

> Love-making and marriage—how could they now be the imagery in which poor Gwendolen's deepest attachment could spontaneously clothe itself? Mighty Love had laid its hand upon her; but what had he demanded of her? Acceptance of rebuke—the hard task of self-change—confession —endurance. If she cried towards him, what then? She cried as the child cries whose little feet have fallen backward— cried to be taken by the hand, lest she should lose herself.

Gwendolen is still young, and in the shock of Grandcourt's death and then of Daniel's imminent departure she is like a child again, momentarily hoping her deepest attachment could be transformed into lovemaking and marriage, but knowing what is now asked of her instead. There follow some touching scenes with her mother, their old relation gone but their love intact and vitally important to both; if she cannot make an entire new life out of that relation, she can make the beginning of one. Gwendolen is still young, and the stuff of daily life is still there, out of which can come new habits and even new hopes, however vague these must be as the novel ends.

James, having pruned and stylized life to a matter of fateful choices, is then forced to ask us to think of Isabel as older than she is, or, in anyone else's novel, could be. We are not asked to think of Isabel's rejection of Goodwood as what, on sensible grounds, it obviously is, the fear of a very young woman who in some ways is still a virgin. Having none of George Eliot's ease in bearing in mind the facts of the situation, having, indeed, only a meagre situation to bear in mind, James seeks effects—such a long novel he has written, it must have a suitably large ending. Even the tearful scene with Ralph was not enough for him, so he tosses up the momentary drama with Goodwood, gratuitous, vulgar, but "strong," and all to keep us from seeing how bare his stage is, how little he leaves for Isabel no matter what she chooses; if we see that we may see how little he has *ever* left for Isabel.

James's big novel was, hardly by coincidence, his George Eliot novel. His other masters did not write big novels, but she did. Not being able to challenge her on her own grounds, he simultaneously had to prune the materials to a notable thinness and write a very long book. He thought he had triumphed, and since many of his readers have agreed with him, there is little need to cavil further. Like most anxious triumphs, it seems a badly equivocal one, and it may have had consequences that neither James nor his admirers have seen. He seems to have become convinced by the success of *The Portrait of a Lady* that his best work would also be his longest. Quentin Anderson may be right when he says that in his largest novels—*The Portrait, The Princess Casamassima, The Tragic Muse,* and the three late self-conscious masterpieces—James expressed most fully his sense of tradition, of his relation to his father. But it does not therefore follow that in these books we see him at the highest reaches of his genius. In his way of conquering George Eliot he had found a model, and in his subsequent presumption that it should be a model for his greatest art he may have deluded himself at least as much as when he dreamed of being a writer of great plays.

Just before writing *The Portrait of a Lady,* James wrote three first-rate short works—*Hawthorne, The Europeans,* and *Washington*

Square. He deprecated these as he wrote them and forever after, so anxious was he to date himself from his big, his George Eliot, novel. All three books are light as a feather, filled with deft touches, like the portrait of Emerson in *Hawthorne,* Mr. Wentworth in *The Europeans,* the closing pages of *Washington Square.* Just after *The Portrait of a Lady* he wrote his queerest and perhaps his best novel, *The Bostonians,* marked most strongly by James's willingness to let matters get slightly out of control, especially in his fascination with Olive Chancellor, his one character that clearly o'ermastered the master.

The apparent consequence of his conquest of George Eliot, however, was that ease, small touches, and a willingness to let matters somewhat shape themselves are absent from the big and self-conscious masterpieces. That the greatest "doing," the greatest acceptance of a difficulty, led to the greatest works became an axiom with James, and it was only his prodigious appetite for writing that led to the considerable array of shorter works in which he could let himself be more at ease and more open. James loved to pick up his material by listening to someone begin to tell a story, by tuning out any continuation he may have been asked to hear, and by letting the virus of suggestion grow. Turgenev worked that way, but he wrote only short stories, sketches, and short novels, while James the conqueror continued to let very long novels grow from these little suggestions of person and place. Which meant he had to be pleased with himself for being able to do so.

As a result, much of James's art became devoted to concealing and revealing, to finding ways to continue the concealing over hundreds of pages. The enigmatic hovering he first employed in *The Portrait of a Lady,* the creation of an air that insists that settling something is a sign of crudeness and saying something straight the mark of a fool—if such hovering is the highest art, then *The Golden Bowl* is his finest novel and *The Ambassadors* is almost as good. I admit to finding both these novels elephantine monsters. But what the end of *The Portrait of a Lady* shows, and what the revised ending especially shows, is James's increasing sense that what was to be concealed and then revealed is sexual, and about the sexual James is limited because for him it is mostly scenario,

secret, the thing to be revealed. What seems a dangerous mistake in the 1881 ending of *The Portrait of a Lady* becomes almost an egregious leer in 1907, Isabel the hapless victim of James's need to reveal a final truth about her.

Nor, I fear, does the attempt to control this impulse help much when all it leads to is a vast extension of the concealing. It takes Lambert Strether hundreds of pages to discover that ordinary Chad Newsome is not returning to America for the ordinary reason that he has fallen for a fin-de-siècle fatal woman—why? For the simple reason that the novel had to be long. Strether is a fine creation, and James poured much of his best love of the observer into his making, but he did all that just for a trip down a river and a hushed scene where Madame de Vionnet dresses like a madonna. And what may seem the one exception to the pattern in James's later writing I have been describing really turns out to prove it. In Kate Croy and Merton Densher in *The Wings of the Dove* we have one of the finest of James's achievements, a man and a woman in love that make most fictional lovers seem sterile or merely breathless. Here there is little concealing and revealing, and unquestionably the novel is the better for it. James, however, could let that happen because the lovers are for him the foreground figures, while it is Milly Theale who receives his lavish, and enervating, acts of concealment revelation.

All this because he had attempted to conquer George Eliot in *The Portrait of a Lady*? I suggest only that that was an important event, perhaps the most important one, in the story of James's coming to be who he was, write as he did. That he was to be the first competitive novelist can be explained in many ways; that this would happen when it did in the history of the novel can be explained by many things that are extraneous to James himself, since a phase of the novel, and of England, was ending about the time James came to London. But James's easy mastery of Hawthorne, his almost casual mastery of Balzac, show that he could enter into the lists without committing himself to the kind of conquering he attempted in his rewriting of *Daniel Deronda*, an assault that had to be massive to have any hope of success while at the same time being limiting and pruning. He wanted to sit in that chair in George Eliot's study and, believing that in writing

The Portrait of a Lady, he had earned the right to do so, he gave himself over to a continued repeating of that kind of effort even when he was no longer competing with a looming predecessor. The effort did not kill him, obviously, but it defined him, committed him, perhaps without his knowing it, to his peculiar kind of conquering. But that he could do this at all, that he could consciously rewrite a major George Eliot novel, that he could then write for another thirty years and produce some of the finest pages of fiction in English, shows that this combat and conquering did not have for him the really crippling consequences it had for so many poets. And if it did considerable damage to James as a theorist of the novel, it seems to have had very little effect on his ability to write well about a large number of other writers, in essays and reviews where, if he is blind, he is blind in a way he would have been had George Eliot never lived.

    ➥➥➥➥Born and bred in darkness, the novel shows many fewer scars than does poetry of battles waged between predecessors and heirs, many fewer signs, indeed, of having or needing a clearly defined sense of its own past. Of the many anxious heirs among novelists, almost all show the grappling of a lesser with a greater talent, followers with a master. In these cases the lesser talents do not seem crippled or deprived because they could not escape the clutches of the earlier, larger talent. The southern Faulknerians are not different in this respect from the Scottish Chaucerians or the Elizabethan Petrarchans, except that their work is not supposed to look like Faulkner's and the debt, therefore, is harder to acknowledge. But this kind of relation is probably as old as written literature, and has not affected the ability of novelists, by and large, to write the novel they wish to write.

What the novel has suffered from is its own advance guard, ever since James delighted in talking with the French literati. The demand for originality, for writers to find their own "voices," was not restricted to poets, and among novelists this has been interpreted as a need to be self-conscious, to be guided by principles or even theories. James sought this, and, in his wake, so did Conrad and Ford, and, not long into this century, the word began to come back from the advance guard that the novel was dying, or dead, and that the only way to avoid or postpone this death was by "experimenting," doing something new with modes of narration, characterization, or surface intelligibility. Joyce, not entirely unwittingly, gave a great impetus to these notions. Not only did he write *Ulysses*, with its last nine chapters each done in a different "style." Not only did he fill Stuart Gilbert's ear with little schemata he had employed while writing the novel, which Gilbert and others could then think were at least as important as the novel itself. Joyce also wrote, after Molly Bloom's final "yes," "Trieste-Zurich-Paris 1914–1921." Novel writing, so the avant-garde then read the matter, was henceforth to be slow, agonizing, calculated, *work, Work in Progress*.

This chatter has continued, on and off, ever since, mostly because it makes good copy in literary magazines and consorts well with literary professorships. The striking thing about the literature itself that has resulted from this need to Experiment is how much more static and derivative it is than other fiction, which has gone on changing as the world changes. The cry for something new keeps turning up something old; its most recent breeding ground has been South America, where a great deal of fiction is now being written based on principles one might most easily label "Paris, 1925," if not "Kentish Coast, 1900." When a really original practitioner of novelistic experiment has come along, a Nabokov or a Borges, one finds no theories or ideas supporting them, and no looming predecessors either. They just do what they do.

Still, in the history of the novel of this century, Anaïs Nin, Lawrence Durrell, Djuna Barnes, John Hawkes, et al. are not going to loom very large; I doubt if even Nabokov or Borges will. The world reduced to the real is always changing and therefore always tossing up new materials, and the novel, when it is not sterilized by test tube or laboratory, changes all the time. In many modern novelists one can see two forces at work—the one to be modern, technically fancy, up-to-date, the other to break free of such restriction and let the materials dictate the form. When I was growing up, the "great" Conrad was *Nostromo*, the "great" Ford was *The Good Soldier*, the most "interesting" part of *To the Light-*

house was "Time Passes," the most "original" parts of *The Sound and the Fury* were Benjy and Quentin, the scenes to know in *Ulysses* were Nighttown and Molly. In each case what one was asked most to admire was the test-tube work; in each case another part of the same book, or another novel by the same writer, was at hand to show something better, funnier, sadder, often more truly accomplished, that was more governed by the writer's impulse and responsiveness to life: *The Secret Agent, Parade's End*, the boeuf-en-daube in Woolf, the Jason section in Faulkner, almost anything in *Ulysses except* Nighttown and Molly (and the newspaper office and the hospital). In the test-tube parts of books, one notices, the writers all seem rather like each other, while in the freer parts they are different, themselves, doing what no one could have shown them how to do.

All this begins with James, and begins, more than any other single place, with *The Portrait of a Lady*. If anyone can be said to have had a "great fund of life," it is James—tireless energy, life-long ability to be absorbed by people, places, books, and the workings of his own mind, and the generosity and loyalty that attend such energy and ability. That he had to be an observer, and celibate, and one who had to be able to patronize in order to love was not, I think, such a terrible limitation, though of course it meant there were things he could not do or write about. But what he had to do to conquer George Eliot cost him. He never would have been a panoramic viewer, an all-walks-of-society writer, someone interested in processes of work, ordinary aspects of the natural world, quirky habits of dress, speech, or daily life, all of which could absorb George Eliot. But he seemed to have to deny himself more than he might have, both in what he did in order to best her, and in the idea of art he had then to invent in order to remain conqueror. Louisa Musgrove can fall off the Cob and break a leg; Hindley Earnshaw can become a drunk; Richard Carstone can become obsessed by Jarndyce vs. Jarndyce; Gabriel Oak and Bathsheba Everdene can hurriedly prepare for a storm that never happens. Accidents, obsessions, circumstances that momentarily overtake, all these happen in other peoples' novels, and in life, but cannot happen in James. The need to prune was with James before he took on George Eliot, but when that need is combined with the need to be massive, and each is then asked to be subservient to an idea of fiction, then more serious limitations result. Such an interesting man, there probably is no work in his very large output without interest, but one sees in instance after instance the same kind of fact I noted about some of the great modern novelists. Book Second of *The Wings of the Dove* is truly great James, the meetings of Kate and Merton that led them to pledge their lives to each other, not just passion and comedy but irritation and worry and misunderstanding. But Book Fourth, Milly's coming to London and the long dinner party with Lord Mark, is insufferable, James dithering, setting things up, pages and pages in which nothing happens because nothing is supposed to happen to the heroine of a long novel so early.

James couldn't kill the novel, or the novelist in himself. So too Conrad, Ford, Woolf, Faulkner, Joyce. But when they gave themselves over to an idea of fiction, which in most cases meant giving themselves over to a received idea, they could sterilize and monotonize their work. Only in Ford and Conrad, really, can one see James himself at work as a limiting influence, but in many other writers we can read and learn the lesson of the master.

6 ° *Now, and Then*

⫸⫸⫸⫸ I want to begin this closing section with a passage from Hans-Georg Gadamer's *Truth and Method*. It is one I could have used in differing ways at many earlier places:

> Thus the meaning of the connection with tradition, i.e., the element of tradition in our historical, hermeneutical attitude, is fulfilled in the fact that we share fundamental prejudices with tradition. Hermeneutics must start from the position that a person seeking to understand something has a relation to the object that comes into language in the transmitted text and has, or acquires, a connection with the tradition out of which the text speaks. On the other hand, hermeneutical consciousness is aware that it cannot be connected with this object in some self evident, questioned way, as is the case with the unbroken stream of a tradition. There is a polarity of familiarity and strangeness on which hermeneutical work is based: only that this polarity is not to be seen, psychologically, with Schleiermacher, as the tension that conceals the mystery of individuality, but truly hermeneutically, i.e., in regard to what has been said: the language in which the text addresses us, the story that it tells us. Here too there is a tension. The place between strangeness and familiarity that a transmitted text has for us is that intermediate place between being an historically intended separate object and being part of a tradition.

This, in its way, summarizes much of what the preceding chapters have concerned themselves with: a tradition that was unbroken for centuries, then broken, and the problems that arose in understanding and interpretation when this happened. The ones doing the understanding and interpreting here are not philosophers but poets, novelists, and literary historians. In many ways, what Gadamer means by hermeneutics is what I mean by literary history.

That this should be so may tell us something about ourselves. That a German philosopher and a decidedly untheoretical American literary historian, using very different means, should be able to arrive at the same "position" is not, on the face of it, likely. Yet, on going back to René Wellek's *A History of Modern Criticism* after reading Gadamer, in order to see how Wellek handles many of the German writers Gadamer discusses, I was struck by Wellek's need to be certain, to be dogmatic, to deny even the possibility of "a polarity of familiarity and strangeness" in our reading of authors long dead. One would not sense, reading Wellek, that we ever have any difficulty in reading older works of literature; nor would he ever call what we share with tradition "prejudices." By comparison, Gadamer seems flexible, knowing our impulses toward dogmatism, toward relativity, toward a historicism that imagines we can go back and read Jonson, or Johnson, or James as their contemporaries did, yet settling, as it seems obvious that we must, in "the place between strangeness and familiarity."

It is not my intention here to try to discover why this seems obvious now, when it did not perhaps as recently as a generation ago. It is, rather, to ask what sense of the past, of history, of forebears or ancestors, can be found in our literature, when to look backward is to be placed between strangeness and familiarity. I want to contrast the contemporary with the modern, and to concentrate on American literature, where that contrast is most fully felt and where, if it is not simply provincial so to say, the greatest contemporary literary achievements are to be found.

The modern (1900–1940) literary view of history is essentially nostalgic, an imagining of a time past when the world was intelligible and whole, to contrast to a time now when the center does not hold, or the world will soon end, with electrical holocaust, or a whimper. Keats, expressing a naive optimism, could write that the world in the time of Milton was awakening from a long age of superstition. A century later, the idea of progress tarnished and knowledge of earlier eras much increased, the modern reversed the emphasis, longed for unified sensibilities, Mont St. Michel and Chartres, custom and ceremony in which beauty and innocence are born. Subsequent history was a nightmare from which Stephen Dedalus and others were trying to awaken. Early in the twentieth century, the old bitch was gone in the teeth, and history was to blame. No more parades.

Much, if far from all, modern literature is self-consciously experimental in a way that consorts with this nostalgia. Though we have learned much about how to read *Ulysses, Parade's End, The Waste Land, The Cantos,* and *Harmonium,* when these appeared they seemed designed to be difficult, to insist that difficulty was a necessary aspect of the craft, to let the past come in as echo, quotation, longing, often jarring with a seedier, forlorn, lost sense of the present. Narrative pace slows, poetic structure becomes static, time shifts, and shifts in point of view break up the received and "old-fashioned" sense of sequence and causation. Nor, when the modern began to pass away after World War II, did it do so entirely. This was so especially in France and then later in South America, where the modern did not seem to take hold until after it had mostly disappeared in England and America. The amazing tour de force of G. Cabrera Infante's *Three Trapped Tigers* of 1971 may not even be matched by *Finnegans Wake;* Cabrera, in assisting his translators, has in effect written three different novels, each with the same title, in three different languages, Cuban Spanish, French, and English, each replete with wordplay, puns, and parody that is indigenous to each language, there being no equivalent in the other languages for "to the manor born," or "Somersault Maugham," or "vice versatile." The modern died hard.

But it has died, at least in the English-speaking countries. Rather than attempt to say just how or when, let me first point to a couple of striking shifts within works, shifts from a recognizable modern manner to something else. First, in Faulkner's *The Sound and the Fury*, here is Quentin just before his suicide, sounding very much like Stephen Dedalus:

> The first note sounded, measured and tranquil, serenely peremptory, emptying the unhurried silence for the next one and that's it if people could only change one another forever that way merge like a flame swirling up for an instant then blown cleanly out along the cool eternal dark instead of lying there trying not to think of the swing until all cedars came to have that vivid dead smell of perfume that Benjy hated so.

Then, a few pages later, in the opening of Jason's chapter, something very different:

> Once a bitch always a bitch, what I say. I says you're lucky if her playing out of school is all that worries you. I says she ought to be down there in that kitchen right now, instead of up there in her room, gobbing paint on her face and waiting for six niggers that can't even stand up out of a chair unless they've got a pan full of bread and meat to balance them, to fix breakfast for her.

In Quentin, a self-conscious static verbal reflexiveness, poetic modern; in Jason a twang, energetic, a force let loose that knows no bounds, knows no past, a very prosaic contemporary. With Quentin, Faulkner looks backward; with Jason, he cannot be said to look ahead since there is no "ahead" for Jason, but he can be said to commit himself to energy, to rolling out with the voice wherever it will go. Having discovered Jason, Faulkner did not, in this novel or elsewhere, simply turn his back on the modern and embrace the contemporary. But we can note the turn, and say that in his subsequent work he tried often to combine the solemnity of Quentin's manner with the comic grotesqueness of Jason's.

Something similar happens within the covers of Robert Lowell's *Life Studies*. Though the point could be made more strikingly if one started with a truly Eliotic early Lowell poem like "The Quaker Graveyard in Nantucket," this, from "Beyond the Alps," shows well enough the modern Lowell, in thrall in part to Eliot and in part to Stevens:

> God herded his people to the *coup de grâce*—
> the costumed Switzers sloped their pikes to push,
> O Pius, through the monstrous human crush . . .
> Our mountain-climbing train had come to earth.
> Tired of the querulous hush-hush of the wheels,
> the blear-eyed ego kicking in my berth
> lay still, and saw Apollo plant his heels
> on terra firma through the morning's thigh . . .

Lowell as Poet, robes on, heavily rhetorical. Then this, from "Skunk Hour," at the end of the volume:

> And now our fairy
> decorator brightens his shop for fall;
> his fishnet's filled with orange cork,
> orange, his cobbler's bench and awl;
> there is no money in his work,
> he'd rather marry.

Again, the shift we can note here is not definitive, though Lowell, like Faulkner, does keep working away from a knotted early literary manner. Here he is less in need of effects, and more willing to trace simply the motions of a sensibility, letting the poetry go where it will:

> One dark night,
> my Tudor Ford climbed the hill's skull;
> I watched for love-cars. Lights turned down,
> they lay together, hull to hull,
> where the graveyard shelves on the town. . . .
> My mind's not right.

Six-line stanzas, each shaped alike, yet there is little sense of pattern, and a strong sense of Lowell, subdued, centrifugal in motion.

One could find many such instances of the same kind of shift, within a single book, within an author's career, and within American literature as a whole as it has moved from the modern to the contemporary in the last generation or so. The most marked turning point comes in the late 1950s and early 1960s. Immediately postwar American literature often seems written according to the dictates of a New Criticism textbook: controlled, ironic, shapely, subtle, as in *All the King's Men*, the early novels of Wright Morris and Frederic Buechner, Lowell's *Lord Weary's Castle*, Richard Wilbur's *Things of This World*, Theodore Roethke's *The Waking*, Saul Bellow's *The Victim*, which Bellow once tellingly called his Ph.D. novel. It is literature that, if it cannot be said that it was written in order to be taught, is eminently teachable should a teacher be interested in identifying irony, texture, point of view, structure.

But then comes *Life Studies*, Allen Ginsberg's *Howl*, Bellow's *Adventures of Augie March*, and suddenly control gives way to motion, extravagance. Marvin Mudrick once alleged that "the modern is America, unbounded centrifugal energy spinning away from the totem of history." He is using "modern" to cover anything in this century, and I would say that, with some exceptions, that is definitely not true of American literature before the late 1950s, but entirely true for American literature after that, especially in the novel. Whatever are the best American novels of the last twenty-five years, among the most characteristic are Joseph Heller's *Catch-22*, Philip Roth's *Portnoy's Complaint*, Thomas Pynchon's *V.* and *Gravity's Rainbow*, Bellow's *Herzog* and *Humboldt's Gift*, Updike's *Rabbit Is Rich*—to use Mudrick's words again, "no spiritual preparations, no coyness, no fainting spells, no Don Juanish palaver; pure profane activity in a new world, out of bounds." Here it is not surprising that, once free, these novelists seem as able as the English novelists of the last century to work without predecessors, to be guided by impulse, to be bursting and lavish rather than clever in language, to let someone else figure out the rules for plot or point of view.

This is not, I think, simply another turn from (to use the language of another time) the Paleface to the Redskin, from cooked to raw. The art of *Catch-22* or of *Herzog* is every bit as sophisticated, even as calculated, as that of *All the King's Men* or *Absolom! Absolom!* But the art of more recent fiction is put in the service of something less in need of votive candles for illumination, more in need of a sense of impulsive exploration in order to be responsive to "pure profane activity in a new world, out of bounds." Furthermore, although it may seem as though contemporary fiction seeks to spin away from the totem of history, and though it is important to these writers to be rid of the modern sense of history, the past is still there. Not as a matter of ancestors casting shadows —one sees no trace of O'Hara, Marquand, or Cheever in Updike, or of Bellow and Malamud in Roth (even when, as in *The Ghost Writer,* both earlier writers seem to appear in Roth's pages). Nor as a matter of nostalgia or a nightmare from which one needs to awaken. Nor, except occasionally, as a matter of the child being parent to the adult. Rather, as history, and history understood as a polarity of familiarity and strangeness.

We can note, first of all, a large number of works of straightforward historical fiction: Mary Renault's retellings of ancient myths and history; Gore Vidal's *Burr* and *1876;* Gladys Schmitt's *Rembrandt* and Marguerite Yourcenar's *Hadrian's Memoirs,* with their unabashed fascination with a single figure; Isaac Bashevis Singer's novels, especially *The Manor* and *The Estate,* where the need is to know the world of one's childhood historically; Paul Scott's similarly motivated tetrology about India gaining independence after World War II; the spate of novels about the Holocaust by people who were not there; Leslie Silko's *Ceremony,* which retells the devastation of her Native American forebears, also immediately after World War II; at an extreme, Jean Auel's *The Clan of the Cave Bear,* where the human and the human's ancestors meet, in a tale of millennia ago.

In most of these novels the aim is to honor both the strange and the familiar. A gap in time is to be leaped, and if the leap is very long, it knows that on the other side are people who did not think, feel, and speak as we do. The problem of idiom is considerable, since we know that Alexander the Great or Thomas Jefferson did not speak a language we easily understand, yet we do not want them to sound as though they were always speaking proclamations, or as though we could not understand them at all. There is also the problem of what we call "psychology" or "motivation" that involves a series of presumptions about the way people act of which earlier centuries were innocent. The writer usually makes a bargain with a reader: in these ways I will emphasize the strange, even the impenetrable, and in these other ways I will seek to make the past familiar. One reason these historical fictions tend to be long is that the writer needs a good deal of space to establish the bargain without making it seem a trick; one mark of success in such fiction is a writer's willingness to be uncompromising once the bargain has been made. On these terms, I would say that Renault's *The Last of the Wine* is almost totally successful, while John Gardner's *Freddy's Book* is a failure. But in any event, it is one mark of contemporary fiction that so much exploration of history is to be found there; when George Lukacs's *The Historical Novel* appeared, it seemed as though he were writing about a kind of literature of which we could not expect many more examples, and in fact the opposite has turned out to be the case. It is as though once free of the modern need always to be relating the Then to the Now, novelists could more freely re-create a Then and invest the energies of Now in matters of idiom in the bargain whereby the polarity between the familiar and the strange is honored.

There is a somewhat different kind of historical fiction which has been very fashionable in the last decade. While I don't think either the fashion or the fictions themselves will prove lasting, the very fact of the fashion is revealing. It is blended fiction, in which figures of the past and their eras are re-created in unabashedly contemporary terms, and in which "real" people mingle with "fictional characters": E. L. Doctorow's *The Book of Daniel, Ragtime,* and *Loon Lake;* D. S. Thomas's *The White Hotel,* Beryl Bainbridge's *Young Adolph,* George Steiner's *The Portage to San Cristobel of A. H.,* Timothy Findley's *Famous Last Words.* In these books Emma Goldman not only meets Evelyn Nesbit, but also some characters invented by Doctorow; Freud treats a patient he never had; Hitler takes a journey he never took; Ezra Pound meets Hugh Selwyn Mauberley, and Mauberley meets the Duke and Duchess of Windsor. The specific aims of these novels vary, of course, but all are marked with a kind of hell-bent inventiveness, an air of "Watch me bring this off." If Eliot in *The Waste Land* is seeking ways to shore up his lands against the ruins, these novels delightedly poke about among those ruins in order to make stick figures, wind-up dolls, and, occasionally, rather portentous history out of the way these figures then move about. Unfortunately, the more portentous the history, the greater the clash with the fictional fun. It may be that if we leave history to mere historians, the past will be lost, and so fictional sport may seem an attractive alternative. But only for a while, I should think. A much denser and more invigorating imagining is available in *annales* history, which is also very entertaining; Fernand Braudel, giving himself whole regions and centuries to create in *The Structures of Everyday Life* and *The Mediterranean,* and Dorothy Hartley, attempting to reconstruct the months of a farming year in *Lost Country Life,* do not write fiction, but they are much more responsive in their imagining than are the blending historical novelists, to say nothing of being more invigorating about their ignorance.

But the contemporary writer who takes plunges into history that make the blending novelists look as though they are afraid to swim is Marvin Mudrick. In his pages one finds a Chinese emperor, Jesus, Voltaire, William of Orange, Aristotle, Johnson and Boswell, Trotsky, P. T. Barnum, Casanova, and it is hard to know what to call the result. His figures, he writes, "look to the mind's eye just like you and me and give the impression of being just as free to choose, hence I needn't pretend they're only an historian's abstracts or a novelist's inventions," since "life is too emphatic to get lost in the words on a page." He allows strangeness only in the sense that life can be strange, not in any acknowledgment that the passing of time has rendered his figures any less clear than anyone alive today. Thus:

> Alcibiades was the talk of the town all his life, born to rank and wealth, brilliant, fearless, shameless, hugely ambitious, courting the populace like a lover ("his curtesies, his liberalities, and noble expences to shewe the people so great pleasure and pastime as nothing could be more") boundlessly sensual, the nonpareil of beauty ("he was wonderful fayer, being a child, a boye, and a man, and that at all times, which made him beloved of every man"), the complete charmer: "his company and manner to passe the time awaye, was

commonly marvelous full of mirthe and pleasure, and he
had suche pleasaunt comely devises with him, that no man
was of so sullen a nature, but he would make him merie, nor
so churlishe, but he would make him gentle."

Mudrick here is quoting from North's Plutarch, as if to insist that
no foreignness in idiom or phrasing can hide his people, and that
it matters little if Plutarch is "right," just as long as Mudrick can
use him to place Alcibiades before us. Just before this passage, he
has set us straight about Shakespeare, *his* Timon, *his* Alcibiades:
"Anyhow Shakespeare's Timon railing at Alcibiades is full of the
usual Shakespearean bullshit and hot air (which boil down to the
usual Shakespearean verb. sap.: Beware the foul fiend Hanky-
panky, from whose crotch and armpit come all diseases—bald-
ness, fallen noses, and severe depression)." Mudrick, we see, is
too emphatic for any brilliance like Shakespeare's to keep him
from seeing what is really happening, what really happened at
any point in the past he happens to be looking at.

Given his wildness, and his determination not to be fooled or
to have anything to do with tradition, it is his work with quotations that keeps Mudrick from being the simply willful writer he
often has been accused of being. "Alcibiades was the talk of the
town all his life" swaggers its contemporary American idiom,
and if North were not amply placed in front of us, only swagger
would result. But, since the North is right there, the result is a
kind of marvelous show, and Mudrick likes to call himself a literary entertainer. In a passage I quoted earlier, he describes the
American modern as "no spiritual preparations, no coyness, no
fainting spells, no Don Juanish palaver; pure profane activity in a
new world, out of bounds." It is not surprising that of all living
writers these words apply most aptly to Mudrick himself, everyone else being just a little bit shy, a little bit respectful of tradition,
by comparison.

When his texts, and therefore his quotations, are energetic and
responsive to the spoken voice, the result can often be a very
happy partnership, as in all he has written on Chaucer, Boswell,
Jane Austen, and Trollope. When he has to work against a heavy
rhetoric or an embellished verbal surface, as he does with Shake-

speare and with all the academics he loves to attack, the result is often very funny, but convincing only if the quotations are in need of being seen through because they really hide some depraved feeling or some vacuity of thought. When he is dealing with the gospels, treating them as though no attention had to be paid to which gospel is in question or the obscure nature of their coming to being and subsequent transmission, he seems rather like a dog barking at a truck, and his Jesus isn't even interesting. Which is why, for all that Mudrick is famous for his attacks, he really is best when he is admiring and praising, his energy and his spoken voice wonderfully able to elucidate the energy and the human complication spoken by his quotations. I hope that his essay on William of Orange, "The Unsung Hero," which seems to me his best single piece of work, will soon be rescued from the obscuring clouds of antagonism that Mudrick's name seems currently to be hiding behind; it should be in any anthology that seeks to represent the best contemporary American prose.

In one respect, at least, there is some merit in saying that Mudrick is a writer who "goes too far." His unabashed defiance of history and tradition may be typically American, but its purity, or its extremity, shows it is not truly representative of our relation to the past while it is a marked sign of that relation that it seems unburdened by the past, and wrestles with no ancestors, that it casts away the modern sense of history as nightmare, there is in much contemporary fiction a tension between Then and Now that is quite absent in Mudrick's entertainments. One finds it in the nostalgia of Updike, in Pynchon's extravagant imaginings of what he calls this tourist century, in Marilynne Robinson's seeking after "the life of perished things" in *Housekeeping*, in the cockeyed revisionism of Heller's *Catch-22*, in Roth's reincarnating Kafka and Anne Frank, in nonce quotations scattered in the concoctions of Donald Barthelme. The emphasis may be on the strange, and may be on the familiar, but always we need to assess the relation between past and present. Of all our writers, the one in whom this relation is richest is Saul Bellow, and of all Bellow's works, the one in which it is richest is *Herzog*. That novel is now twenty years old, but I know of none that more clearly or fully articulates what I take to be the contemporary sense of then and now.

The past in *Herzog*, the nonpersonal historical past, is mostly a matter of argument and speculation, Herzog working his way among the big European names of the last few centuries, always wanting to know where their Then leaves him and us Now. Herzog, though, is not just historian by trade but by reason of his own past: "So we had a great schooling in grief," he remembers, thinking of the night his father, an incompetent bootlegger in Montreal, returns home, beaten by thugs and his resources stolen; "I still know those cries of the soul." Herzog also remembers that Dr. Johnson had said, "Grief, Sir, is a species of idleness," but while he can castigate himself for his idleness, Herzog cannot give up his past:

> These personal histories, old tales from old times that may not be worth remembering, I remember. I must. But who else—to whom can this matter? So many millions—multitudes—go down in terrible pain. And, at that, moral suffering is denied, these days. Personalities are good only for comic relief. But I am still a slave to Papa's pain. The way Father Herzog spoke of himself! That could make one laugh. His *I* had such dignity.

So Moses, heir to the pain, seeks dignity for his *I*, but is afraid he is only providing comic relief. Of his affair with Sono Oguki he says "I lacked the strength of character to bear such joy," and of his life "I rose from humble origins to complete disaster." It is with the force of a "therefore" that he then says of history: "To be free is to be released from historical limitation. On the other hand, GWF Hegel (1770–1831) understood the essence of human life to be derived from history. History—memory—that is what makes us human, that, and our knowledge of death."

It is a comic anguished swirl of a novel, so intricately constructed that what Herzog is muttering or shouting at any point in the book is deepening something said earlier or showing the way to something later, and yet the sense of swirl, of a mad and aimless Herzog, is never lost. In a suitcase are stacks of unsent and unfinished letters, and a manuscript, *The Phenomenology of Mind*, which is about "the importance of 'the law of the heart' in Western traditions, the origins of moral sentimentalism and related matters." Bucking the trends of his get-with-it-and-into-America Reality Instructors, who "tout the void as though it was so much salable real estate," Herzog seeks a life of moral sentiment and moral suffering, but usually gets no closer than a comic martyrdom. He buys a house in the Berkshires in order to finish his book, brings with him his second wife, the redoubtable Madeleine. He spends a year fixing the house, the Herzogs have a daughter, Moses frets Madeleine's frivolous furnishing of the house and her extravagance; he fosters the friendship of Valentine Gersbach, who proceeds to spirit Madeleine and the daughter away as he gives Herzog advice on how to handle it all. Moral sentiment and moral suffering? The book goes into the suitcase and Herzog's life goes smash, not for the first or the last time.

Herzog's argument about our history goes something like this: the Romantics inherited from earlier centuries an idea of the "inspired condition" and accompanying ideas of transcendence and generosity. They thereby became the first bourgeois aristocrats. Then modern technology had made democracy possible and made us all heirs to the Romantics. Yet the value given to that technology led the Reality Instructors to the conclusion that moral sentiment was a dead issue and that "the law of the heart" is just another monstrous selfishness or else a form of madness.

Thus Herzog writes to the monsignor who converted Madeleine to Catholicism:

> Very tired of the modern form of historicism which sees in this civilization the defeat of the best hopes of Western religion and thought, what Heidegger calls the second Fall of Man into the quotidian or ordinary. No philosopher knows what the ordinary is, has fallen into it deeply enough. The question of ordinary human experience is the principal question of these modern centuries. As Montaigne and Pascal, otherwise in disagreement, both clearly saw—the strength of a man's virtue or spiritual capacity measured by his ordinary life.

Herzog wills himself heir to everything except that aspect of modernism that thinks the best hopes of Western religion and thought have been defeated. He wishes to be a marvelous Herzog, measured not by any achievement other than the quality of his ordinary life as a midcentury American.

Yet in remembering the monsignor, Herzog thinks back to the year he was courting Madeleine. After the letter ends, the next sentence is: "Herzog tragically sipping milk in Philadelphia, a frail hopeful lunatic, tipping the carton to quiet his stomach and drown his unquiet mind, courting sleep." Bellow's genius is right there, in the juxtaposition of the lofty thought with the ordinarily living thinker, especially in the exquisite "tragically sipping milk in Philadelphia," which gives Herzog honor and reveals his confusion and folly. Let Herzog rise up, try to give his *I* a dignity: "The occupation of a man is in duty, in civility, in use, in politics in the Aristotelean sense." Then let Herzog measure the thought by ordinary life:

> Now then, why am I arriving here, in Vineyard Haven, on a *holiday* no less! Heartbroken, and gussied up, with my Italian pants and my fountain pens, and my grief—to both pester poor Libbie, and exploit her affections, forcing her to pay off because I was so kind and decent when *her* last husband, Erikson, went off his rocker and tried to stab her and take the gas himself? At which time, yes, I was very helpful. But if she hadn't been so very beautiful, sexual, and obviously attracted to me, would I have been such a willing friend and helper?

And so, having invited himself to Vineyard Haven, Herzog discovers the moment he arrives that he must flee, back to New York and frantic letter writing.

In the examples discussed earlier from Faulkner and Lowell, we see a motion from the modern to the contemporary, and if, in their works, this is not a single move taken once and for all, in them we do not have anything like what Bellow offers: the contemporary in dialogue with the modern, and, often using the ideas of a pre–twentieth-century Europe, the contemporary keeps asking: how are we to live *now*? Bellow does not stack the deck by turning his Reality Instructors into monsters. Himmelstein, Simkin, Madeleine, and Gersbach are nothing if not impressive and unfreaky; they too have lives, and are part of a recognizable history. No one knows better than Bellow the pure profane power of America, and he can envy those who scorn his, and Herzog's concerns, and are free to be profanely powerful. No one, thus, is better placed for making the plea that memory demands: "My God! Who is this creature? It considers itself human. But what is it! Not human of itself. But has the longing to be human. And like a troubling dream, a persistent vapor. A desire. Where does it all come from? And what is it? What can it be? Not immortal longing. No, entirely mortal, but human." Not free of historical limitation, Herzog becomes what he calls human by remembering, by being willing to be a historian. Then, in this novel, speaks to Now, and Now answers as best it can. The past is gone, tradition is tattered or broken, but because gone does not mean dead, neither are we.

"Hermeneutical consciousness," Gadamer writes, "is aware that it cannot be connected with this object [any older literary text] in some self evident, questioned way, as is the case with the unbroken stream of tradition." As I suggested earlier, literary history is my name for what Gadamer calls hermeneutics; Herzog needs no other words then "remember" and "the longing to be human." What I find striking about this collocation, or what I would like most to stress about it by way of conclusion, is the way in which something called hermeneutics, something called literary history, and something called being human all can rest comfortably inside an awareness that instead of inheriting a tradition we must be historians, but that this now is a liberating and not an oppressive or anguished task.

In the terms offered by this book, the real break in tradition comes in the middle of the eighteenth century. If another tradition can be said to have come out of that break, a tradition usually called Romantic, it is my sense that one reason it so often had to be anguished was that it did not understand the older tradition or its relation to it. It is also my sense that, after the eighteenth century, the most important work is done in the novel, which has always had a much weaker sense of tradition than poetry. In these terms, then, the modern is primarily a later stage of Romanticism, especially in its need to see history as a struggle of the new against the old, its craving after originality.

The essential mark of the contemporary, then, is that it does not feel this sense of struggle. If this is truer in America than elsewhere, it may be because the modern was essentially a European phenomenon, and, for some time now, American writers have been able to work without feeling Europe as a looming parent but more as something one does not wish to be entirely done with, as in *Herzog*. But it is remarkable that a German philosopher like Gadamer (and, insofar as I understand him, Jauss), working diligently within a received inheritance of that philosophy in the last three centuries, can emerge with a sense of task and of history that seems to me as different from its predecessors as the American contemporary is from its. I earlier compared Gadamer with René Wellek in this regard; he might also be compared with E. R. Curtius who, having constructed his monument to the old culture, falls at the end into the old Shelleyean hankering after lonesome mountaintops, in this case named Dante, Shakespeare, and Goethe. It is hard to imagine Gadamer falling like that.

It is not accidental, however, that in attempting to locate contemporary possibilities for history I have relied primarily on novelists and not on more self-conscious (and academic) historians and critics and theorists, and for the reason that contemporary novelists seem freer in their way of relating Then and Now, less anxious to worry about tripping over a predecessor, less in need of making sure that the predecessors one wants dead stay dead (as with Harold Bloom and Eliot). The whole hue and cry about "texts" and "writing" as opposed to authors and human consciousnesses strikes me as being, more often than not, a latter-day modernism that cannot quite rid itself of a sense of the past as potential oppressor. Even most deconstructive criticism I am aware of, though born of the desire to be free of such oppression, and potentially able, I should think, to gain a free relation with the literature of the past, often makes the cry of freedom seem like a rattle of chains. Though Bellow and Herzog are far from happy, their relation to history seems, by comparison with so much contemporary literary history and theory, both sensible and enabling.

In writing about the Renaissance, I cited William Kerrigan's essay in which Kerrigan postulates that the great energy and ambition of so many Renaissance writers result from a weaning from the native mother language, an intense training in Latin, the father language, followed by a return to the mother language that was made powerful by an integration of the two parents. I would like to think that something similar is now becoming possible, especially in America: the original training in American culture, followed by as deep an immersion as possible in the older European culture, and then followed by a return to the American in which, one may hope, an integration takes place. Because the tradition is broken, one cannot expect the results to be more than analogous. We can remember, however, that one source of the energy and ambition of the Renaissance was that Latin was no longer a living language, and it had to be learned as we have had to learn those and later European writers. If Jonson and Milton could gain a sense of their tradition from Horace and Vergil, and if we cannot expect really to gain a traditional relation to Jonson and Milton, we can, as historians, attempt something similar. We can, at the very least, keep remembering that they gained their relation not by inspiration but by labor—that was, rightly, Carew's praise of Jonson—and we can labor too.

Notes

◊◊◊◊ I have used what I hope are simple means: quotations from the standard or an easily available edition; line numbers for long poems and plays, page numbers for prose works, chapter numbers for novels where many editions are available, days of entry for Boswell's *Life*, exceptions noted.

1. INTRODUCTION

The work of Harold Bloom I most have in mind here is *The Anxiety of Influence* (New York, 1973) and *A Map of Misreading* (New York, 1975); see also W. Jackson Bate, *The Burden of the Past and the English Poet* (Cambridge, 1970). Two books that work with an idea of inheritance similar to mine, but with totally different writers, are Donald Davie, *Thomas Hardy and British Poetry* (Oxford, 1972) and John Barrell, *The Idea of Landscape and the Sense of Place 1730–1840* (Cambridge, 1972).

For the F. R. Leavis cited here, *Revaluation* (London, 1936), pp. 19, 32; for William Empson, *Some Versions of Pastoral* (London, 1935), pp. 189–91.

E. R. Curtius, on *auctores*, *European Literature in the Latin Middle Ages* (New York, 1953), p. 51; on the line of the flower flora, p. 202 n; for Baudri of Bourguiel, see p. 363.

Marvell and Keats are quoted from the Oxford editions of H. M. Margoliouth and H. W. Garrod.

2. CAREW AS COMPOSER

Shelley, *A Defence of Poetry*, in *The Poetical Works of Shelley*, ed. Newell F. Ford, Cambridge edition (Boston, 1974), p. 610.

Ben Jonson's poetry is cited from *The Complete Poetry of Ben Jonson*, ed. William Hunter (New York, 1968). Jonson's plays (*Volpone* 3.7.157–64, 175–78, and *The Alchemist*, 1.1.107–10 and 2.5.36–44) are from *The Complete Plays of Ben Jonson*, ed. G. A. Wilkes (Oxford, 1982), based on that of Herford and Simpson. Hugh Kenner on Jonson and Camden, is from *The Schools of Donne and Jonson* (New York, 1964), p. 68; later, on Waller, p. 387.

William Kerrigan, "The Articulation of the Ego in the English Renaissance," is in *The Literary Freud: Mechanisms of Defense and the Poetic Will*, ed. Joseph Smith (New Haven, 1980), pp. 261–308.

Carew's poems, and the letter by James Howells, are cited from the Oxford edition by Rhodes Dunlap. Leavis on Carew, *Revaluation*, pp. 16–17, 36. See also one of the few serious essays on Carew: Rufus Blanshard, "Thomas Carew's Master Figures," *Boston University Studies in English* 3(1957): 214–27.

For Beatrix Potter on the lesser work of great artists, *The Journal of Beatrix Potter*, ed. Leslie Linder (London, 1966), p. 67.

Nashe's "Preface" to Greene's *Menaphon*, from *The Works of Thomas Nashe*, ed. Ronald B. McKerrow (Oxford, 1958), 3:311, 315.

Citation of "To William Wordsworth," the edition of E. H. Coleridge; of "The Welcome to Sack," that of L. C. Martin; "Satire iii," that of W. Milgate; of "Astrophil and Stella 19," that of William A. Ringler, Jr.; of "Loves Deitie," that of Helen Gardner.

Christopher Ricks, "Allusion: The Poet as Heir," is an essay that comes as close to any I know to doing the kind of literary history incorporating the idea of inheritance that I attempt in this book. It is in *Studies in the Eighteenth Century, III: Papers Presented at the Third David Nicol Smith Memorial Seminar* (Toronto, 1973).

Pope, *Dunciad*, 2, 1–5, Herbert Davis's edition (Oxford, 1965). The poems and essays of Dryden are quoted from *Dryden: A Selection* (London, 1978); the passage from the *Essay on Dramatic Poetry* is on p. 530.

3. JOHNSON IN DARKNESS

Boswell's *Life of Johnson* is quoted from the Hill and Powell edition: on "ancient" and "modern" times, April 30, 1783; on religion "now" and "formerly," and on our response to the suffering of others, October 19, 1769; on big words and little matter, August 6, 1763; on the *Dictionary*, October 10, 1779; the recitation of *The Dunciad*, October 16, 1769; on Vergil's being less talked of than Pope, April 29, 1778.

Leavis on *The Dunciad*, *Revaluation*, p. 29.

Passages from *The Lives of the Poets* are quoted from the Everyman edition, volume 2; from "The Life of Thomson," pp. 286–87; from "The Life of Pope," on the grotto, p. 172; on Pope's choice of friends, pp. 205–6; on *Dunciad* 4, p. 197. Volume 7 of the Yale edition of Johnson has the "Preface" to Shakespeare; the passage is on p. 77.

The *Dictionary*, which has at last been reprinted, may be the least read and discussed major work in English; it is typical that James Clifford's *Dictionary Johnson* says very little about the work itself, much about the Johnson of those years. My citations are from the sixth edition (the one I own), which is little different from the more authoritative fourth.

"The Vanity of Human Wishes" and "On the Death of Mr. Robert Levet" are quoted from the Oxford edition of D. Nicol Smith and E. L. McAdam. Christopher Hollis's statement about the latter poem is in *Dr. Johnson* (London, 1928), p. 194.

Marvin Mudrick is unfailingly interesting on Johnson and Boswell. The essay quoted here is "Boswell's Johnson," *Hudson Review* 33 (1981); 279–87.

Quotations from Pope are from Davis's edition: *Imitations of Horace*, 2, 1, 115–33; *Epilogue to the Satires*, 1, 151–70; *Dunciad* 1, 55–78, and 4, 149–60, 465–76, 251–52, 235–38, 653–56, 50–70; *Essay on Man*, 1, 87–88; "To a Lady," 53–68.

Spenser's stanza is *The Faerie Queene*, 4, 10, 32; Gibbon on Commodus is from the Everyman edition of *The Decline and Fall of the Roman Empire*, 1:84 (ch. 4).

"Idol-Worship or the Way to Preferment" can be seen on p. 146 of Maynard Mack, *The Garden and the City* (London, 1969). For Reuben Brower on *Dunciad* 4, see *Alexander Pope: The Poetry of Allusion* (Oxford, 1959), ch. 10.

The passage from Fielding's *Joseph Andrews*, ch. 8.

4. WORDSWORTH'S CENTURY

Quotations from Shelley are from Ingpen and Smith's edition; *Peter Bell the Third*, 4, stanzas 7–10; 5, stanzas 7–8; "The Triumph of Life," 248–55, 332–42; "Mont Blanc," stanza 1. "Hymn to Intellectual Beauty," stanza 2.

All quotations from Wordsworth's poetry are from the de Selincourt Oxford edition; *The Prelude* 5, 584–605; 12, 232–69; 1, 410–14; 12, 272–80; 3, 177–93; *The Excursion* 1, 910–64. I have, of course, added italics to the quotation from "Tintern Abbey." The "Reply to 'Mathetes' " is cited from W. J. B. Owen and Jane Worthington Smyser's Oxford edition of the prose, 2:9–10.

The quotations from Schiller's "Naive and Sentimental Poetry" are from the work of an unknown translator of *Essays Aesthetical and Philosophical* (London, 1875), pp. 264, 285–86, mostly because it was in this book that I first read Schiller's essays; a more recent translation, very little different, by Julius Elias, is more widely available.

Harold Bloom on "Tintern Abbey," *Poetry and Repression* (New Haven, 1976), pp. 80–81; later, on Keats's "Hyperion," p. 116–23; Geoffrey Hartman's canonical reading of "Tintern Abbey" is in *Wordsworth's Poetry 1787–1814* (New Haven, 1964). Let me name here two less well-known books that helped me with Wordsworth: David Ferry, *The Limits of Mortality: An Essay on Wordsworth's Major Poems* (Middletown, Conn., 1959), and Christopher Salvesen, *The Landscape of Memory* (London, 1965); Jonathan Wordsworth makes what seems to me the proper emphasis on the child as parent in *The Borders of Vision* (Oxford, 1982); perhaps the best reader of the spots of time is Jonathan Bishop in his *ELH* article of 1959. Neil Hertz, "Wordsworth and the Tears of Adam," is in *Studies in Romanticism* 7 (1967):

15–33. Empson on nineteenth-century poets is in *Seven Types of Ambiguity* (London, 1947), p. 17.

Santayana on Shelley can be found in *Selected Critical Writings* (Cambridge, 1968), 1:159.

Keats's poems are cited from Garrod's edition; the passage from "The Fall of Hyperion" is 256–63. Keats's letters are from Hyder Rollins's edition, volume 1, for Keats to Reynolds on Wordsworth (February 3, 1818) and to Reynolds on the mansion of many apartments (May 1818); volume 2 for the letter to George and Georgiana Keats (February–May 1819), the quotations being from 1:97, 102, and 2:104.

Quotations from *Great Expectations* are from the Oxford Illustrated Dickens, chs. 8 and 49; Louis Crompton's comment is in a note in his reprint of the novel published by Bobbs-Merrill. For me the classic reading of the novel is that of Robert Garis in *The Dickens Theatre* (Oxford, 1965).

5. HENRY JAMES

Quotations from James's letters are from Leon Edel's edition, as follows: to William on HJ's French ways, 2:58; to Alice on his visit to John Cross, 2:337; to William citing F. T. Palgrave, 2:103.

The passages from James's notebooks are from the edition of F. O. Matthiessen and Kenneth Murdock, pp. 25–26.

There is, alas, no good collection of James's criticism, which must therefore be found in partial selections and more fugitive sources. Edel's grouping, *The House of Fiction* (London, 1957), has the essay on Trollope (see pp. 90–91), the review of *Middlemarch* (see pp. 259, 267), and of *Our Mutual Friend* (see p. 253), and "The Lesson of Balzac," with the devastating remarks on Austen (pp. 62–63) and the Brontës (p. 64). The review of *Far From the Madding Crowd* is in *Literary Reviews and Essays*, ed. Albert Mordell (New York, 1957), pp. 293–94. *Partial Portraits* (Ann Arbor, Mich., 1970) has the review of Cross's *Life of George Eliot* (pp. 56–57) and "*Daniel Deronda*: A Conversation" (pp. 72–73). The review of *The Legend of Jubal* is from "The Poetry of George Eliot," *Views and Reviews* (Boston, 1908), pp. 148–49. For James on Hawthorne's sense of sin, *Hawthorne* (London, 1880), pp. 58–59.

Edel's biography is essential for the years in question; "It is from that that I myself shall pretend to date," *The Conquest of London* (London, 1962), p. 405.

The Norton Critical edition of *The Portrait of a Lady*, ed. Robert Bamberg (New York, 1975) has the 1907 preface (for passages quoted here, see pp. 7, 9), the 1907 text with variants listed from the 1881 text, from which I quote except where noted. The earlier text is currently available in a Signet edition. In the selection of criticism is William Gass's "The High Brutality of Good Intentions." Passages quoted from the novel are from chs. 4, 6, 24, and 26.

Daniel Deronda (Gloucester, Mass., 1973) reprints an 1883 Edinburgh edition and has an introduction by Leavis; passages quoted are from chs. 4, 12, 14, and 66.

Leavis's *The Great Tradition* (London, 1948) often seems grotesque in its attempt to bring "the English novel" to heel, but its was the first good work on the relation of *Daniel Deronda* and *The Portrait of a Lady*; on the "tradition of the English novel," see p. 5; on Isabel's choice of Osmond, pp. 109–12.

Passages from Hawthorne are from the Library of America edition; *The Scarlet Letter*, ch. 6; *The Marble Faun*, ch. 16.

The passage from *Washington Square* is from the Scribners' edition of 1880, ch. 26; from *Roderick Hudson*, on the motive that aches like a wound, the 1907 Scribners' edition only, ch. 19.

Quentin Anderson, *The American Henry James* (London, 1958) is one of the few consistently interesting books on James; the passages quoted here are on pp. 50, 186, 186–87.

Cynthia Chase's "The Decomposition of the Elephants: A Double-Reading of *Daniel Deronda*," *PMLA* 93 (1978): 215–27, attempts a (to my mind, unsuccessful) deconstruction of this text.

6. NOW, AND THEN

Hans-Georg Gadamer, *Truth and Method* (New York, 1975) is painstaking and sane; the passage here cited is on pp. 262–63.

The passage from the Quentin section is on pp. 194–95 of the Modern Library edition of *The Sound and the Fury*; from the Jason section, p. 198.

"Beyond the Alps" is the first and "Skunk Hour" the last poem in Robert Lowell's *Life Studies* (New York: Farrar, Straus and Giroux, 1959), pp. 13–15, 61–62. Reprinted by permission of the publisher and Faber and Faber, Ltd.

Marvin Mudrick on the modern, "The Modern and How It Grew," *Hudson Review* 18 (1965): 313–20; on himself, and on Alcibiades, *Nobody Here But Us Chickens* (New Haven, 1981), pp. 103–4.

Saul Bellow, *Herzog* (New York, 1964); since it is not always easy to find one's way around: "These personal histories . . ." (p. 149); "I lacked the strength of character, . . ." (p. 169); "To be free is to be released . . ." (p. 162); "who tout the void . . ." (p. 93); "Very tired of the modern form of historicism" and "tragically sipping milk in Philadelphia" (p. 106); "Now then, why am I arriving here . . ." (p. 94); "My God! Who is this creature . . ." (p. 220).

Index